DISABILITY TH
MODERN DRAM..

MW00627969

Kirsty Johnston is associate professor in the Department of Theatre and Film at the University of British Columbia, Canada, and author of *Stage Turns: Canadian Disability Theatre* (2012), which received the 2012 prize for best book in Canadian Studies from the Canadian Studies Network. Her research focuses on intersections between disability and performance and has been published in such journals as *Modern Drama*, *Theatre Topics* and *The Journal of Medical Humanities*.

DISABILITY THEATRE AND MODERN DRAMA

RECASTING MODERNISM

Kirsty Johnston

Series Editors: Patrick Lonergan and Kevin J. Wetmore, Jr.

Bloomsbury Methuen Drama
An imprint of Bloomsbury Publishing Plc

B L O O M S B U R Y
LONDON · OXFORD · NEW YORK · NEW DELHI · SYDNEY

Bloomsbury Methuen Drama

An imprint of Bloomsbury Publishing Plc

Imprint previously known as Methuen Drama

50 Bedford Square	1385 Broadway
London	New York
WC1B 3DP	NY 10018
UK	USA

www.bloomsbury.com

BLOOMSBURY, METHUEN DRAMA and the Diana logo are trademarks of Bloomsbury Publishing Plc

First published 2016

Reprinted 2016

© Kirsty Johnston and contributors, 2016

Kirsty Johnston has asserted her right under the Copyright, Designs and Patents Act, 1988, to be identified as author of this work.

British Library Cataloguing-in-Publication Data
A catalogue record for this book is available from the British Library.

ISBN:	HB:	978-1-4081-8449-3
	PB:	978-1-4081-8478-3
	ePDF:	978-1-4725-0638-2
	ePub:	978-1-4725-1035-8

Library of Congress Cataloging-in-Publication Data
A catalog record for this book is available from the Library of Congress.

Series: Critical Companions

Typeset by RefineCatch Limited, Bungay, Suffolk
Printed and bound in Great Britain

CONTENTS

ACKNOWLEDGMENTS

For helping me to imagine this project I thank Erin Hurley. For their encouragement, support and flexibility, I am grateful to Bloomsbury Methuen Drama editor Mark Dudgeon and assistant editor Emily Hockley and copy-editor Ian Howe. The thoughtful criticism shared by series editor Kevin J. Wetmore also greatly improved this volume. Colleagues in the International Federation for Theatre Research Disability Performance Studies Working Group have offered timely and valuable feedback on earlier iterations of the ideas shared here. I offer particular thanks to Yvonne Schmidt and Mark Swetz for their establishment and support of that rich and rewarding group. In that context and others, Petra Kuppers has kindly shared many rich insights for which I would also like to offer thanks. I am also grateful to the Canadian Association for Theatre Research and the Society for Disability Studies for the many valuable dialogues and debates concerning disability, drama, theatre, and performance over time. The generous contributors to this volume—Michael Davidson, Ann M. Fox, Terry Galloway, M. Shane Grant, Ben Gunter, Carrie Sandahl, and Jenny Sealey were a pleasure to work with and they all have my sincere thanks. I would also like to acknowledge the financial support of the Social Sciences and Humanities Research Council of Canada during the tenure of this project. Michael Davidson's chapter in Part II of this book is a revised and updated version of his earlier essay "'Everyman his Specialty': Beckett, Disability and Dependence," first published in *The Journal of Literary and Cultural Disability Studies*, Vol. 1, No. 2 (2007), pp. 55–68. We are grateful to the journal for allowing us to republish this revised version here. For their helpful assistance and keen attention to details I thank research assistants Kelsey Blair, Rebecca Gold, Julia Henderson, and Parie Leung. As always, I am grateful to Matthew and Maggie for their love, laughter and patience.

INTRODUCTION

Writing in 2012, the late and highly influential disability studies scholar
Tobin Siebers posed a provocative question:

> To what concept, other than the idea of disability, might be referred
> modern art's love affair with misshapen and twisted bodies, stunning
> variety of human forms, intense representation of traumatic injury
> and psychological alienation, and unyielding preoccupation with
> wounds and tormented flesh?[1]

This book, largely inspired by Siebers' question and research, extends the
reach of this question to modern drama and its many invocations of
"misshapen and twisted bodies" (e.g. the band of mendicants in Brecht's
Threepenny Opera), "stunning variety of human forms" (e.g. the cast of
Beckett's *Endgame*), "intense representation of traumatic injury and
psychological alienation" (e.g. Williams' *The Glass Menagerie*, Wedekind's
Spring Awakening), and "unyielding preoccupation with wounds and
tormented flesh" (e.g. Büchner's *Woyzeck*).[2] Readers will no doubt be able to
add further modern plays to these examples. Moreover, the many manifestos
associated with modern drama and modern theatre offer further evidence in
support of disability's central place in their aesthetics.[3] Siebers' question
presses us to recognize how the idea of disability animates so much
modern drama and other theatrically oriented writing. For Siebers, the idea
of disability is best understood as central rather than incidental:

> Disability is not therefore, one subject of art among others. It is not
> merely a theme. It is not only a personal or autobiographical response
> embedded in an artwork. It is not solely a political act. It is all of these
> things, but it is more. It is more because disability is properly speaking
> an aesthetic value, which is to say, it participates in a system of
> knowledge that provides materials for and increases critical
> consciousness about the way that some bodies make other bodies
> feel.[4]

Contemporary theatre artists, audiences, critics, and scholars are all connected to disability's aesthetic value, for all participate in the systems of knowledge and culture that Siebers describes. This is true whether or not an individual makes explicit claims to be a disability artist, a disabled patron seeks theatre accessibility, or a critic encounters work under the label of "disability theatre." Indeed, artists, audiences, critics, and scholars who have no connection to any of these modes of theatre engagement are equally involved in disability aesthetics, for theatre has long contributed to "the way that some bodies make other bodies feel." Aesthetic value may be felt in terms of who gets to attend the theatre or not, whose sensory experiences are privileged in the theatre or not, who has been able to receive theatre training to take on professional roles or not, who is cast or not, who finds their bodily experiences shared onstage or not, who finds such stage offerings resonant with their own bodily experience or not, and who finds beauty in the theatre or not.

It is likely that anyone who participates in contemporary theatre will encounter at least one if not many disabled figures, themes, or tropes onstage. As disability studies scholars Carrie Sandahl, Victoria Ann Lewis, and others have pointed out, disabled figures and disability themes have haunted western theatre and drama for millennia (we can think of swollen-footed Oedipus's blindness, Isabella's *commedia dell'arte* mad scenes, Shakespeare's fashioning of Ophelia's madness and Richard III's "deform'd" and "unfinish'd" body) and continue to appear regularly (consider Sam Shepard's *Buried Child*, Mark Medoff's *Children of a Lesser God*, Martin McDonagh's *Cripple of Inishmaan*, David Auburn's *Proof*, Maria Irene Fornes's *Mud*, Tracy Letts' *August: Osage County* and *Bug*, and Sarah Kane's *4:48 Psychosis*).[5] Most western theatre artists, patrons, critics, and scholars will therefore likely encounter many such figures, characters, themes, and tropes in their lifetime. Further, whether such artists, patrons, critics, or scholars are experienced with cognitive, sensory, mobility, and/or other physical disabilities or are what disability activists call TABs (the "temporarily able-bodied"), most will also likely find themselves as or among disabled people in theatre, notwithstanding prevailing barriers to the full participation of disabled people both on and offstage.[6]

As many disability artists, scholars, and activists before me have urged, it is important to think about theatre's role in the "system of knowledge that provides materials for and increases critical consciousness about the way that some bodies make other bodies feel."[7] When directors make choices about play selection, venue, casting, design, marketing, and accessibility, whom do they imagine in their artistic teams, communities, and audiences? When critics assess works, do they imagine readers with lived disability experience? When actors perform onstage, how are their bodies and performance choices read, understood, and felt? These and many related questions are asked often among disability theatre and performance artists, activists, critics, and scholars. As we shall see, a robust and growing scholarship has emerged around disability theatre and performance, offering evidence and insight about its challenges, successes, and potential in a range of international contexts. This book will draw from this lively scholarship but also turns on a more particular set of questions concerning disability and modern drama. Chief among them is why disability is so often invoked in modern drama and what a critical disability studies and disability arts perspective has brought or might bring to understanding and producing these plays for contemporary stages.

This book engages then with two contested terms and fields of study: disability and modern drama. Modernism and disability theorist Janet Lyon has recently described "disability" as "an unstable, capacious" term and in Chapter 1 we will relate her assertions to the shifting ground and models associated with the term over time.[8] It is important to note here, however, that defining modern drama has also been an increasingly and generatively difficult challenge for scholars. Some have argued for modern drama as a particular aesthetic, rejecting or defamiliarizing traditional subjects and forms; others have tied it to a profound conceptual shift associated with modernity and "a climate of thought, feeling, and opinion"[9]; still others have associated the term with particular playwrights, periods, and plays. From the realism of Ibsen, often called the father of modern drama, to the naturalism of Zola and Strindberg to various "isms" (e.g. formalism, expressionism, surrealism, symbolism, futurism) of the avant-garde and the epic dramatic form and defamiliarization techniques of Brecht, what holds together such a broad and amorphous concept like modern drama is not always evident or clear.

Take, for salient example, the 2003 collection *Modern Drama: Defining the Field*, in which editors Ric Knowles, Joanne Tompkins, and W.B. Worthen gathered essays from a 2000 conference on the same topic, all of which sought to make sense of the word pairing in the new millennium.[10] In the volume's introduction, Knowles notes an earlier era in which scholarship concerning modern drama referenced European and American dramaturgies since 1850, "as though the so-called Modern Age (or modernist 'style') arrived everywhere at the same time and extended, always, to the present."[11]

He outlines how the term "modern drama" becomes much less transparent when read through scholarship that questions the stability of periodization associated with modernity, challenges "historical master narratives" and takes seriously the implications of globalization, interculturalism, and postcolonialism.[12] He concludes by suggesting that the volume announces "for the field of modern drama studies, what the editors hope is a new openness to questionings of period and generic boundaries; to questionings of scholarly and generic privilege based on class, race, nation, ethnicity, gender, and sexuality; and to questionings of all kinds, especially those that haven't yet been thought of or understood."[13]

In this same spirit of openness and questioning, this volume adds disability, using the term as leading disability historian Catherine J. Kudlick suggests, "not as an isolated, individual medical pathology but instead as a key defining social category on a par with race, class and gender."[14] Disability artists and scholars have been interested to discover what a disability perspective might bring to the analysis and stage production of those modern plays which return so often to contemporary western stages in urban professional theatres, regional and repertory theatres, university, college and conservatory training theatres, festival theatres, community theatres, and other regular producers of western drama-based theatre. Accordingly, this book is most interested in modern drama that has returned again and again to these stages, haunting culture and shaping the ways in which disability is performed and understood.

Referring to Ibsen as the most influential dramatist of the modern European theatre, theatre historian Marvin Carlson expands a commonplace assertion among Ibsen scholars that all of Ibsen's plays, not just his 1881 text, might be called *Ghosts*.[15] Building from the influential insights of scholars Herbert Blau and Richard Schechner, Carlson argues that, insofar as they are all haunted by memory of past performances, all plays might be called *Ghosts*.[16] Theorizing theatre as a memory machine, he considers the physical theatre to be one of human culture's most haunted structures, "a site of the continuing reinforcement of memory by surrogation."[17] It therefore has been and continues to be important for those interested in theatre and those interested in disability to query the legacy and enduring currency of this drama, particularly in terms of its role in shaping how disability is felt and perceived, understood and experienced, hailed and resonated. For example, introducing her groundbreaking play anthology, *Beyond Victims and Villains: Contemporary Plays by Disabled Playwrights*, Victoria Ann Lewis cites cultural critic Terry Eagleton's oft-quoted claim that "Most of any present is made up of the past."[18] She underlines how contemporary engagement with disability in theatre must contend with a long history of disability representation. Glossing this history, she explores the legacies of the eponymous victims and villains of her title (e.g. Tiny Tim as victim and Richard III as villain) and the longstanding practice, particularly in classic melodrama, of signaling moral character through visual markers of disability (e.g. the use of hooks, peg legs, and eye patches), or of using disabled characters to drive plots of personal transformation and heroic or otherwise inspirational overcoming.[19] The metaphor of disability that haunts western theatre, she argues, "has been so successful in the imaginative arena that it now functions as real."[20]

Emphasizing disability's critical place in modern drama, a growing number of scholars and critics have pointed to such examples as W.B. Yeats' Blind Man in *On Baile's Strand,* J.M. Synge's blind Mary and Martin Doul in *The Well of the Saints,* Henrik Ibsen's syphilitic Oswald in *Ghosts,* Bertolt Brecht's silent Kattrin in *Mother Courage,* Tennessee Williams' limping Laura Wingfield in *The Glass Menagerie,* Samuel Beckett's blind Hamm and his bin-dwelling parents in *Endgame,* and Sophie Treadwell's neurasthenic Young Woman in *Machinal.*[21] The list goes on.

The work of Tobin Siebers presses us, however, to think that the remarkable number of disabled figures and themes is not an accident of chance. Rather, he argues, disability holds a critical place in modern aesthetics. Modern artists have demonstrated a particular awareness and use of disability, finding in it "a powerful tool for rethinking human appearence, intelligence, behavior and creativity."[22] Siebers distinguishes between a commercial culture interested in marketing human beauty and a western aesthetic culture developed over centuries that has increasingly understood human variation as "the motor that drives the appearance of the beautiful."[23] In his pivotal book *Disability Aesthetics,* Siebers locates disability at the center of this motor and modern aesthetics:

> Since human feeling is central to aesthetic history, it is to be expected that disability will crop up everywhere because the disabled body and mind always elicit powerful emotions. I am making a stronger claim: that disability is integral to modern aesthetics and that the influence of disability on art has grown, not dwindled, over the course of time. If this is the case, we may expect disability to exert even greater power over art in the future. We need to consider, then, how art is changed when we conceive of disability as an aesthetic value in itself. In

particular, it is worth asking how the presence of disability requires us to revise traditional conceptions of aesthetic production and appreciation.[24]

While Siebers pursued these questions largely through compelling case studies of modern sculpture, painting and performance art, in this book we will extend the focus to drama. Why have disabled figures and disability themes been so central to modern drama? What role has disability played in their continuing endurance as oft-produced plays in educational, commercial and alternative theatre venues around the world? Most importantly, how and why have disability theatre artists and critics intervened more recently to reimagine disability's place and function in these plays?

Pursuing these questions helps us to address Ann M. Fox's observation that while the field of disability performance studies has grown and enriched scholarship over the past decades, "[m]odern and contemporary drama in particular have been largely underexplored from a disability studies perspective, with the few critical projects extant mostly emphasizing either problematic or progressive portrayals."[25] Fox presses disability scholars to complicate their readings of such plays and others "not written from within disability culture or with an explicit 'message.'"[26] She calls for disability and other scholars to move beyond only assessing stereotypes, or valorizing representations as more realistic or progressive. Generative criticism, she argues, citing the examples of Michael Davidson, Ato Quayson, David Mitchell and Sharon Snyder as well as Tobin Siebers, has followed from asking, "What paradigms can best assist those of us doing this work in tracing disability's presence, depiction and function within a text?"[27]

Fox's question aligns with this book's primary focus on what a critical disability studies and disability arts perspective brings to the study and production of modern drama. Mingling the perspectives of practitioners and scholars here presents a critical opportunity to brush theory across the grain of practice and vice versa. Sometimes unforeseen practical encounters can present stark evidence in support of theory.

Throughout his book *Concerto for the Left Hand: Disability and the Defamiliar Body*, Michael Davidson employs "the trope of aesthetic defamiliarisation as it was applied to the modernist avant-garde to speak of the ways that disability lays bare the body as an unstable, uncontainable site."[28] Just as modernist avant-garde artists argued that art exists to "lay bare the bones" of the familiar, quotidian, and unnoticed, Davidson argues that "we might say that disability becomes the ethos of the social insofar as it exposes cultural assumptions about the corporeality of the social body … disabled bodies, far from occupying roles at the margins of aesthetic discourse, are constitutive of cultural productions in general."[29] Davidson cites for example a French advertising campaign that featured non-disabled people having to navigate an urban landscape designed solely to serve disabled people (e.g. walking people sidelined by speeding wheelchairs, sighted people frustrated by libraries that only have books written in Braille, hearing people frustrated by attendants who only speak sign language).

Many of the disability theatre productions considered in this book similarly defamiliarize drama and its cultural assumptions. In Part II, Jenny Sealey, Artistic Director of the leading UK disabled-led theatre company Graeae, explains how, as someone practiced in thinking about access for Deaf and hearing-impaired artists and audiences such as herself, she made assumptions about Sarah Kane's controversial 1995 text *Blasted* that she pursued through production and that ultimately rendered it strange and new for others:

> With *Blasted*, the most curious thing was that I didn't understand what Sarah Kane meant when she said in her opening notes, everything in round brackets functions as a line. I thought, wow, Sarah Kane is way ahead of her game. She is writing audio-description, because most of the things in the round brackets were saying what people were doing: Ian gulps down a gin. Cate takes off her dress. Cate looks around the room. Ian gets his gun. And I thought, well, that's audio-description, that is wonderful. So, that's exactly what I did in my naïveté. I had the actors voicing those very lines. … What this pairing and its effect did for me was exactly what I thought Kane wanted. She did not want anyone to escape. Every single word she had to say was about our apathy and our lack of engagement with Bosnia and also our own wars at home. Our production of *Blasted* forced everyone to hear or see every single word. It became so claustrophobic, you couldn't switch off.[30]

Sealey's directorial techniques thus defamiliarized Kane's text by making its dramaturgical devices explicit. As Davidson reminds us, when Victor Shklovsky coined the term "defamiliarization" in 1917, he argued that "[t]he purpose of art is to impart the sensation of things as they are perceived and not as they are known. The technique of art is to make objects 'unfamiliar,' to make forms difficult, to increase the difficulty and length of perception because the process of perception is an aesthetic end in itself and must be prolonged."[31] Sealey's choices in service of disabled bodies and her company's aesthetics literally added difficulty and length to the perception of Kane's blistering text. In the chapters that follow, we will explore further examples of ways in which disabled artists, scholars and activists defamiliarize what is modern and dramatic in modern drama.

Organization of the Work

This Critical Companion aims to highlight the critical value of disability studies precepts and disability theatre practices for contemporary theatre practice and study. I was drawn to this project as someone who, through training and employment, has spent significant time in academic theatre settings and urban environments wherein modern drama is regularly taught and produced, most often without engaging disability theatre precepts. Conceived and written for the Critical Companion series, the structure of the book aims to engage with scholars, students, and practitioners who are either new to or familiar with the debates occasioned by the pairing of "disability" and "theatre." Part I includes four chapters that build on each other to introduce disability theatre practice, its precepts and debates, and some key examples of its engagement with modern drama. Chapter 1, "What is Disability Theatre?" begins by tracing the rise of disability arts and culture and the disability movement to provide historical context for thinking about disability theatre's primary principles, critical terms, internal debates, and key challenges to mainstream theatre practice. Chapter 2, "Critical Embodiment and Casting," focuses on the question of casting, a vexed topic in relation to which there has been a great deal of public debate, critical discussion, and advocacy in support of training and casting disabled actors. This chapter engages with ideas shared by leading disability performance scholars, critics, and artists to understand how questions of casting are inextricably bound up with demands for accessible theatre training and other professionalization opportunities. The chapter also includes references to resources aimed at developing and supporting the full inclusion of disabled people in theatre, from training and auditioning to casting and performance. Chapter 3, "Staging Inclusion," extends the logic of the prior chapters to examine another foundational aspect of disability theatre practice: the provision of inclusive and accessible space. What inclusion strategies, accessible built environments, and adaptive technologies have disability theatre artists experimented with and favored? How do these kinds of inclusion and accessibility choices inform aesthetics? The final chapter of Part I, "Inherited Plays and New Approaches," investigates specific choices in a range of important and distinctive disability theatre productions of modern drama. The analysis centers on two recent touring co-productions involving Graeae Theatre Company: in 2014, Bertolt Brecht, Elisabeth Hauptmann and Kurt Weill's *The Threepenny Opera*; and, in 2015, Federico Garcia Lorca's *Blood Wedding*. The chapter also investigates Theatre Workshop Scotland's 2007 production of Samuel Beckett's *Endgame* directed by Robert Rae and starring leading UK disability theatre artists Nabil Shaban and Garry Robson. Each production provides a valuable means to uncover how, in the words of prominent disability studies scholar Simi Linton, disability has been rethought, rewritten, and recast.[32]

Part II of this book begins with two critical essays by leading disability studies scholars on the topic of modern drama. In " 'Every Man his Specialty': Beckett, Disability, and Dependence," Michael Davidson argues that Beckett's pairing of characters as co-dependents—from Hamm and Clov in *Endgame* to Vladimir and Estragon in *Waiting for Godot*—binds them together in desperate, sometimes tragi-comic relations which challenge communitarian ideals of mutual support and charity while "dismodernizing" notions of liberal autonomy and agency. His readings of Beckett's drama and other work thus reference two influential disability studies discourses: Lennard Davis' coinage and articulation of "dismodernism" and a robust scholarship concerning disability and dependency generated by Albert Memmi, Martha Nussbaum, Michael Berubé, Eva Kittay, and Alasdair MacIntyre. Beyond close readings of Beckett's *Waiting for Godot, Happy Days, Endgame*, and *Rough for Theatre I*, Davidson's analysis also engages the larger context of Beckett's *oeuvre*. In each case he finds compelling evidence that, instead of disability acting as a metaphor for something else, in Beckett's work it is "the constitutive feature of the social contract."[33] While acknowledging that Beckett would not have been focused on "the claims of disability on social justice," Davidson focuses on the co-dependent relationships and disabled characters throughout Beckett's *oeuvre*, arguing provocatively that, in Beckett's plays, the human condition "*is* living with disability and dependence, however abject their portrayal may be."[34]

Where Davidson explores several of Beckett's texts, in the chapter that follows, "Reclaiming the Ordinary Extraordinary Body: Or, The Importance of *The Glass Menagerie* for Literary Disability Studies," Ann M. Fox offers a historically contextualized analysis of a single play, Tennessee Williams' *The Glass Menagerie*. She builds from Davidson and other disability theorists

Tobin Siebers and Ato Quayson's respective calls for analysis that does not simply read drama and other texts as progressive or regressive in the context of a self-conscious disability culture. She argues rather for an expanded sense of disability theatre, one that goes beyond the work of playwrights with clear ties to disability culture. Demonstrating such plays' importance for disability history, she identifies a hitherto lost opportunity for the field, posing critical questions to help frame a new approach: "What could a reconsideration of the most canonical images of disability in dramatic literature model for directors, teachers, critics, and audiences? What could it do—if anything—to help us reconsider literature's role in portraying disability history and offering challenges to ableism?"[35] In pursuit of these questions, she revisits prior disability studies approaches to studying *The Glass Menagerie*, including her own, and wonders "if we might use a reconsideration of Laura as a model for a more nuanced deployment of disability. In so doing, we can come to see that modern drama, particularly that which was popular, is another source of disability history to which we all might productively attend."[36] Through her analysis of the play in its historical context, its attending scholarly criticism and some provocative recent productions involving disabled artists whose insights she shares, she models exciting critical and artistic possibilities for those interested in both the play and disability: "we can find examples of disability representation that, when more carefully parsed, suggest that disability has been an integral subject and part of social protest for longer than we might suspect, distracted by the superficial disability drag of characters who seem too untrue to be any good."[37] Fox emphasizes the value of this approach for those familiar with disability studies as well as newcomers to the field in that it prompts a reclaiming of disability history that appreciates disability's presence as "generative, innovative, and creative" without disavowing ableism and oppression.[38]

The final two entries in Part II break from the essay form and explore the relationships between disability and modern drama from artistic perspectives. The first is an interview with Jenny Sealey, Artistic Director of the UK's Graeae Theatre Company since 1997. The pioneering disabled-led theatre company has been drawn to modern plays since its earliest days in the 1980s. While we explore some of these productions in the context of the company's history in the closing chapter of Part I, here, in "Access Aesthetics and Modern Drama: An Interview with Jenny Sealey on Graeae Theatre Company's *The Threepenny Opera* and *Blood Wedding*," Sealey shares her sense of the aesthetics, practical choices, and impulses driving the company's work. She reflects particularly on the company's touring productions of Brecht's *The Threepenny Opera* in 2014 and Lorca's *Blood Wedding* in 2015, offering critical insights about how their trademark "access aesthetics" functioned practically in these works.

Following the interview is a provocative play entitled *Shattering the Glass Menagerie* by celebrated disability artists and scholars Terry Galloway, M. Shane Grant, Ben Gunter, and Carrie Sandahl. Although the play form of the final chapter distinguishes it from others in this volume, its creative and dramatic structure extends the spirit of artistic intervention and critical re-interpretation of modern plays demonstrated by disability performance artists cited earlier. The play turns around a conversation between Galloway and Sandahl as they re-enact, question, mock, delight in, argue, and otherwise wrestle with Williams' text in light of disability scholarship and activism, crip and queer identities, as well as their own personal connections with the narrative. Mingling key scenes from *The Glass Menagerie* with their own critical and creative interventions, they demonstrate diverse disability experiences of the text. Like the chapters that precede it, the play reads modern drama through a disability studies and activist perspective. Speaking back to the metaphoric treatment of impairment, the script provides further evidence in support of Michael Davidson's account of "Disabled artists and activists [who] have attempted to reverse this pattern, turning their cameo appearances in such theaters back upon the audience, refusing the crippling gaze of an ableist society and reassigning the meanings of disability in their own terms."[39] Complementing Fox's earlier arguments and the other prior chapters, the play resists any definitive placing of Williams' play on a continuum of progressive or regressive texts, inviting instead an understanding of disability aesthetics in relation to disability history and an awareness of disability history as archived in the play itself.

PART I
CRITICAL SURVEY OF DISABILITY THEATRE AESTHETICS, POLITICS, AND PRACTICES

CHAPTER 1
WHAT IS DISABILITY THEATRE?

The questions concerning disability theatre and modern drama that drive this book emerge in the wake of several decades of Western-based disability activism, disability studies scholarship, and artistic innovation. Disability theatre is one branch of a wider international disability arts and culture movement which seeks to address and redress the very idea of disability in the modern arts and, by extension, society. Undermining stereotypes and stigma on the one hand, and pressing the boundaries of aesthetic convention on the other, disability theatre is thus both activist and artistic in orientation. To make sense of the term disability theatre, we begin here by exploring its place in the disability arts and culture movement, and illustrating some of the ways in which diverse artists have appealed to and created disability theatre practices and aesthetics. Recognizing that words and terminology matter, we conclude the discussion by explaining a series of neologisms which are widely used in disability arts, culture, and studies but which may remain obscure to others. It is best to start, however, by examining the key concept at the heart of this endeavor—disability.

Disability has a long and complex cultural history that raises fundamental questions about identity, definitions of normalcy, and the social conditions of everyday life. Although some argue that disability "has existed throughout human history, cutting across time and space," others would locate its emergence as an idea in western modernity.[1] Drawing on Michel Foucault's lectures about the "abnormal," Sharon L. Snyder and David T. Mitchell argue that disability's origins may be found in the eighteenth century when the emergence of a notion of an abnormal body coincided with the development of networks of knowledge and power which classified, measured, and imposed cultural diagnoses on bodies.[2] In a related but different vein, Lennard Davis insists that any understanding of the disabled body must take into account the concept of the norm or normal body and he highlights the "rather remarkable fact that that the constellation of words describing this concept—'normal,' 'normalcy,' 'normality,' 'norm,' 'average,' 'abnormal'—all entered the European languages rather late in human history ... It is possible to date the coming into consciousness in English of an idea of the 'norm' over the period 1840–1860."[3] As the idea of a *normal person* emerged, Davis suggests, degrees of abnormality could also be considered, even measured. With the rise of the eugenics movement in the late nineteenth century, abnormality came to be considered as a sign and cause of wider social dysfunction in which medical science was misdirected "to the designation of pathology as a transmissible characteristic of human biology."[4] This provided the rationale, Snyder and Mitchell contend, for a shift from curative to more coercive and "custodial" practices of a pervasive "diagnostic regime" to discipline disability.[5] Pointing to the countless ways in which people are measured and disciplined according to norms from birth to death, Davis demonstrates how the idea of the normal "permeates our contemporary life"; the product of a historical moment, it "is part of a notion of progress, of industrialization, and of ideological consolidation of the power of the bourgeoisie. The implications of the hegemony of normalcy are profound and extend into the very heart of cultural production."[6]

While tracing the concept of the normal helps to explain the emergence and evolution of disability as a cultural idea, it is also important to recognize that contemporary activist understandings of disability emerged from a relatively recent period of political struggle and organization. Although one can trace advocacy for particular disability experiences to the early twentieth century through such organizations as institutes for the Blind or organizations for the handicapped, a wider spectrum of disability identity and political interest emerged in western countries in the late 1960s and 1970s. Modeled partly on contemporary civil rights campaigns from which it drew inspiration, a modern disability movement emerged which identified common cause across different disability communities and experiences. In the United States, for example, the independent living movement, founded by Ed Roberts in Berkeley in the early 1970s, argued for the right of persons with disabilities to control the conditions of their own lives and expressed a basic belief that persons with disabilities should wrest control over their circumstances from charities, experts, and institutions. At the national level disability activists argued for the extension of civil rights to persons with disabilities in important pieces of legislation, such as the 1973 Rehabilitation Act in the USA. In the same period, the Union of the Physically Impaired Against Segregation organized in the UK as a strong voice for disability advocacy, lobbying for a new social perspective on impairments as physical conditions which were made disabling by inaccessible environments and exclusionary attitudes and policies.[7] Disability activism in this period thus sought to express common cause among different impairment communities and advocate for social and political change.[8]

In variegated fashion, different governments conceded ground to disability rights advocates—taking their views into consideration in major moments of constitutional evolution in Canada in the early 1980s, for example, and passing legislation to support independent living for persons with disabilities in the UK and USA in the 1990s. Two landmark pieces of legislation, the Americans with Disabilities Act (1990) and the UK's Disability Discrimination Act (1995), addressed disability at national levels and provided education and employment supports for persons with disabilities.[9] Internationally, the United Nations provided a focus for discussions about disability during the International Year of Disabled Persons in 1981 and recognized disability rights through the Convention on the Rights of Persons with Disabilities in 2008.[10] While the funding of services for persons with disabilities has been an ongoing battle, legal and diplomatic changes such as these marked a fundamental shift in the cultural and legal articulation of disability.[11]

As in other civil rights movements, disability activists have focused thoughtfully on society's language for hailing disabled people, wresting back words from ableist understanding. For example, in *Beyond Victims and Villains: Contemporary Drama by Disabled Playwrights*, Victoria Ann Lewis explores how the movement and the plays in her collection champion the term "disabled." She points to the activist work in the 1970s at Berkeley, "when a group of significantly disabled young people, calling themselves the 'Rolling Quads,' decided to throw off the invisibility cloak of shame and reclaim the negative term 'disability' as a badge of pride and power."[12] Reclaiming the terms "disability" and "disabled," Lewis argues, against such euphemisms as "differently-abled," "handi-capable," or "special," was a self-conscious strategy: "Disability oppression, advocates argue, will not be erased by a more sensitive etiquette, but rather by a recognition of the social and economic conditions that characterize life lived with a disability."[13] Whether using the term "disabled people" or "people with disabilities," the word "disability" itself has therefore been remobilized by advocates for its power to reference disabling social and economic conditions, building connections among an otherwise strikingly diverse and vast complement of people through their shared experience of oppression.

Disability activism also left its mark on academic research and gave rise to the field of disability studies. Just as disability activists argued for new ways of understanding disability and impairment experiences, disability studies scholars began to define new ways to conceive of disability as a social and cultural phenomenon. Much of this work developed against what came to be called "the medical model," an understanding of impairment that "renders disability as a series of physiological, psychological, and functional pathologies originating within the bodies of individuals."[14] Coming from a range of different perspectives, disability studies scholars argued that the medical model problematically treated disability as an individual condition while ignoring the social and cultural context in which it existed. From this critique emerged the highly influential social model, which distinguishes impairment from disability, connecting the former with the individual, private body and the latter with the structural and public body.[15] Mike Oliver explains the fundamental difference between these conceptions: "Models are ways of translating ideas into practice and the idea underpinning the individual [or medical] model was that of personal tragedy, while the idea underpinning the social model was that of externally imposed restriction."[16] Like gender, race, and class, disability is thus understood as a social category, one that historian Paul K. Longmore ascribes to "deep-seated, pervasive cultural devaluation and systemic institutionalized discrimination."[17] The recognition among some disability activists of a shared common experience, particularly, as Longmore argues, in the US context, also prompted the development of a minority model of disability.

Signaling the connection to other civil rights campaigns, the minority rights model argued that the social experience of disability led to political action that in turn produced a shared identity. In *Disability Theory*, Tobin Siebers explains that, "[t]ired of discrimination and claiming disability as a positive identity, people with disabilities insist on the pertinence of disability to the human condition, on the value of disability as a form of diversity, and on the power of disability as a critical concept for thinking about human identity in general."[18] While important distinctions were made between the focus on the social conditions of disablement in the social model and the positive identification of disability identity in the minority rights model, Longmore rightly notes that both "paradigms shift[ed] the focus from individuals and pathologies to institutions and ideologies."[19]

After the turn of the century, new questions began to be raised about the usefulness of these social claims about disability from within the field itself. In 2001, for example, Tom Shakespeare and Nicholas Watson provocatively entitled a critical essay "The social model of disability: An outdated ideology?"[20] They raised questions about the kinds of dualisms that circulated within the field between disablement and impairment and called for a more critical approach to the meaning of embodiment. Others emphasized the need for a more complex reading of disability identity, rent by other forms of identity, difference, and inequality, as well as culturally and historically diverse embodiments. These critical questions ultimately turned on notions of embodiment and identity, giving rise to a new cultural model of disability.

In *Cultural Locations of Disability*, David Mitchell and Sharon Snyder note that proponents of the social model have long distinguished "between disability and impairment, arguing that the latter term is a neutral designator of biological difference while the former represents a social process termed 'disablement.'"[21] Seeking to blur this clean distinction between the terms, Snyder and Mitchell align themselves with Sally French, Simi Linton, Susan Wendell, and other scholars who "recognize disability as a site of phenomenological value that is not purely synonymous with the processes of social disablement."[22] Moreover, they argue, the cultural model finds in impairment "both human variation encountering environmental obstacles *and* socially mediated difference that lends group identity and phenomenological perspective."[23] To make sense of this "*and*," especially given that our primary point of cultural reference here is drama, it is revealing that their explanation of the cultural model's benefits cites *Oedipus Rex*; "where the limping Oedipus solves the sphinx's riddle *because* of his experience with mobility impairment. ... This insight shifts disability from either a medical pathology or signifier of social discrimination into a source of embodied revelation."[24] Their reading reminds us not only of how very long some cultural narratives of disability have been haunting western culture but also of the ways in which critical disability studies opens up such narratives to readings that demand fuller engagement with embodiment, disability experience, knowledge, and history.

Further, and illuminating of the "phenomenological perspective" that Mitchell and Snyder outline above, disability theatre takes up a particularly critical role in this model. In her 2010 book *Theatre and the Body*, Colette Conroy explains the link:

> Phenomenology is an important reference point for many scholars and practitioners of disability theatre. There is a huge difference between talking about "the body" and its experience of a theatre performance and talking about "bodies" and their experiences. *The body* supposes that there is an ideal or assumed body and that all people gain access to the pleasures of performance in broadly the same way. When we think about *bodies* as entities that see, feel and

move in radically different ways, as in disability theatre, the idealized *body* becomes disparate *bodies*. We can't suppose that the play offers one overriding "meaning" or a single coherent performance.[25]

As we will explore more fully in Chapter 4 when we examine contemporary disability theatre approaches to modern drama, just as a play can open up to multiple experiences and cultural interpretations, so too bodies themselves might experience and interpret disability differently.

In her recent summary of the term "disability," theorist Kanta Kochhar-Lindgren has emphasized the scholarly advances made by understanding disability as a cultural problematic rather than a fixed category. She also notes, however, persistent challenges in uniting what is otherwise a remarkably diverse complement of people under the term.[26] Sociologists who have studied disability cultures emphasize differences arising from particular gender, race, and class experiences of disability as well as the variegated engagement with a culture that many encounter for the first time in later life and from different disability experiences.[27] Socio-economic status, gender, sexuality, and age have the capacity to "exacerbate or modify" disability experience, experiences that can be further distinguished by their various connections to distinctive cognitive, sensory, and other physiological impairments, ages of acquisition, stigma, pain, severity, transience or intractibility, visibility or invisibility.[28] Simi Linton offers a vivid account of the sheer diversity of bodily experiences driving the impulse to "claim disability":

> We are everywhere these days, wheeling and loping down the street, tapping our canes, sucking on our breathing tubes, following our guide dogs, puffing and sipping on the mouth sticks that propel our motorized chairs. We may drool, hear voices, speak in staccato syllables, wear catheters to collect our urine, or live with a compromised immune system. We are all bound together, not by this list of our collective symptoms but by the social and political circumstances that have forged us as a group.[29]

As Linton suggests, the political power in coalition is undeniable but Kochhar-Lindgren and others are also keen not to lose the specificities of individual experience. As she neatly summarizes, "the ongoing challenge will be to identify disability as a discrete category, while also pluralizing our understanding of its manifestations."[30] To this end, she highlights the growing number of disability scholars—from Mairian Corker to Tobin Siebers—whose works emphasize the particular value of "reclaiming individual bodily experience through art, performance, and literature."[31] She points to greater engagement with disability art, performance, and literature as a primary means to "recuperate a more embodied reference point for disability and to claim a more visible social space in the public sphere."[32] In pursuit of these ends, the disability arts and culture work of the past decades has been crucial.

Disability arts and culture

In several respects, the disability arts and culture movement coincided with, contributed to, and drew upon the rise of disability rights activism. Emerging first in the UK and USA in the 1980s, the impulse to link art and activism made the aesthetic and cultural political: by claiming a place for disability experience in the arts as worthy and valuably different, the movement took aim at hackneyed stereotypes and the recurring use of disabilities as metaphors for something else. Contributors to the lively opening debates on and discussions of disability arts and culture decried false media images, advocated for greater participation and inclusion of disabled people, and sought to create art that expressed and explored disability as a valued human condition. Disability theatre was part of this ferment, addressing the displacement of persons with disabilities from audiences and the stage, and critiquing directly and powerfully the casting of disabled roles with non-disabled performers and the representation of disability in drama, theatre, film, media, and performance. As with the wider disability arts and culture movement, disability theatre artists engaged in both critiques of dominant modes of performing disability and explorations of new ways to put disability on stage.

While the disability arts and culture movement sprang from disability rights activist programs primarily in the UK and USA, in subsequent decades it became increasingly international in reach and orientation. New communications technologies, the unwinding of public institutions under neo-liberal policies and increasing international collaborations around disability arts and culture all played a role in shifting the scale of activity. As a result, the foundations of disability arts and culture at the local and national scale contributed to a new level of activity beyond the nation. Local disability arts groups built coalitions, attended international symposia, festivals, and conferences, and began to construct their own institutions and communications in a form of alter-globalization—or globalization that adopts the tools of new global communications to subvert the logic of the market. While these new collaborations did not displace or replace the active local fields of artistic exploration, they have nevertheless connected it in important and challenging ways and increased the broader field's international reach and recognition.

National and international disability arts festivals played a major role in connecting disability arts communities with local, national, and international colleagues. In many cases, they sought to "kickstart" disability arts, in the words of Canadian artists and activists who founded in 2001 the kickstART! celebration of disability art and culture series in Vancouver and Victoria, British Columbia.[33] Festivals in the UK which emerged as part of this trend included DaDaFest Celebration of Disability and Deaf Culture, DEGENERATE International Festival of Disability Art (Theatre Workshop, Edinburgh) and the Xposure festival.[34] The High Beam Disability Arts Festival in Adelaide, Australia as well as the Giant Leap Festival in New Zealand also focused on presenting disability artists. In Canada, Toronto's Workman Theatre Project started the Madness and Arts World Festival series in 2003 which focused on presenting disability art connected to the experience of mental illness; from 2001 to 2012, Calgary's Stage Left Productions also ran an annual, internationally connected disability arts festival entitled Balancing Acts. Bodies of Work: The Chicago Festival of Disability has likewise presented disability artists and speakers. This is far from an exhaustive list but it offers some sense of the range of events and their diversity.

For disability theatre artists, festivals have offered particularly valuable means to share their work and connect with like-minded artists outside their region. Being able to share the costs of accessibility, space, and marketing under a festival banner is a boon for most theatre artists given the often high levels of capital and labor needed to produce theatre. Further, sharing ideas about art as well as strategies around best professional practices with others who are already familiar with the particularities of disability theatre has been tremendously valuable and energizing over time. Connecting discrete pockets of disability arts activity with the larger, more-connected hubs like London, Chicago, San Francisco, Toronto, and Adelaide, festivals have also provided valuable forums for critical exchange about the language and political dimensions of disability arts and cultural work.[35]

Although the national, formal, economic, and other contexts for these various efforts are diverse, they are linked by a shared interest in legitimating experiences of disability. In his valuable survey of disability and art practices in the UK, Paul Anthony Darke distinguishes *artists with disabilities* from the more politically charged category of *disability artists*. The latter, he argues, are connected to disability art, an activist practice "based upon legitimizing the experiences of disabled people as equal within art and all other cultural practices ... Disability Art is a challenge to, an undermining of (as a minimum), traditional aesthetic and social values."[36] He is concerned that disability artists who might achieve mainstream success need to be careful not to undermine the activist aims that gave rise to disability arts in the first place. For some disability arts activists, however, the lines are less clearly drawn. For example, while she is a firm advocate of the activist aims Darke expresses, disability artist and filmmaker Bonnie Klein nonetheless argues that simply "to give permission to the artist in your body is an outrageous act of defiance."[37]

Further questions arise among those who would seek to include and those who would seek to distinguish or exclude Deaf arts from disability arts and culture. In "Deaf People: A Different Center," Carol Padden and Tom Humphries argue that the label of "disabled" has "historically not belonged to Deaf people. It suggests political self-representations and goals unfamiliar to the group. When Deaf people discuss their deafness, they use terms deeply related to their language, their past, and their community. Their enduring concerns have been the preservation of their language, policies for educating deaf children, and maintenance of their social and political organizations."[38] Although it has been an uneasy history, they argue, over time some Deaf community members have strategically coalesced with disability groups, but, they insist, "'disabled' is not a primary term of self-identification, indeed it is one that requires a disclaimer."[39] With strong claims to unique and independent histories, languages and cultural forms, and in some cases refusing to understand deafness as an impairment, Deaf culture advocates have not always sought or welcomed a strong connection with disability arts and culture. Others, by contrast, have found strong rationales for alignment.[40]

As these kinds of debates and concerns about naming and inclusion suggest, finding a coherent and fixed definition of disability culture is challenging. Insisting that "disability culture is no monoculture," Petra Kuppers has drawn from her extensive exposure to and involvement with disability arts practices around the world.[41] In her 2012 award-winning book *Disability Culture and Community Performance: Find a Strange and Twisted Shape*, she argues for thinking about disability culture as a polyvalent process:

Disability culture: there is a fine line here, between exclusionary essentialism on the one hand, and, on the other, the desire to mark the differences that disability-focused environments (which can include both non-disabled and disabled people) offer to mainstream ways of acknowledging bodies and their needs. I do not think that disability culture is something that comes "naturally" to people identified or identifying as disabled. And I do not think that disability culture is closed to non-disabled allies, or allies who do not wish to identify as either disabled or not. To me, disability culture is not a thing, but a process. Boundaries, norms, belongings: disability cultural environments can suspend a whole slew of rules, try to undo the history of exclusions that many of its members have experienced when they have heard or felt "you shouldn't be like this." At the same time, disability cultural environments have to safeguard against perpetuating or erecting other exclusions (based on racial stereotypes, class, gender, economic access, internalized ableism, etc.). This is all a lot of work, trying to think without victimization and exclusion, forgiving others and oneself when it is not yet working well, and being aware of the many different forces of privilege and power that mark how we got here, into this workshop, or onto the pages of this book. It needs an ongoing flow of contact, touch, questioning and affirmation, a flow of love.[42]

I include Kuppers' remarks at length here for her sense of disability culture as a series of processes filled with promise, delight, and frustrations when things are "not yet working well" resonate both with my own experiences and those shared by many others in the field. For example, in their introduction to the collection *Points of Contact: Disability, Art and Culture*, editors Susan Crutchfield and Marcy Epstein reflect back on their coordination with Joanne Leonard of the University of Michigan's spring 1995 This/Ability interdisciplinary conference on disability and the arts and its related art exhibit "Vis/Ability: Views from the Interior." They note that the conference was the first to assemble national disability activists, scholars, and artists for discussion of disability in the academy and its relationship to the arts. They also helpfully share that accommodation problems shaped people's experiences of both the conference and the exhibit, producing frustration and learning. For Crutchfield and Epstein, both the problem and solution in the earlier event lay partially in "the recognition among participants that we were practicing a relatively new discipline and experiencing a complex political struggle over the identity of the people attached to its development."[43] They also emphasize, however, the profound struggle of blending aesthetic and academic concerns with what they describe as the "powerful notion of *culture*—in the 'them and us' division that comes as we try to create a space for a disabled subject who has for centuries been the object of culture."[44]

It is a struggle that continues, as I witnessed twenty years later at a 2015 Toronto event entitled "The Republic of Inclusion," co-curated by Alex Bulmer and Sarah Garton Stanley as part of that year's Progress International Festival of Performance and Ideas.[45] The discussions involved scholars, local and visiting disability artists, other artists, and community members, all of whom were interested in thinking about building greater inclusion in Toronto's performing arts community. While much effort and care went into creating an inclusive space for participants and performers, part of the day's main discussion period was oriented toward thinking through collectively what it would mean to build a truly inclusive event. Thus, while the gathering produced excitement about its creative and practical inclusion efforts, organizers and participants afterwards were still able to highlight many important ways in which significantly greater inclusion might yet have been possible. Collectively, Kuppers, Crutchfield and Epstein, and the 2015 event demonstrate that the stakes are too high not to engage in disability culture's processes of negotiation, respecting its complexity, encouraging further experimentation while anticipating problems, mistakes, and renegotiations. Theatre and other live performing arts are of particular value in this process, driven as they frequently are to build shared space in which performers and audiences are co-present, mutually informing, and in communicative process.

Disability theatre

As part of the larger disability arts and culture movement, a movement with different origins in different national contexts, disability theatre is broadly connected to impulses for social justice in the face of ableist ideologies and practices as well as a profound recognition of disabled lives and experiences as inherently valuable, particularly in their connection to the full expression of what Mitchell and Snyder describe above as "human variation."[46] Disability theatre, drama, and performance have emerged as important sites in the movement. Theatre scholars Joan Lipkin and Ann M. Fox argued in 2002 that "[t]o speak of disability theater as an entity is to speak of a self-conscious artistic movement of roughly the last three decades, during which time writers and performers within disability culture have moved to create art as multifaceted as the community from which it emerges."[47] Disability theatre may thus be best understood as a kind of theatre-making that draws from disability culture's challenges to ableism and comprises a growing international field of practice remarkable for its political force, artistic re-imagining of theatre traditions, and lively aesthetic debates.

The rich international field that exists today emerged from diverse and often disconnected points of origin. One of the ways to make sense of disability theatre is to survey a diverse complement of those companies associated with the name. As many of the companies focused upon later in this book operate in the UK, here the focus expands to include examples from elsewhere to underline the form's broader international reach, breadth, and range. To begin, consider the early history and *oeuvre* of two important disability theatre companies—Phamaly, based in Denver, Colorado and Back to Back Theatre in Geelong, Australia.

Phamaly

Phamaly is a Denver-based disability theatre company that produces musicals, theatre, and training workshops. Founded in 1989 as the Physically Handicapped Actors and Musical Artists League by a group of five friends who had met at the Boettcher School, the company's mandate originally focused on producing "traditional theatre in nontraditional ways (i.e. with disabled performers), not necessarily [producing] theatre about disability."[48] More recently, the company has redefined itself as an inclusive theatre open to actors of any disability, with a central mission "to inspire people to re-envision disability through professional theatre."[49] Since its first production in 1990, the company has pursued Broadway musical hits from *Guys and Dolls* to *Beauty and the Beast*, as well as canonical modern and popular plays.[50] In 2014, for example, Phamaly produced Tennessee Williams' *The Glass Menagerie*.

Phamaly's productions seek to develop inclusive staging practices to meet actors' needs. Actors are cast for roles, not for disabilities. In an interview with trade magazine, *Stage Directions*, past artistic director Steve Wilson explained, "We're looking for actors. We'll figure out a way to work with any challenge, but you'd better be interesting on stage."[51] Or, as Erin Ramsey, a fight choreographer and stage manager on several Phamaly productions, put it, "The rule is, 'If an actor has a disability, their character has that same disability."[52] To fulfill this goal, the company has used a seeing-eye dog as Toto to guide a blind actor performing the role of Dorothy in *The Wiz*, developed innovative sound technology to facilitate the voice and singing roles of Deaf performers, and substituted clapping for tapping in the musical *Anything Goes*.[53] Jason Dorwart, who has been involved in various facets of Phamaly's work as well as studied the company's history and policies, observes that "Phamaly productions integrate disability into the world of the play."[54] Today Phamaly operates its own theatre space and performs a lively annual season of plays and musicals, both in Denver and through tours in the region.

Back to Back Theatre

One of the more internationally known companies among both disability arts and mainstream theatre festival communities is Australia's Back to Back Theatre. Producing work since 1988, the company's productions have toured from Helsinki to Weimar, New York to Vancouver, Tokyo to Berlin, and throughout Australia. The productions for which they are best known are their devised works, *small metal objects*, *Food Court*, and *Ganesh Versus the Third Reich*. The company is also the subject of a 2013 collection edited by Helena Grehan and Peter Eckersall entitled, *"We're People who do Shows": Back to Back Theatre: Performance, Politics, Visibility*.[55] Here, Grehan and Eckersall explain that Back to Back Theatre "is the only full-time professional acting ensemble in Australia at the moment. As an ensemble they can work on a show for up to thirty-six months and this gives the company the capacity to develop a deep connection to and understanding of the material that they are working with."[56]

Belying this exceptional professional status today is a hard-scrabble origin story that parallels those of many disability theatre companies. Back to Back grew from the grassroots efforts of individuals working as staff and volunteers at a disability services center. In this case, the book's editors explain, these individuals included theatre-maker Cas Anderson, musician Robin Gador, and visual artist Noel Hart, all of whom met through the Geelong (Victoria, Australia) disability service provider Corilong, a day center for people with intellectual disabilities. Over the past twenty-five years the company has had four successive artistic directors: Cas Anderson, Barry Kay, Ian Pidd, and Bruce Gladwin. The latter has been artistic director since 1999. The company's comparatively lengthy history parallels the emergence of the self-conscious disability arts and culture movement.

Although the broad origins stretch to the mid-80s, Pidd notes that under his artistic directorship, in 1997, they turned Back to Back "into its own thing. We insisted that this wasn't some sort of disability support organization—that it was a professional theatre company."[57] Gladwin has explained that the company does not describe its performers as disabled, preferring to use the term "perceived disability."[58] As Gladwin explains, "We often don't know what the [performing artist's] disability is. If your employer asked you what your genetic condition was it would be an outrage. The only prerequisite is that they are able to apply for a disability pension."[59] Although "theatre" is central to the company name and history, the company's relationship with the term has been mixed. As Bryoni Trezise and Caroline Wake argue in their account of *Food Court*, the company's first conventional theatre-based production,

> For the most part, Back to Back Theatre have avoided the field and framework of disability theatre, preferring instead to position themselves within the context of contemporary performance. To clarify the difference between disability theatre and disability performance, we might say that while the former contemplates relations between actor and representation, the latter interrogates the "re" in representation and works instead from the basis of the presentational.[60]

Trezise and Wake argue that *Food Court* plays on the very expectations of disability theatre, mingling representational and presentational choices and noting that, for Gladwin, the play with conventional theatre trappings (proscenium arch, orchestra pit, curtains) was a meaningfully risky enterprise for the company.[61]

The examples of Phamaly and Back to Back Theatre raise several important dimensions concerning the idea of disability theatre. First, both can trace their activity through several decades, some of which prefigured the self-conscious designation of disability theatre. Second, over time the language associated with company members' variety of lived disability experiences has shifted and, so too, the means for referencing or, importantly, not-referencing that experience in relation to the theatre or performance work has become more self-consciously political. Third, the difference in repertoire evident between the companies, from an ongoing commitment to exploring mainstream extant works at Phamaly to a preference for avant-garde devised performance at Back to Back, demonstrates some of the remarkable breadth and range of theatre interest and enterprise associated with the label "disability theatre." Finally, while neither company engages with these impulses exclusively, it is possible to distinguish Phamaly's long-standing commitment to developing regional talent, regional audiences, and a fixed place in the Denver community from Back to Back Theatre's courting of international audiences and more itinerant approach to staging venues. In these ways, Phamaly and Back to Back Theatre demonstrate some of the multifaceted nature of disability theatre that Fox and Lipkin noted above.

A further example of this multifaceted nature includes playwright and director Joan Lipkin's own work in the context of the DisAbility Project. Founded in 1995, the company is "a grassroots St. Louis theater ensemble that creates and performs work centered around disability culture."[62] Organized first to work toward a single performance event, the project, now known as "That Uppity Theatre Company," evolved into a multi-award-winning ensemble that has performed in a wide variety of venues.[63] Integrating disabled and non-disabled members, Lipkin notes that, over time, the company has included members with "paraplegia, quadriplegia, AIDS, multiple sclerosis, cerebral palsy, stroke, blindness, bipolar disorder, cancer, spina bifida, muscular dystrophy, spinal cord injury, asthma, polio, epilepsy, amputation, depression, cognitive disability, and alcoholism."[64] I cite this broad representation of disability experience to contrast the company's work with others like the UK's Extant Theatre company, which attend to a narrower range of disability experiences.

Formed in 1997 by "a group of professional visually impaired artists, for the emergence of a new dynamic space, intended to redress our invisibility as artists and explore new creative territories," Extant Theatre chose its name in opposition to the word extinct.[65] The company is dedicated to serving blind or visually impaired audiences and artists. Artistic Director Maria Oshodi has described how the company's production process imagines a visually impaired perspective from the start, emphasizing a rich sonic environment that unifies the audience. Given this book's primary focus on disability theatre and modern drama, it is also interesting to note that, having earlier devised their own work, in 2014 they elected to produce their first classic text, Eugene Ionesco's *The Chairs*. Since encountering the play as a student, Oshodi had "imagin[ed] from the start how casting blind performers might refresh an interpretation of the piece." Indeed, she argues,

Paradoxically, it has taken working on this classic play to finally find a true forum where we can engage Extant's years of research with visually impaired actors into more authentic performance practices on stage. Absurdism is the natural theatrical port of call for visual impairment. Our casting of blind actors lends itself to the absurdist's belief that theatre is an intersection between reality and an artificial representation.[66]

Oshodi's ideas resonate with those we will consider more fully in Chapter 4: a sense of mutually revitalizing power found in the encounter between modern drama and disability artists. Here, however, the company exemplifies a different kind of production model associated with the idea of disability theatre.

Beyond Extant are further companies that pursue a more focused engagement with artists and audiences defined by a specific disability or impairment experience. In their 2010 survey of international disability arts companies, Rose Jacobson and Geoff McMurchy noted that "in the US there are at least 12 Deaf theatre companies which offer professional productions, seasons, tours and performance training. The National Theater of the Deaf: Hartford Connecticut through its almost 40 year history has given over 100 national tours, performances in all 50 states, on all the continents and 31 international tours."[67] As with the broader Deaf and hearing impaired communities noted above, Deaf arts are also on a continuum of involvement with disability theatre. Some Deaf and hearing impaired artists—Graeae Theatre Company Artistic Director Jenny Sealey in the UK for example— have connected with disability theatre while other Deaf or hearing-impaired people have resisted the term, rejecting the idea of deafness as an impairment and citing Deaf culture's unique and independent history, cultural forms and language.[68]

In a similar way, some artists with mental illness experiences or diagnoses have also sought to distinguish their work from disability arts. In Canada, Toronto's Workman Arts grew from a "theatre company of eight member artists to a multidisciplinary arts organization with over 280 member artists." Founded by former psychiatric nurse Lisa Brown in 1987, over time the company has fostered the professional theatre development of many company members, people who self-identified as having had experiences with mental illness diagnoses or addiction experiences. Like some Deaf culture artists, however, the company has developed outside formal disability theatre claims, in part because mental illness experiences have not always found an easy place within disability activism. The group has nonetheless toured its shows and connected internationally with other disability theatre practitioners.[69]

A suggestive but far from exhaustive list of other prominent disability theatre companies beyond the UK examples we will consider later and those already cited above might include Germany's Theater Thikwa and Theater RambaZamba, New York City's Theater Breaking Through Barriers and The Apothetae, San Francisco's Sins Invalid, Canada's Stage Left Productions and Realwheels, the UK's Birds of Paradise Theatre, New Zealand's A Different Light and South Africa's FTH:K (From the Hip: Khulumakhale). Each has made distinctive choices about theatre processes and their means of involving and describing the work of disability artists. Importantly, however, insofar as they are connected by disability arts and culture, each also presumes purchase in an open-ended identity rooted in disability experience that "rejects the notion of impairment difference as a symbol of shame, and stresses instead solidarity and a positive identification."[70]

Beyond the work of disability theatre artists, disability theatre and performance studies scholars have also emphasized the importance of theatre and performance as critical sites wherein audiences and performers bring together their material, human bodies, confronting firsthand the very variations in which Siebers locates the central motor of modern aesthetics. In their award-winning 2005 collection *Bodies in Commotion: Disability and Performance*, editors Carrie Sandahl and Philip Auslander explain that while early disability studies scholars were wary of the arts, "seeing them mainly as purveyors of negative images of people with disabilities," a remarkable shift in the other direction was notable in the mid-1990s as more and more scholars attended to the arts and theatre.[71] The shift was unsurprising, they argue, "given the theatricality of disability and the centrality of performance to the formation of disability cultures and identities."[72] The importance of disability theatre has long been recognized by its proponents, as the 1982 comments of the UK's Graeae Theatre Company co-founder Richard Tomlinson attest:

> [t]he very act of controlling the particular medium for a certain time in front of a largely passive, captive crowd, actually does allow for the possibility of clearing away much of the mythology that has been created about disability . . . So performance gives power. The very fact of power creates status. In general the status of disabled people in society is low . . . There are other reasons why theatre is such an important medium for disabled people. It allows for enlightenment and education; it is a tool whereby the reality of disability and the realities of people who have disabilities can be introduced, demonstrated and discussed.[73]

Further, as Kochhar-Lindgren notes above, theatre is a prime means through which to stake claims for disability experience in the public sphere and recuperate more embodied reference points for disability.[74] As we have seen in the cases of Phamaly, Back to Back, Extant, Workman Arts and other companies, to claim such stakes rests to some degree on language. The words we use when we speak about disability and disability theatre, therefore, matter.

Keywords

Disability activists and disability studies scholars have generated new concepts to challenge ideas about disability. To some extent, this has involved reclaiming words found to be limiting and stigmatizing by persons with disabilities. Kuppers emphasizes the particular value of this work for artists:

> [In art practice] many disabled people I know like to feel a bit more lift under their wings. Try to write a poem with "people first" language: "people with disabilities." That's quite a mouthful. So in our own shorthand, artists often use different terms. Some of these are terms with a longer history and a richer resonance than those used in our legal and civil rights struggles, our encounters with the bureaucracies, and the march through institutions.[75]

In other directions, this work has involved devising new language to theorize embodied performance and cultural representation of bodies. Since some of these terms or particular understandings are not yet in general circulation, it is well to signpost and explain a few keywords before proceeding.

Against the longstanding use of the term "cripple," disability activists and scholars have also reclaimed and mobilized the term and its shorthand, "crip." For example, prior to the company's official founding in 1980, in 1974 Graeae's founding artists toured their devised show *Ready Salted Crips*.[76] The term's continuing resonance can be seen in David Mitchell and Sharon Snyder's 1995 documentary *Vital Signs: Crip Culture Talks Back*.[77] Petra Kuppers, by contrast, favors the word "cripple" and in her above-noted book includes rap and poetry built around the word and its meanings "not only because of its strong emotional impact, but also because of the way the word has history, within and without the English language, because of the resonances and vibrations that surround it when spoken slowly, rippled across a tongue."[78] Reclamation of the terms "crip" and "cripple" can claim kinship with the political activism and scholarship of other identity-based groups. In her analysis of the solo autobiographical work of four queer crip performers, for example, Carrie Sandahl demonstrates parallels between queer theory and activists' uptake of the term "queer" and disability studies and activists' uptake of the term "crip." In both cases, she argues, those who use the terms do not seek to "pass" or otherwise minimize their differences, preferring instead to "appropriate and rearticulate labels that the mainstream once used to silence or humiliate them and that the liberal factions of their subcultures would like to suppress."[79] She also references the influential work of poet and essayist Eli Clare, who argues that "*Queer* and *Cripple* are cousins: words to shock, words to infuse with pride and self-love, words to resist internalized hatred, words to help forge a politics."[80] Both Clare and Sandahl link "crip" to disability activism that is deeply invested in processes of reclamation in the service of a radical disability culture. Sandahl explains that she would prefer to "replace the term *disability studies* with *crip theory* or *crip studies* to represent its radical edge."[81] Thus, while the term "crip" has undeniable currency, her remarks serve as a helpful reminder of the competing ideas and internal debates within disability politics, activism, arts, and culture.

An important keyword that has also emerged from disability studies scholarship is Rosemarie Garland-Thomson's term, "normate." She traces valued and devalued positions in the social hierarchies of embodiment, offering "normate" as the mutually constituting figure of disability.

> This neologism names the veiled subject position of cultural self, the figure outlined by the array of deviant others whose marked bodies shore up the normate's boundaries. The term *normate* usefully designates the social figure through which people can represent themselves as definitive human beings. Normate, then, is the constructed identity of those who, by way of the bodily configurations and cultural capital they assume, can step into a position of authority and wield the power it grants them.[82]

Coined in part as a means to avoid such simple binaries of physical difference as able-bodied/disabled, Garland-Thomson's term relies on careful analysis of the social processes and assumptions that find so many bodies trying to wrestle themselves into a position of power and authority available to so few. To illustrate her argument, she cites Erving Goffman's famous example of the only "complete unblushing male in America: a young, married, white, urban, northern, heterosexual, Protestant father of college education, fully employed, of good complexion, weight and height, and a recent record in sports."[83] As we shall see throughout this book, however, the concept of the normate is particularly valuable for laying bare the body's myriad contingencies and instabilities. Moreover, as Michael Davidson argues both in *Concerto for the Left Hand* and later in this book, "[t]he defamiliarisation of the normate body is also the generative force in new cultural production."[84] As Davidson suggests, it is a concept that has resonated for both scholars and artists, as is evident in playwright Chuck Mee's contemporary notes on casting:

> There is not a single role in any one of my plays that must be played by a physically intact white person. And directors should go very far out of their way to avoid creating the bizarre, artificial world of all intact white people, a world that no longer exists where I live, in casting my plays.[85]

Garland-Thomson has also connected the idea of the extraordinary body to freakery, another key idea both for disability studies and the period of drama and performance that interests us here. In the introduction to *Freakery: Cultural Spectacles of the Extraordinary Body*, she notes the transition from the visually extraordinary body as a subject of monstrosity and wonder to a figure of spectacle and horror in modernity.[86] Focusing on the figure of the freak over the period from 1850 to 1950, she demonstrates the significance of performances of extraordinary bodies in dime museums, travelling circuses, and freak shows. In such venues, extraordinary bodies were put on display, costumed, staged, and performed for popular audiences. The entertainment played on oppositions—of tall and short, large and slim—and presented anomalous bodies such as bearded ladies or armless men as signs of horror and humor. As in Snyder and Mitchell's analysis, Garland-Thomson identifies the freak show as a fundamental, necessary opposition to an emerging notion of the normal. Unlike Snyder and Mitchell, however, she connects the discourse of abnormality/normality or freakery and the normate body within the context of popular performance.

While few would identify the freak show in the canon of modern drama, from a disability studies perspective it matters that the genre was contemporaneous with the origins of modern drama. As Garland-Thomson argues, "the extraordinary body is fundamental to the narratives by which we make sense of ourselves and our world."[87] More recently, in her book *Disability,*

Public Space, Performance and Spectatorship: Unconscious Performers, Bree Hadley has cited the number of books of the past three decades that have recognized and analyzed the role of freakshows in "defining, categorizing and controlling the disabled body," particularly in the late nineteenth century when new technologies, media, and touring circuits saw "the freakshow's motley cast of characters ma[k]e their way into mainstream theatre, literature and cinema, offering an ever-expanding audience a warning of what can happen when the body goes awry."[88] Thus, both Garland-Thomson and Hadley remind us that audiences who attended the theatre and embraced modern plays, as well as their many disabled characters, had other reservoirs of cultural reference from which to draw to make sense of extraordinary bodies on modern stages.

Like "crip," "normate," and "freakery," "disability theatre" is rooted in a kind of cultural provocation, in this case a word pairing that rests on the hard-won recognition of disability arts and culture's place and stake in theatre. Disability theatre, then, does not designate a single pattern, model, site, disability experience, or means of theatre production. Rather, the term has emerged in connection to the disability arts and culture movement at a particular moment in the re-imagining of the term "disability" in many different geographical, socio-economic, and otherwise diverse cultural contexts. Different artists have embraced and resisted both sides of the term. Some have sought to highlight specific disability experiences while others favor kinds of performance that lie outside the scope of theatre's more traditional framings. Despite the ongoing negotiations, the term persists in artistic and academic discourses, from grant applications to festival marketing, academic journal articles to media arts criticism. That modern drama as well as modern conceptions of the "extraordinary" and "normate" reach well into the twenty-first century is undeniable. Disability theatre is interested in troubling their associated performance traditions, first and foremost with who is in the theatre, onstage and off, and what they hope to find there.

CHAPTER 2
CRITICAL EMBODIMENT AND CASTING

In Bertolt Brecht's *Messingkauf Dialogues*, the dramaturg's speech about casting reminds directors, producers, actors, audiences, and critics about the dangers of casting to a pre-conceived "type," particularly when the tradition seems cut off from the full range of offstage realities.

> Parts are allotted wrongly and thoughtlessly. As if all cooks were fat, all peasants phlegmatic, all statesmen stately. As if all who love and are loved were beautiful. As if all good speakers had a fine voice ... Then actors must be able to develop. Here is a young man who will make a better Troilus once he has played Amtsdiener Mitteldorf. Here we have an actress who hasn't the lasciviousness needed for Gretchen in the last act: can she get it by playing Cressida (whose situations demand it) or Grusha (whose situations rule it out completely)?[1]

Brecht's oft-quoted remarks also emphasize the importance of actor training and professional opportunities to develop.

In this chapter we will survey disability performance studies and activist discourses concerning theatre casting and actor-training practices, both central concerns in the field. Brecht's *Messingkauf Dialogues*, written between 1938 and 1942, remind us of theatre practitioners' and theorists' longstanding interest in questions of casting, conversations that continue in a range of heated forums today. Who gets to be on stage? How does a disabled actor prepare for the stage? Who has been and who ought to be cast in modern drama's many rich roles, its disabled characters and otherwise? How, when, and why does it matter if a disabled character is played by a non-disabled actor? How, when, and why does it matter if a non-disabled character is played by a disabled actor? From one perspective, as we shall explore, the challenges facing the diverse group of theatre artists and audiences who have strategically coalesced in relation to disability follow a particular and distinctive trajectory. From another perspective, these questions form a critical part of a larger interrogation of theatre inclusion and diversity. Indeed, as many readers will likely know firsthand, few theatre topics have raised and continue to raise the passion and ire of practitioners, scholars, critics, and audiences more than casting.

Over the past decades the pressing need for more innovative, expansive, and diverse casting practices has prompted many to lobby for change. A particularly strong US-based example of leadership in this vein can be found in the 1986 founding by Harry Newman and Clinton Turner Davis of the Non-Traditional Casting Project (NTCP). The NTCP drew its name and mission from its response to a four-year Actors' Equity Association (AEA) study released in January 1986 which indicated that "over 90 percent of all the professional theatre produced in this country—from stock and dinner theatre to the avant-garde to Broadway—was staged with all-Caucasian casts."[2] Newman has explained that the report galvanized their organization and they took their name from AEA precepts: "To address the lack of participation of their black, Hispanic, Asian, and native American membership, AEA conceived of non-traditional casting, which they formally defined as the casting of ethnic and female performers in roles where race, ethnicity or gender are not germane to the character's or play's development. (The NTCP later expanded this definition to include performers with disabilities)."[3] For Newman, the industry currency of the term, its provocative qualities and the fact that it points to its own end were strong advantages: "In time we hope that—like our organization—the phrase will disappear, and 'non-traditional' casting will become the performing arts' new tradition."[4] Newman also noted, however, the term's inadequacies.

Theorists Angela Pao and Daniel Banks are among those who have surveyed these inadequacies and offered histories of non-traditional casting. In *No Safe Spaces: Re-Casting Race, Ethnicity, and Nationality in American Theatre*, Pao discusses the term's potential reification of discredited racial categories reliant on "visual and visible distinctions."[5] Given the tensions raised by visibility and invisibility, passing and staring in disability experience, Pao's concerns extend easily to disability culture. In his article "The Welcome Table: Casting for an Integrated Society," Banks notes that the organization's name did indeed change in 2006 when it became known as the Alliance for Inclusion in the Arts (AIA).[6]

Visiting the website of the Alliance for Inclusion in the Arts today, the organization explains that it

promotes and advocates for full inclusion of artists of color and performers with disabilities at all levels of production in theatre, film, television, and related media. Our work also extends to audiences, particularly those belonging to underserved and historically excluded communities. Principal programs include the Advocacy, Consulting and Information Program; the Disability Initiative, which includes Disability in Entertainment and Arts Link (DEAL); and the National Diversity Forum. Through these activities, Inclusion in the Arts has become the primary catalyst for and facilitator of increased diversity and inclusion on a national level.

Our principal aim is to achieve full inclusion in American arts and entertainment, such that what we see on our screens and stages truly reflects the society in which we live; where each artist is considered on his/her merits as an individual; where the stories being told are drawn from authentic and diverse experiences; and where our individual humanity can be celebrated. To this end, we actively engage artists and decision makers, forge partnerships, and create opportunities.

The only organization of its kind in the United States, Inclusion in the Arts serves communities that have traditionally been denied equitable professional opportunities, including those who identify as African American, Asian Pacific American, Caribbean Black, South Asian, Latino, Arab American, Persian American, Native American, Deaf and hard of hearing, blind and low vision, have mobility, physical, developmental or intellectual disabilities.[7]

I cite the description in full to emphasize disabled people's place alongside other groups seeking equitable opportunities and participation in the arts. Further, although casting remains a primary concern, the organization has broadened its scope to recognize casting's place within a complex network of interrelated artistic choices. Their advocacy therefore now extends to building equity in all levels of production, whether in theatre, film, television, or other media. In the early days, the project began to assemble what has since become a national talent bank that currently comprises over 400 actors with disabilities.[8] The AIA has also developed industry ties by providing consultation and organizing panels, meetings, and symposia. Speaking with interviewer Betsy Goolian after the organization won a 2011 Tony Honor for Excellence in the Theatre, Sharon Jensen, who became the NTCP's executive director in 1989 and continues in this role today at the AIA, explained:

"We've done more in disability in recent years because the need is so huge ... and because there have been opportunities to make a difference ... Historically, disability has been primarily written about by people who are not disabled and don't have a lived experience of disability ... It's often an idealized or sentimental script. It's usually about the cure: making the blind person see or the person in the wheelchair walk. People with disabilities have been seen as having limitations that can't be gotten beyond ... It's still common for people who are non-disabled to play roles that are disability specific.[9]

Goolian extends this insight and notes that "the losses are threefold—for the disabled actor, who has the same training and background and has worked just as hard; for the ensemble, to be exposed to what the lived experience of disability is; and for the audience, to see a portrayal of what the authentic experience of disability is."[10]

An important project of the AIA that focuses on addressing these losses is their Disability in Entertainment and Arts Link (DEAL), described on their website as

a collective of arts and entertainment professionals dedicated to the full inclusion of people with disabilities—physical, developmental, intellectual, and sensory—in all sectors of American arts and entertainment ... DEAL was expressly created to serve writers, directors, producers, technicians, network and studio executives, casting directors, and disabled artists at every stage of the creative process—from development of the initial idea through production, marketing, and public presentation.[11]

Through the links on the AIA website, industry professionals can find a "Glossary of Terms and Preferred Language" as well as other resources linking to and explaining "standards and practices in programming, hiring, casting, production, and the accessibility of physical structures and modes of communication used in theatre, film, and television, and related media."[12] A list of DEAL affiliated participants is also offered as a means to "develop projects that reflect the changing landscape of disability, introduce provocative ideas about disability, and put forth a more authentic representation of what it means to be a disabled person in the 21st century."[13] Among the core assumptions about casting that inform this work are that disabled artists require equal opportunities to participate and that the industry should support "realistic portrayals, authentic representations, accurate content, information, and language when presenting disabled people and ideas about disability."[14] A further link on the AIA website entitled "Listening with an Open Eye" is part of an intended "series of resource guides focusing on Deaf and hard of hearing actors and actors with disabilities."[15] Published online in 2002, the guide includes explanations of Deaf Culture and American Sign Language (ASL) and covers such topics as working with consultants as well as planning and executing a production. It aims "to provide employers background and practical information with respect to working with Deaf and hard of hearing actors in auditions."[16]

That such information was valuable to industry professionals became clear through two events a few years later which leading disability performance scholar Carrie Sandahl later described as a "watershed moment" with "the industry beginning to pay more positive attention to disabled artists."[17] In November 2005, Sandahl found herself participating in an open discussion between disabled theatre artists and what she describes as "nearly 150 entertainment industry professionals. This audience included directors, designers, writers, producers, funders, actors, and casting agents in not only theatre but film and television as well."[18] Facilitated by New York City's Public Theater, the event was led by the Disability Initiative, a group formed by Jensen of what was then still known as the NTCP, and leading disability studies scholar, Simi Linton, founder of consulting business Disability/Arts. For Sandahl, the gathering was remarkable in large part because it was both voluntary and included more than the "usual suspects."[19] Rather, she reports, both panelists and attendees demonstrated exceptional candor about their concerns, past shortcomings, and successes. A significant group also made a commitment to more conversation. This led to a further event in April 2006 held at HBO's New York headquarters entitled "Written on the Body: A Conversation about Disability," a transcript of which is available on the AIA website.[20] Among a range of topics directed at raising the number of disabled actors featured in theatre, film, and television, professional writers, directors, actors, scholars, producers, writers, and others discussed how best to avoid such clichéd narratives as "the blind seer," "the inspirational overcomer" or "the cure." Many also shared ideas about casting, including *Sesame Street* writer Emily Perl Kingsley, who underlined its importance: "The message has to get out to casting people that people with disabilities can be ordinary. They can be the lawyers, they can be the judges, they can be the background people in the scenes who are not involved with disability issues. They can be just plain members of the community."[21] Others explained how important actors' relationships to writers and other theatre professionals can be for generating valuable acting opportunities, ones that could run the gamut from the "ordinariness" called for by Kingsley to the distinctive textured features of particular disability experiences noted by disability artist and scholar Victoria Ann Lewis. Clark Middleton, for example, noted that he had had parts written for him by Quentin Tarantino and Sam Shepard; Daryl "Chill" Mitchell's relationships from his acting career prior to becoming disabled helped colleagues to press the industry in order to cast him. Further discussions explained key disability activist and studies precepts and pointed to valuable resources for those who wanted to take these up in their writing or producing. For Sandahl, these events offered rare but critical opportunities to explain "why disability identity matters to an audience that had the power to put our arguments directly into action by changing the exclusionary practices of the entertainment industry's business-as-usual."[22]

Sandahl has been a leader in bringing disability studies perspectives to bear on questions of casting and actor training. Her explanation of disability activists' use of the term "cripping up" emphasizes the double-edged problem facing disabled performers who seek to find roles that resonate with their experience but do not limit them:

> In the disability arts and activist communities, casting non-disabled actors as disabled characters is called pejoratively "cripping up," referencing the outdated practice of white actors "blacking up" to play African American characters.[23] In "cripping up" . . . an actor is cast to play a character from a less dominant social position. Rarely is an actor of color, a woman, or a disabled person cast against type to play a character from a more dominant social position. Actors from marginalized groups must battle on two fronts, then: to be cast in roles that resemble their own identities and to be cast in roles that do not."[24]

Disability activists and scholars' use of the term "cripping up" has also gained traction in broader critical and cultural spheres. In 2015, for example, citing Eddie Redmayne's award-winning film turn as Stephen Hawking in *The Theory of Everything* and Daniel Radcliffe's award-winning stage turn as a disabled orphan in Martin McDonagh's *The Cripple of Inishmaan*, Frances Ryan wrote a piece in *The Guardian* titled "'We wouldn't accept actors blacking up, so why applaud 'cripping up'?" Ryan argues that the rationales offered in favor of these "cripped up" casting choices (e.g. Redmayne's ability to perform Hawking prior to his disability experiences; producers' need to draw on Radcliffe's star power) would fail and prompt outrage if "made for white actors 'playing black.'"[25] Ryan is not the first to make the analogy with blackface minstrelsy. For example, in 2001 playwright and performer Cheryl

Marie Wade argued on a panel dedicated to thinking about disability and performance that

> non-disabled actors think that disability *is* the character. (*general assent*) That's what they're busy paying attention to playing. So all of the attention and the emotion goes into having their head postured right, or their wrist lax, or whatever. It's playing a mannerism rather than playing a human being. To some extent, that's like a white guy putting on blackface. It's just as offensive.[26]

In response to Wade, Joan Lipkin agreed and argued that "part of the issue is that non-disabled actors are operating from a place of resistance and fear."[27]

In a 2014 article for *The Atlantic Monthly* entitled "Disability Is Not Just a Metaphor," playwright Christopher Shinn echoed these remarks, arguing that casting non-disabled actors in disabled character roles is connected to "society's fear and loathing of disability" as it is reassuring to see able-bodied actors portray disability convincingly and then re-emerge as able-bodied. In other words, the actor's able-bodiedness is a central rather than incidental feature of such representations' success in that they

> provide us with the comforting assurance that we are not witnessing the actual pain and struggle of real disabled human beings; it is all make believe . . . Able-bodied actors can listen to the disabled, can do research, can use imagination and empathy to create believable characters. But they can't draw on their direct experience. That means that audiences will be able to "enjoy" them without really confronting disability's deepest implications for human life . . . Disabled characters are often seen as symbolising the triumph of the human spirit, or the freakishness we all feel inside. That may be another reason disabled actors are often overlooked—they don't allow disability-as-metaphor to flourish as easily.[28]

Shinn cites influential disabled playwright John Belluso as his source for this theory. In addition to his central and animating presence in the 2005 conversation described by Sandahl, Belluso also contributed to the oft-cited "We Are Not a Metaphor: A Conversation About Representation" panel introduced and moderated by Kathleen Tolan and published in 2001 in *American Theatre*. In this context he argued,

Having had both disabled actors and non-disabled actors interpreting roles in a play that I've written, I've found that the experience is like night and day. When you have a non-disabled actor playing the role, the curtain goes up at the end, the lights come up, it's time for the curtain call. And the actor will stand up out of the wheelchair and take a bow, and suddenly everything that has come before has just been erased. The audience is let off the hook. Suddenly this isn't social history; this is just artifice. Whereas when the lights come up and there is someone who is still sitting, and they take their bow in the wheelchair, it helps the audience understand this is bigger than the topic of a play. This is part of a movement. This is part of social history.[29]

In this argument for casting disabled actors, to do otherwise risks disavowing or erasing the accomplishments of the disability movement in order to privilege artifice or illusion. As panelist Susan Nussbaum argued, however, the problem is vexed in theatre precisely because the form "*is* artifice."[30] The tension she raises is akin to one raised often in forums concerned with re-imagining casting practices to promote greater diversity on stage.

It is important to remember that theatre casting and representation are generally fraught with contradiction, argues Daniel Banks, in that, "[u]nless a person is playing herself in an autobiographical performance, all theatre is cross-casting of some sort. For decades, people advocating for better representational practices on the US stage have queried why a person with a different skin color than a playwright intended should be any less believable than a person born in a different century or on a different continent."[31] Like Nussbaum, Banks underlines the rhetorical weakness in arguments that disavow the artifice at play between character and actor.

A similar argument was offered in 2012 at the Theatre Communications Group Fall Forum on Governance focused on diversity and inclusion. The AIA's Jensen moderated a panel entitled "Diversity Models in Theatre," and speaker Kwame Kwei-Armah, Artistic Director of Baltimore's Center Stage, explained that a particularly effective way to press for inclusive theatre practices is to argue that "theatre is the last place that should be literal and we cannot be literal . . . if theatre cannot be the place where I can leave literalism at the door and enter into the magic then where am I?"[32] His question aims to highlight theatre's impulses for transformation, artifice, and illusion. Even the most iconic theatre, in which signs seem most like that which they seek to represent, involves some level of artificiality or transformation. Kwei-Armah's rhetorical strategy for promoting greater diversity and inclusion on stage, relevant for our analysis of casting here, insists that it is most critical that race, gender, disability, and other categories of human diversity be equally amenable to theatre's anti-literal play; individuals should be cast for their powers of transformation, their ability to "enter into the magic," not for who they literally are.[33]

An individual actor's powers of transformation do not exist in a vacuum, however, and we are reminded here of Brecht's earlier assertion about actors' needs to develop. For disabled actors first to understand theatre as a valuable art form to which they can contribute meaningfully, second, to have the drive and confidence to compete for roles and, third, to feel valued professionally when they are cast, training, audition, and professional practices must be organized in accessible, inclusive ways. As Victoria Ann Lewis argued in the "We Are Not a Metaphor" panel,

> Things need to change in the area of training. We need to aggressively recruit disabled artists for the professional training schools. The theatres need to recognize disability as part of the diversity agenda. And our casting practices need to reflect those of other minority communities, in which every effort is made to provide employment for qualified actors with disabilities.[34]

The call resonated with others on the panel. For example, Father Rick Curry, founder in 1977 of the National Theatre Workshop for the Handicapped, explained that he founded the school "directly out of a political slap-in-the-face—I wasn't even allowed to audition for a mouthwash commercial because I don't have a right forearm. The absurdity of that propelled me into offering a course for people with disabling conditions."[35] In a similar vein, Sandahl cited the inaccessibility of many theatre department classrooms, something she had noted in her academic workplace: "[W]e have one classroom where we do movement training that is at the bottom of a flight of stairs. So I see that from a very early stage in a young actor's career, they're getting excluded from the curriculum, from the classroom and from the stage, because of a lack of roles and opportunities."[36] Barriers to training, both attitudinal and physical, are important to remember in the face of what Sandahl has described as the most commonly cited reason for casting non-disabled actors over disabled ones: the limited pool of professionally trained actors.[37] In many movements, the lack of minority representation in coveted positions of leadership and influence can be linked to longstanding training patterns and professional accreditation systems in which barriers to the minority groups are imbricated in the system. In addition to physical and attitudinal barriers, Sandahl has also argued that disabled actors seeking greater representation in western professional theatre must contend with exclusionary and potentially damaging actor-training models.

In "The Tyranny of Neutral: Disability and Actor Training," Sandahl provides an insightful and historically contextualized analysis of the challenges facing disabled actors who seek professional training and opportunities to be cast in contemporary theatre roles.[38] She references the legacy of inaccessible theatre and theatre training architectures as well as "demeaning, stereotypical roles" for disabled actors, many of whom are told by directors that "their impairments would detract from the playwright's or director's intent for a nondisabled character."[39] Further, citing the abundance of disabled characters that she notes fill the dramatic canon, she notes a comparative lack of trained disabled actors to take them on.[40] Drawing in part from her own university-based actor training experiences and broader research into the genealogy of current dominant principles for actor training in western contexts, she demonstrates how core aspects of western acting curricula can repel disabled actors and further entrench some of theatre's largest barriers. She criticizes some of the primary metaphors at play in current acting pedagogy, a field in which she argues most can trace their ideas to some interpretation of Stanislavsky's "method" and the voice and movement principles drawn from renowned physical actors like Jacques Copeau, Étienne Decroux, and Jacques Lecoq.[41] She demonstrates the rootedness of key acting terms in late nineteenth and early twentieth-century precepts about the body that privilege and presume the normate body as humanity's baseline.

The first term Sandahl queries is "neutral," a state idealized in actor training as free from the actor's idiosyncrasies, a flexible platform from which to build a character. She notes the various ways the concept is rigorously addressed through training, "[w]hether called neutral, divine neutral, zero position, or relaxation, most of today's acting programs spend many hours working with students to achieve this state, since it is considered the absolute foundation of the actor's work no matter what the style of performance."[42] After tracing the concept's history and noting that most instructors recognize neutral as a necessarily unachievable ideal, she demonstrates the ways in which the metaphor poses particular problems for disabled actors.

[T]he concept of neutral emerged in the late-nineteenth-century industrial age, an age when bodies were studied and trained for efficiency, standardization, and normalcy. Words that recur in this eclectic collection of training methods include *control*, *efficiency*, *balance*, and *symmetry*. Whatever the acting style, the notion that actors' bodies should first be stripped of individuality and idiosyncrasy as a prerequisite to creating a role undergirds them all. Bodies are considered damaged physically and emotionally from the process of living, and those bodies capable of cure are suitable actors. Disabled bodies, though, cannot be cured. They may tremor, wobble, or be asymmetrical. Implicit in the various manifestations of the neutral metaphor is the assumption that a character cannot be built from a position of physical difference. The appropriate actor's body for any character, even a character that is literally disabled or symbolically struggling, is not only the able body, but also the extraordinarily able body.[43]

The second term Sandahl queries is "the emotional body," her coinage for the training principle that physicality develops from past emotional experiences. Although she follows this idea to its roots in nineteenth and early twentieth-century theories of psychology, it is useful here to consider the example she includes from David Alberts' 1997 movement textbook that offers six basic body types (normal, dependent, self-defeating, self-possessed, self-denying, and schizoid), each tied to key dramatic characters and each with a set of corresponding physical and psychological traits. Sandahl notes Alberts' casting of Laura Wingfield in *The Glass Menagerie* as a "dependent" type characterized by "feelings of loss, helplessness, despair and inner emptiness," traits which Alberts argues manifest physically: 'Long, thin body. Weak, underdeveloped muscles, particularly in the legs and arms ... Sway back and an inflexible spine ... Emotional pain equals physical pain'.[44] Sandahl is careful to note that Alberts and others who have articulated their work in this manner propose such types only as stepping stones toward a more fully realized character, but Sandahl offers a valuable summary of the damage that such steps risk for disabled actors-in-training:

> [A]ttributing basic emotional and psychological traits to certain body types encourages stereotypical acting choices. Perhaps these stereotypes become even more pernicious because actors make them appear more fully rounded and lifelike. Additionally, simulation exercises can humiliate the disabled actor on a couple of fronts. First, the notion that physicality develops from our inner emotions and

psychology does not make sense to a person who was born with or acquired an impairment that causes a limp, a curved spine, muscle spasms, or asymmetrical features. Having to participate in or even observe one's classmates "trying on" disabled or deformed bodies and reporting what emotions are evoked can be painful. Second, simulation exercises in which students are asked to pose as deviant bodies as means of conjuring up their "innate" feelings are not an objective process. Strong value judgments about disabled bodies, such as fear and pity, are ingrained in our popular culture, dramatic canon, and in the acting textbooks themselves. These prejudices cannot help but influence the emotions such simulations will evoke.[45]

Whether or not Alberts' textbook has currency within a specific program, Sandahl demonstrates that much contemporary actor training is rooted in unquestioned assumptions about the body that do little to help an actor playing Laura or any other disabled character step away from ableist framings of disability experience. Her analysis urges those involved in actor training and those disabled actors who seek such training to think critically about the potentially ableist assumptions that underpin some standard approaches and activities. Victoria Ann Lewis echoed this call in 2010 when she argued that,

[w]ithout an awareness of the social and historical redefinition of disability that has occurred over the past twenty to thirty odd years, the theatre educator will be ill-equipped to resist the force of centuries of tradition assigning meaning to the disabled figure in dramatic texts and in performance. Educators are encouraged to become as familiar with the prevailing stereotypes of disabled characters (victims or villains) as they are with those of African American depiction (crooks or clowns) or those of women (Madonna or whore).[46]

Sandahl and Lewis's respective calls to tackle the vexed problem of casting at the level of training align with a number of activist educational initiatives. An important example of a relatively large-scale initiative to address the problem of training began in 2006 with Arts Council England's (ACE) creation of the *Into the Scene* project. ACE worked with a team from Graeae Theatre Company which included playwright, actor, and vocal coach Alex Bulmer in the role of project coordinator. Bulmer explained the impulse for the project:

Arts Council England set it up through their London office in order to address a very uncomfortable truth. Very, very few disabled people were graduating, attending or even applying to performing arts institutions. So the main questions were why is this the case and what can we do about it? . . .The Arts Council recognizes that the professional profile or status of actors with disabilities is far more likely to be improved if educational opportunities are available. There is a real concern that disabled actors at the moment do not have the same access to skill development as non-disabled performers and in order to compete in the industry with graduates from three-year programmes they need to be equally skilled.[47]

Bulmer has explained that the project was particularly interested in addressing attitudinal barriers to training and employment opportunities. She had experienced these during her own theatre training when, two years into a three-year conservatory program in Toronto, her worsening degenerative eye condition coupled with a lack of understanding of how she might then navigate the program meant she did not complete her third year there. Rather, she credits an "exceptionally visionary teacher," David Carey at the Central School of Speech and Drama, for finding unobtrusive and effective means to support her completion of the Advanced Diploma in Voice Studies a few years later.

Bulmer's experience is similar to that of other prominent disability theatre artists. In her 2010 essay "Disability and Access: A Manifesto for Actor Training," Victoria Ann Lewis shares details of the barriers she faced starting out as a disabled actor and draws from her thirty years' experience as a working actress, producer, and theatre educator to offer a close analysis of the faulty assumptions and practices that prevent disabled people from seeking and receiving performance training. Through case studies focused on movement training, vocal training, and casting, she builds toward five primary recommendations for improved access. First, she recommends that the onus be taken off the individual student to fight for access: "The university needs to step up, enforce the laws, explore disability as a cultural and historical phenomenon, and actively recruit and welcome disabled students—because without some leadership at the top, whether in regional theatre or the academic theatre, these initiatives are doomed."[48] In terms of training program structures, she also advocates for an adjusted sense of time and progress that accommodates disabled people as well as a more flexible approach to skill training, one which would ideally also include disabled artists as training mentors and examples. In view of "the significant barriers that prevent young people with disabilities from even dreaming about a career in theatre," her fourth call is for more active recruitment of disabled people into programs and audition opportunities, perhaps through explicit notation in public advertisement.[49] Noting that "a lack of expectations has been identified as one of the main barriers for disabled students in all fields," her fifth recommendation presses for the application of critical standards throughout training.[50]

Her arguments in this final regard resonate with those expressed by Canadian actor James Sanders who, during his third semester in theatre school in 1990, became quadriplegic from a spinal cord injury. The website of the multi-award-winning theatre company he founded, Realwheels, notes some of these experiences:

> After a year of rehabilitation [Sanders] returned to school to complete his training. What he found far more profound than the physical changes to which he needed to adapt were the shifts in perceptions he experienced from his peers and instructors. For the first time in his life he was being told what he could or could not do before he even tried. He quickly learned that the attitudinal barriers he would experience as a person with a disability would be much more difficult to navigate than the physical barriers.[51]

Sanders left his original program to attend Simon Fraser University's theatre training program in Vancouver and graduated as valedictorian in 1998. A significant part of his company's work now involves "nurtur[ing] and develop[ing] emerging talent in the disability community."[52]

In this mentoring work, Realwheels follows the path of Graeae Theatre Company and many other disability theatre companies that offer theatre training and mentoring opportunities to emerging disabled artists. For example, in 2006, following a year-long Graeae-led project in UK schools that participate in the Learning and Skills Council Dance and Drama Awards (DaDA), the company developed "The Missing Piece" with London Metropolitan University, a "bespoke programme for disabled students to train in acting skills."[53] Taking an average of twelve students each year, the program ran for five years. Graeae's subsequent work with the *Into the Scene* project experimented with and ultimately created a practical model for mentorship. From their work on these projects and another called *Scene Change*, the company has created a handbook and DVD for teachers, both available through their website. Teachers involved in the project helped the organizers to understand that "adjusting their teaching methods or finding ways to make lessons inclusive was not an issue. It was the assessment of progress and achievement that would need to be examined."[54] As individual instructors must conform to institutional assessment criteria and examination processes, the *Into the Scene* project began to identify key governing bodies (e.g. "external validation boards, degree committees and the Conference of Drama Schools") with whom to develop inclusive practices that individual instructors could follow while still upholding standards for achievement.[55] Auditioning boards are a particularly powerful set of governing bodies insofar as they are the first to determine who will gain access to training. Working with the Royal Academy of Dramatic Art (RADA), the project pressed the auditioning board to think past the disabled applicants' potential teaching and assessment hurdles in order to build instead from the principle that "if we accept this applicant on the basis of their talent then what do we need to do to make our course accessible?"[56] Auditioning boards thus play a pivotal role in helping instructors, audiences, artists, and future students re-imagine the place of disabled performers both in schools and in theatre more broadly. Expanding their sense of possible paths through curriculum that do not shortchange the program or the student in terms of maintaining high achievement standards is a critical step in fostering a critical mass of professionally prepared disabled actors.

Bulmer also emphasizes casting disabled actors in mainstream theatre roles as a means to kindle the desire to pursue theatre among disabled people:

Nicola Miles-Wildin is in *The Glass Menagerie* at Ipswich and Tim Gebbels is with the Oxfordshire Touring Company. But I would like to see engagement in a wider sphere of theatre activity, in lighting and stage management. I would like to see disabled actors in front-line roles, the detective rather than the victim, in positions of power, playing classic roles, playing Shakespeare. But there is a high level of skill needed for these bigger roles and that comes back to training. With high-profile roles and greater visibility will come a change at secondary school level. Students with impairments who show enthusiasm and potential will, as a result of this higher visibility, be encouraged to take part in drama at school and then to apply to performance programmes.[57]

Bulmer's remarks usefully summarize the need for interconnected efforts to bring disabled actors to the stage. Where discussions with the AIA focused on disabled actors' need to build relationships with writers, producers, and casting agents, the *Into the Scene* project focused on the public promotion of disabled actors in lead acting roles as a means to generate the desire for professional training among a new generation of disabled theatre artists.

It is striking that Bulmer's remarks about Graeae actors, like Sandahl's and Alberts' arguments noted earlier, reference Williams' *The Glass Menagerie*. As both Ann M. Fox's essay and the play *Shattering the Glass Menagerie* in this book's second part demonstrate, the play offers strong means for thinking generatively about the place of disability in drama and theatre. The question of who might best be cast as Laura, however, turns on the above-noted concerns about disabled access to actor-training and auditioning processes, the kind and quality of acting championed in these processes, the long-lauded yet deeply problematic tradition of "cripping up," and the need for actors to develop and showcase their powers of transformation, particularly within the demands of theatrical realism.

Embodying realism

Arguably, realist and naturalist aesthetics pose the strongest challenges for disabled actors who seek to embody non-disabled characters or for non-disabled actors who seek to play disabled characters. Due at least in part to realism's pivotal place as one of if not the dominant aesthetic mode in modern western theatre following the Second World War, these same aesthetics have prompted a great deal of scholarly and practical debate over the past few decades. In their 2012 analysis of "unsafe realisms," scholars Roberta Barker and Kim Solga trouble the thirty-year critical tradition that discounts realism as the ineluctable tool of hegemonic cultural practice. They chart the emergence of realism and naturalism in *fin de siècle* Europe, these aesthetics' growing cultural currency and dominance over the twentieth century, and the series of compelling critiques against the form's political complacency launched by feminist and other critics in the later twentieth century. They note that "[o]ver the last thirty years realism has come primarily to be defined by political failure, especially in its representations of gender and of queer and minority subjectivities."[58] Certainly, many of the critiques from disability scholars and activists cited above have imagined realist theatre in their rhetorical framing, highlighting casting choices that either fail or succeed in representing on stage the real, authentic experiences of disabled people.

In 2010, the AIA challenged the casting of Academy Award nominee Abigail Breslin in the role of Helen Keller in the Broadway Circle in the Square Theatre remount of *The Miracle Worker*. The production aimed to mark the fiftieth anniversary of William Gibson's realist play and the 1959–61 lauded Broadway run starring Patty Duke as Helen Keller and Anne Bancroft as Annie Sullivan. The AIA's Sharon Jensen was quoted in the *New York Times* ArtsBeat blog by author Patrick Healy as opposing the producers' decision not to audition actors for the part of Keller who shared Keller's disabilities:

> We do not think it's O.K. for reputable producers to cast this lead role without seriously considering an actress from our community … I understand how difficult it is to capitalize a new production on Broadway, but that to me is not the issue. There are other, larger human and artistic issues at stake here.[59]

Against this logic, Healy includes lead producer David Richenthal's explanation of the commercial imperatives that drove him to insist on a star in the role of Keller. Healy also notes that Jensen and the AIA had protested a few weeks earlier over the casting of a hearing actor in the role of the Deaf character Singer in New York Theatre Workshop's stage adaptation of Carson McCullers' *The Heart is a Lonely Hunter*. Healy neatly summarizes the catch-22 facing disabled actors:

> So, first Singer and now Helen Keller: Should producers and directors audition and hire whoever they see fit for these seminal roles? Or, as Ms. Jensen asserts, if deaf or blind child actors do not start getting work that will turn them into stars, how will there ever be any for producers like Mr. Richenthal to audition?[60]

The incident prompted a great deal of discussion on blogs and in the comments sections of related articles. Imbricated in the arguments, however, is an assumption that there is an iconic correspondence between what is real and what is represented. Fantastical and avant garde aesthetics interested in shocking or defamiliarizing audiences are less concerned with keeping the ratio of this correspondence small and stable. Realism delights precisely, however, in the paradoxical tension of an actor seeming very much to be the character represented but not, crucially, being the character represented.

Critics of realism, Barker and Solga assert, have been keen to show the distance between the real and the represented, particularly in terms of who assesses what is real on either side of the equation. They cite Michael Vanden Heuvel's summary of the critics' concerns: "Realism simply replicates existing—and therefore arguably bourgeois, patriarchal, racist, oppressive, and oedipal—discourses, and functions as a mode of conciliation, assimilation, adaptation, and resignation to those discourses."[61] To Vanden Heuvel's list of existing discourses disability scholars add "ableist" and likewise seek to trouble rather than resign themselves to realism's conventions. For Barker and Solga, however, the form has been over-maligned and decontextualized. They seek to reassert the form's political potential, returning their readers to early realism's political roots and entanglement in the paradoxes of the "real":

> At its inception, realist performance may have been defined less by a univocal world view—the most consistently damning, and consistently repeated, argument against realist theory and practice—than by a series of fundamental paradoxes that created deliberate tension between page, stage, and world and provoked both audience discomfort and public debate.[62]

Barker and Solga's interest in realism's paradoxes and political promise led them to include in their collection an essay by Natalie Alvarez that I think may be generative for scholars and practitioners interested in rethinking casting from a disability studies and activist perspective.

In "Realisms of Redress: Alameda Theatre and the Formation of a Latina/o Canadian Theatre and Politics," Alvarez offers a detailed examination of the paradoxes and fraught politics imbricated in casting policies that insist on realism's iconicity. Alvarez explains:

> When it comes to the question of the representation of minorities in realist frameworks, iconicity presents an unwieldy problem. On the one hand, for minoritized subjects, iconicity provides a vocabulary for identifying what is wrong when, for example, a heterosexual woman plays a lesbian or a white actor plays a Latino ... On the other hand, the appeal of continuity between actor and character in the logic of iconicity runs the risk of re-entrenching essentializing representations and obfuscating difference.[63]

In other words, when Latina/o actors insist that only Latina/o people can play Latina/o characters, they uphold realism's insistence on the strongest resemblance between actor and character, its iconic logic. By extension, however, they also risk re-entrenching the idea that those are the only roles they can play, cutting away their opportunities to take up a greater variety of realist roles and risking the sidelining of their artistry within a silo apart from mainstream opportunities. Alvarez summarizes the problem thus: "The question that iconicity poses is how to form a theatrical culture that recognizes difference without making oneself *reducible* to that difference and obfuscating what Alicia Arrizón describes as 'the cultural plurality that defines the configuration of Latina/o identity'?"[64] These remarks resonate here in part because disability identity is also defined by plurality, comprising as it does people who connect to the term through a myriad of different means (for example, as people with lifelong or acquired disabilities, as individuals who experience cognitive, motor, physical, and/or sensory impairments on a continual or intermittent basis, as people whose disabilities are visible or invisible etc.).

In face of the longstanding debates concerning realism's value for hitherto marginalized artists, Alvarez offers an alternative: indexical realism or realism that follows the logic of the indexical sign rather than the strictly iconic one. In such a system, she argues,

> Latina/o and other "visible minorities" can participate in realism's aesthetic criteria without having to render themselves "illegible" within its sign system, but also without ceding to a referential system that always already governs the scene of recognition. There is, as the debates outlined in this paper have demonstrated, something productively recalcitrant about "race"[65] within the conventions of realism and its repertoire. The inability of visible minorities to be subsumed within realism's dynamics of iconicity and therefore preserve its illusionism suggests that visible minorities on realist stages inevitably introduce indexical forms of representation. The contingent "fact" of one's race is always being indexed within realism's illusionism precisely because it is a contingent fact—one to which one belongs but to which one doesn't wish to be reduced.[66]

As a case study for her arguments, Alvarez considers a production of Carmen Aguirre's *The Refugee Hotel* in which the role of Cristina, an Indigenous Mapuche of south-central Chile, was played by Cheri Maracle, a First

Nations actor. Alvarez credits this casting strategy to Aguirre, who wanted to index the continuity between the challenges faced by the Mapuche and First Nations in their discrete contexts.

Thinking toward a similar practice in theatre involving disabled actors, we might imagine a production of *The Glass Menagerie* wherein the actor playing Laura has cerebral palsy or a production of *The Miracle Worker* wherein neither of the actors playing Helen and Annie are visually impaired but each is disabled in her own particular way, indexing disability but not reducing character or actor to its fact. Alvarez explains further how such choices would serve as a realism of redress:

> An indexical realism would embrace this facticity and the radical singularity of the Latina/o [or disabled] actor who stands before the audience with all of her "irreducible specificities," apart from the referential "idea" of Latinidad [or disability] culture that the realist text might otherwise prefigure. This "failure" to live up to the notional might serve as a ground upon which realism's politics of visibility are revised, enjoining the spectator to take account of what is always missing and never wholly recuperable in presentation ... Perhaps an indexical realism might allow us to renegotiate not only realism's aesthetic criteria, but also how ethnicity is "read" in realist performance, presenting a critical opening for a truly viable "realism of redress."[67]

As we have seen above, many disability studies scholars, activists, and artists have sought equally redressive action for realist theatre's long tradition of mining disability experience but casting non-disabled actors. They have expressed frustration at the laurels heaped on non-disabled actors who perform disability, arguing that such actors have often paid attention to mannerisms over fully developed characters. They have also highlighted and challenged the usurping of roles from disabled actors and the perpetuation of a performance tradition in which disabled people have not been central in representing their experience. Strikingly, Sandahl's helpful summary of these demands for redressive action concludes in a manner open to the kind of indexical realism described by Alvarez, a continuity rooted in shared disability experience and identity rather than the specific "facts" of the body:

> In terms of aesthetics, disabled actors argue that non-disabled actors, no matter how good their technical skill at imitating the physicality of a disabled character (and most often verisimilitude is not achieved) or

how good their research into the lives of disabled people, they lack the lived experience of disability necessary to bring these characters fully to life. Non-disabled people, even fine actors, understand the disability experience primarily through stereotypes available in mainstream media. These actors often focus on getting the outward shell of the characterization right (how a disabled person might move, speak, carry the body, etc.) but have little access to the lived experience of disability. Experiences such as being stared at, using personal assistants for activities of daily living, living with pain, dealing with access issues, and navigating social services and the medical establishment are unavailable to most non-disabled actors. Even if a disabled actor has not personally experienced all of these situations, it is likely that he or she has better access to them because of related disability experiences or ties to the disability community in general.[68]

Sandahl, like Alvarez, points to the potential political power and redressive action available to those who cast disabled actors indexically for the wealth of character-related experience their artistry and bodies bring to realism's enterprise.

Given realism and naturalism's central place in modernism, we will have more opportunities to think about casting choices in specific instances in the chapters ahead. In Part II of this book, Ann M. Fox takes up such casting possibilities in specific terms. Exploring some key examples of disabled actors cast in the lead roles of *The Glass Menagerie*, she shifts the primary question from "to what degree a non-disabled actor might imitate Laura's limp" to consider instead how "casting a disabled actor in the role shifts things entirely, and in ways we might not entirely expect..."[69] In the next chapter, as well as in Fox's, we will consider several prominent disability theatre productions of modern plays, examining casting choices amid other process and production decisions.

We began this chapter with Brecht's mid-twentieth-century call for questioning and attention to the actor's need to train and grow. As we have seen, casting and actor development choices can perpetuate or defamiliarize theatre traditions. It is well to conclude with the 2012 remarks of celebrated disabled screen and stage actor Nabil Shaban that so clearly resonate with Brecht's:

In addition to possessing a means to convey a belief, to be an actor you have to have certain other contributory prerequisite qualities:

imagination, passion and a capacity to learn. What you don't have to have are two arms, two legs, two eyes and a so-called "pretty face". You don't have to be physically dexterous or mobile as defined by the dominant able-bodied culture. For too long, disabled performers have been denied access to the great mirrors of life. This very denial renders the reflected visions distorted and cracked. The medium of theatre, with a few exceptions, has rarely grown beyond an impotent infancy with its facile and fallacious belief that physical beauty equals the good. The romantic leads, the heroes and heroines, are inevitably played by the so-called handsome and beautiful, and yet, in life, neither love nor greatness is the preserve of the physically perfect. Because the performing arts have been responsible for this lopsided portrayal of history and society, people with disabilities have felt inferior and excluded. And when, on occasion, they are included, it is rarely on their own terms. With the active and self-governing involvement of people with physical and mental differences in the performing arts, there is a chance that the more truly representative visions of the world will more effectively lead the world to a greater maturity, tolerance and safekeeping. Disabled performers, like other minority artists, are creating their impact, either as independent operators within the mainstream or by provoking consciousness-raising through organized disability theatre.[70]

CHAPTER 3
STAGING INCLUSION

This chapter extends the logic of prior chapters to examine another foundational aspect of disability theatre practice: the pursuit of inclusive and accessible space and staging. Moving forward from the demands for accessible actor training and casting noted in the last chapter, here we query access in relation to a broader range of theatre participation that includes theatre artists alongside producers, technicians, managers, audience members, and critics.

In her 2011 monograph, *The Question of Access: Disability, Space, Meaning*, Tanya Titchkosky centers her analysis around potent scenes that reveal how the idea of access is always an invitation to ask questions.[1] Following Titchkosky, I also begin with three scenes, each of which has the potential to prompt further inquiry into access. In light of the last chapters, the first scene imagines a production of Beckett's *Endgame* in which disabled people neither participate in the artistic creation process nor attend because the production does not support touch tours or audio-description technologies and is sited in a space without ramps, flexible viewing spaces, or accessible washrooms. The production is thus inaccessible to patrons who, perhaps like Clov, cannot sit or, perhaps like Hamm, cannot stand or see. Is it plausible that such a production has occurred or does it resonate with readers' past experiences? In a less imaginative vein, the second scene recalls a 2012 critically praised stage adaptation of Dostoevsky's *The Idiot* in which strobe lighting effects were incorporated into the design elements as effects to signal the eponymous hero's epileptic seizures. While the production as a whole was innovative and featured strong performances, this particular artistic choice challenged the ability of patrons with photosensitive epilepsy to see safely this production concerning one of fiction's most famous figures with epilepsy, becoming in this way inaccessible to both patrons as well as artists with epilepsy, like modernist forerunner Dostoevsky himself.[2] The final scene draws from the 2009 production in Toronto called *The Book of Judith* in which late inclusion activist and artist Judith Snow performed alongside Graeae-affiliated director, playwright, and actor Alex Bulmer as well as a choir comprising many artists with a range of disabilities. In explicit protest at the lack of accessibility in Toronto theatres, the company erected for their performances an evangelical revival-style white tent on the lawn of a mental health center, aligning the production's design elements with the performers' needs and the needs of patrons in wheelchairs.[3]

Together, these three scenes point to the many ways choices about access influence theatre production and reception, whether they are consciously or explicitly engaged with questions of access or not. Whom do artists seek in their theatres when they produce work, whether the work engages with disability or not? When work explicitly engages with disability, is it particularly important to include those whose disability experiences are represented? When this does not happen, how and why have the choices been explained or rationalized? Are such questions of disability content in the production relevant or distracting in a broader fight for access? How, when, where, and why do disabled artists and patrons gain access to theatre sites? What responsibilities do theatre companies have to be explicit about accessibility in their marketing, and theatre critics to address accessibility in their reviews? What kinds of built environments, staging techniques, adaptive technologies, audience management and supports, pre- and post-show activities, marketing strategies, ticketing policies, and other material theatre choices inform how access is queried and practiced? What inclusion strategies have disability theatre artists experimented with and favored? How do these kinds of inclusion and accessibility choices inform aesthetics? As we shall see, answers to these questions are varied and complex but, most of all for our purposes here, they are highly generative for thinking about theatre aesthetics.

At the end of her 2002 article "Considering Disability: Disability Phenomenology's Role in Revolutionizing Theatrical Space," Carrie Sandahl explains that "[i]f this essay has read like a manifesto, that is because it is."[4] Throughout, she argues forcefully that theatre aesthetics have, to their detriment, too long understood disability as a "pathological aberration" rather than a critical dimension of human diversity, leaving untapped vast reservoirs of creative possibility and community.[5] She demonstrates how, by moving beyond stigmatized understandings to recognize disability experiences as inherently generative in and of themselves, a fuller scope of human variety and experience emerges, prompting the provocative question, "How might consideration of disability transform the aesthetics and use of theatrical space altogether?"[6] This chapter takes up the central terms of this critical question, a question that disability performance theorist Victoria Ann Lewis has since described as *the* question, "the one that brings the disabled body to center stage in the 21st century."[7] Like the questions raised by casting practices considered in the last chapter, how disabled people, whether artists, patrons, staff, or otherwise, are interpellated into and able to find voice and place in theatre spaces is a primary concern of disability arts, studies, and activism.

That Sandahl lays claim to the manifesto genre for her arguments forges a further link between the two central concerns of this book: modernism and disability theatre. Likewise, in her 2004 article "The Theatrical Landscape of Disability," Lewis also cites modernist manifestos:

> I begin with Marinetti's Futurist manifestos published in the teens of the last century, which called for the banishing of all previous theatrical forms and the creation of a totally new drama ... Perhaps there is a clue here for how to transform the narrative of disability in playtexts, given the deep roots of the convention of the disabled figure in drama.[8]

While Sandahl embraces the manifesto genre, however, Lewis analyzes emerging disability performance and new disability drama to highlight how very difficult it is to create something wholly new. Ultimately, she argues that "dramaturgical reform, like architectural reform, is not accomplished through a modernist heroic departure, the individual in exile from the entire canon of dramatic literature."[9] That there is tension between Sandahl's and Lewis's rhetorical use of the manifesto form is perhaps a function of the form itself and a further suggestion of disability theatre's ties to modernist impulses, forms, and frameworks.

In *Manifestoes: Provocations of the Modern*, Janet Lyon connects the history of the manifesto genre with the emergence of political modernity. She argues that the manifesto form has "much to teach us about the problems of modernity."[10] For example, she argues that the manifesto

> exposes the broken promises of modernity: if modern democratic forms claim to honor the sovereignty of universal political subjecthood, the manifesto is a testimony to the partiality of that claim. Manifestoes chronicle the exclusions and deferrals experienced by those outside the "legitimate" bourgeois spheres of public exchange; the manifesto marks the gap between democratic ideals and modern political practice. At the same time, however, the manifesto promulgates the very discourses it critiques: it makes itself intelligible to the dominant

order through a logic that presumes the efficacy of modern democratic ideals. However paratactic or irreverent or systematic a manifesto may be, it nonetheless operates by putting the case of a particular group into a context that honors the *idea* of a universal political subject.[11]

Such an idea is clearly at play in Sandahl's urging of the value for all theatre of engaging disability's generative potential. Arguably, serving an abiding commitment to universal political subjecthood despite the hitherto profound dehumanizing and social exclusion of disabled people is a primary engine driving access discussions. If, as we have noted in prior chapters, the social model of disability locates disability not in the individual body but in the failure of the social environment to serve and enfranchise non-normate bodies, then it is also centrally concerned with the myriad ways that the built environment might best be accessed by and enable the participation and expression of the full range of human bodies.

The idea and problem of access have been a major focus of critical inquiry within disability studies and disability activism, arts and otherwise. Arguing for the understanding of access as, fundamentally, an act of perception, disability studies scholar Tanya Titchkosky suggests that any time access is discussed or acted upon, an important opportunity emerges "to reveal how access is a form of perception and thus a space of questions."[12] Although Titchkosky's focus is on university access, the example and questions she offers in support of this claim resonate with those cited and asked by many contemporary theatre practitioners and patrons, many of whom encounter theatre and theatre training spaces built long before the productive demands of disability activists:

For example, a common expression that arises as people struggle to secure physical access is, "Look, disability just wasn't a concern when this building was built." "Look" is a recent expression which does the interactional work of pointing out what should be obvious and beyond question. Still, this declaration and certainty hosts many questions. Who are "we" such that disabled people are excluded? Who are disabled people such that "they" can be overlooked in the past? Who do we become when such a past is used as a justification for the present state of affairs? How might the space we find in our workplace socially organize what is thinkable and doable there? How is it that what access means for you and what it means for me are different, and what might these different interpretations do for inclusion, for exclusion, and the intermingling of the two? Finally, that we are asked—told, actually—to "look" at the issue implies it could be understood in other ways.[13]

The questions Titchkosky raises are just as easily applied to inaccessible theatre and performance sites. Equally relevant here are how the scenes of access around which Titchkosky builds her arguments provide "opportunities to address questions such as *who* belongs and *how*; *what* do representations of disability mean; *when* does interest in disability become elided so as to not yet figure as a necessary participant; and *where* does this all happen?"[14] In the structure of what follows I borrow from Titchkosky's insistence that discussions of access continually question the premises behind the term. I begin, therefore with examples of how theatre-relevant disability rights policy has understood and articulated access. Second, I investigate principles of universal design in light of their understandings of access and relevance for theatre. Third, I consider the generative potential at play in theatre's unresolved questions concerning access. Finally, I note key research resources available to artists, patrons, producers, scholars, and activists who continue to ask the many questions of and pursue answers for theatre access.

It is well beyond the scope of this chapter to offer a full and global history of disabled access advocacy and provision across different national contexts. It is possible, however, to highlight key examples of how theatre-relevant disability rights policy has understood and articulated access over time and in different national contexts. Taking up this work in July 2015, the media is filled with references to US President Obama's White House celebration of twenty-five years of the Americans with Disabilities Act (ADA). In this context Obama claimed, "Thanks to the ADA, the places that comprise our shared American life—schools, workplaces, movie theaters, courthouses, buses, baseball stadiums, national parks—they truly belong to everyone."[15] In his article "Why I wrote the Americans with Disabilities Act" that ran in the *Washington Post* on 24 July 2015, disability rights scholar and legal advocate Robert L. Burgdorf Jr. summarized the historical context for the creation of the ADA: "The ADA was a response to an appalling problem: widespread, systemic, inhumane discrimination against people with disabilities."[16] In a further article shared on the website for the University of the District of Columbia David A. Clarke School of Law, where Burgdorf Jr. is Professor Emeritus, he explains that "[a] key part of the ADA is its Title III that prohibits discrimination on the basis of disability in 'public accommodations.' Public accommodations can be defined broadly as facilities or services in commercial use and open to the general public."[17] Theatres are covered in this Title and requiring that they and other such public sites be accessible to disabled people is a significant part of what Burgdorf Jr. emphasizes as the act's "profound, albeit imperfect, impact in ameliorating discrimination against people with disabilities and furthering their integration into society in America and elsewhere in the world."[18]

Although he acknowledges large gaps in implementation and legal enforcement, Burgdorf Jr. summarizes and highlights some of the ADA's major areas of impact and increased accessibility for disabled people under the categories of mass transportation, telecommunications, state and local government services and public accommodations, hiring practices, HIV discrimination, and international effects. His further notes concerning the category of "Buildings, Facilities and Thoroughfares" are particularly instructive here as we query the idea of theatre access:

> The accessibility provisions of the ADA have changed the face of American society in numerous concrete ways. A vast number of buildings and other structures have been affected by provisions of the ADA that require newly designed or constructed places of public accommodation or other commercial facilities to be readily accessible to and usable by people with disabilities. Flat or ramped entrances into buildings are becoming the rule rather than the exception, and curb cuts/curb ramps on sidewalks are now commonplace. As a result of ADA mandates, designated disability parking spaces have become a standard feature of parking lots and garages. Due to all these improvements, today it is common to encounter people using electric and manual wheelchairs, or crutches, or white canes or service animals, or with prosthetic devices, on sidewalks and in parking lots, at malls and shopping centers, in airports and train stations, in stadiums and theaters, in parks and playgrounds, and at most other public places.[19]

Against the historical context of discrimination against and social isolation of disabled people recounted by Burgdorf Jr., the relatively newfound and widespread access to public sites that many non-disabled people take for granted is indeed a move forward. Importantly, however, as disability activists will be quick to argue, the gaps between law and practice, changes to the built environment to include access and full social inclusion persist in often overwhelming ways.

Working to close these gaps in contemporary theatres, argues Victoria Ann Lewis, involves a complex "weaving of social, spatial negotiations" that draw from policy, individual, and collective action.[20] She cites examples of inconsistency and hostility toward inclusion of disabled people in cultural and works settings, arguing that "The absence of disabled people from these spaces or the invisibility or misinterpretation of their social roles in those spaces establish the very rigid boundaries which separate disabled people from the arts whether as working artists, students or audience members. Gaining access is a complex process, precisely because it is social, civic and aesthetic."[21] As an example of this complexity, Lewis traces how Los Angeles' prestigious Mark Taper Forum, after thirty-five years of operation, came to offer for the first time in 2001 an accessible "performance stage as well as backstage dressing rooms."[22] While playwright Tony Kushner credited the newfound accessibilities to the groundbreaking work of talented young disabled playwright John Belluso, whose play ran during this period and involved disabled artists both backstage and onstage, Lewis expands this narrative to trace a longer history of change. While not wishing to undermine the achievements of Belluso, she explains her impulse to account for access history at one theatre as a means to

> emphasize the complexity of the politics of location, the importance of the disability community's involvement with cultural institutions and the extraordinary changes, however frustratingly slow, that have been achieved by disabled artists, academics, and advocates in the re-imagination of the disabled body in performance. I will be talking about the structures of cultural life, such things as licensing contracts, the myriad of specific social relations that control performance space.[23]

Thus, while individual efforts are meaningful, Lewis demonstrates that they are threads that cannot be understood outside a more complex tapestry that includes, for example, the Mark Taper Forum's place in a network of regional theatres funded by the National Endowment of the Arts and thus dependent on public funds in ways that force compliance with Section 504 of the Rehabilitation Act of 1976 and the ADA in such titles as those noted above.

The US context and the ADA offer but one rich set of examples amid the larger international context of disability rights activism around the question of access. For further example, writing in the summer of 2015 also prompts me to cite the current forceful activism of Stop Changes to Access to Work, the UK advocacy group against the termination of the Independent Living Funding and the scaling back of the Access to Work program.[24] Artistic Director of Graeae Theatre Company Jenny Sealey, whose company's productions are discussed further in the next chapter, and who offers insights in an interview later in the book, is the group's national spokesperson. She advocates in the media in support of the programs that she demonstrates have been fundamental contributors to the UK's widely recognized international leadership in the field of disability arts and culture. Canadian artist Alex Bulmer, for example, moved to London precisely because of the country's Access to Work program. Although she had had several successes as a performer and playwright in Canada, persistent and overwhelming inaccessibilities in the workplace pressed Bulmer in 2003 to look for opportunities elsewhere. She explained her choices to interviewer Diane Flacks when she returned to Toronto to work on *The Book of Judith* in 2009:

> Essentially, if you are an employed disabled person, this program funds you to purchase equipment or person time. So, basically, I get a seeing-eye person. They work with me—and unlike a seeing-eye dog, I don't have to take them out to poo! It's great! . . . No one could turn me down for work because I'm disabled . . . For my job, I get loads of new scripts that I have to read and I run workshops to develop new plays. My computer reads the script with me. But in a workshop, you have to be able to say, "flip to page 30," "refer back to page 12," "make a note," "cut this line" and people act out a scene and there is a lot of non-verbal action. My seeing-eye person is trained in audio description.[25]

As we noted in the last chapter, the Access to Work program supported Bulmer in her work with Graeae Theatre Company as Literary Manager. It also allowed her to teach voice and inclusive theatre practice as well as pursue other directing, playwriting, and screenwriting opportunities, co-writing, for example, a six-part comedy series commissioned by Britain's Channel 4, called *Cast Offs*, starring six disabled actors.

In her advocacy work for Stop Changes to Access to Work, Jenny Sealey likewise makes clear the critical role of the program in her own career, a career that has included co-directing the Paralympic Opening Ceremonies as well as directing many professional theatre productions such as those discussed in the next chapter. Writing for *The Guardian*, Lyn Gardner outlined the challenges of the cuts facing Sealey:

> As a result of the profile created around the Paralympics there was significant interest in the skills of deaf and disabled people in international co-productions. But those co-productions cannot get off

the ground if there is no access to sign language interpreters and other support. Sealey has been told to reduce her hours and that only scientists—not artists—are allowed access to the highest level of interpreters. She is also having her hours reviewed on a month-by-month basis, which makes it impossible to plan ahead. In a really bizarre twist, the Access to Work application is now only by telephone. Because Sealey is deaf, she does not use the telephone.[26]

In addition to understanding theatre as a public artistic space in need of an accessible built environment for patrons and performers, understanding theatre as a workplace raises questions of access that pertain to communication between theatre workers throughout the process of artistic collaboration and creation. Where Burgdorf Jr. emphasized the now more commonplace engagement of disabled people in such public sites as theatres, the examples of Bulmer and Sealey demonstrate that access also involves committing to supporting disabled people's professional and artistic work through such means as the provision of trained personnel and adaptive technologies for communication.

A further relatively recent example of how theatre-relevant disability rights policy has queried and articulated access can be found in "Accessing the Arts: A Symposium presented by Selfconscious Theatre and Abilities Centre," a June 2014 conference in Whitby, Ontario, Canada.[27] The conference was offered in conjunction with evening productions of the aforementioned *The Book of Judith* and all events took place on the site of Whitby's Abilities Centre, a center built in 2012 in close proximity to public transit that self-describes as "fully accessible" and "state of the art." On its website, the center explains that it "serves local, national and international communities by providing resources and research tools that promote inclusivity and accessibility, while enhancing quality of life."[28] What exactly inclusivity and access might look like for Canadian disability artists was the subject of the day-long symposium that included keynotes, panels, and "artbursts" with a range of disabled and Deaf artists from across Canada.

The event opened with a keynote conversation between Alex Bulmer and Judith Snow. In addition to her work in the UK, Bulmer has long been involved in Canadian disability arts and cultural activism. She opened her speech by noting that she had just spoken with another conference attendee with whom she had run a similar event twenty years earlier. Noting what they felt were limited changes since the previous conference, she said they wondered if the day's conference was going to be the beginning of real, substantive change. The conversation between Bulmer and Snow continued with the artist/activists' respective struggles with the word "disability," a term that frustrates them but that they mobilize differently in different contexts. Bulmer explained that at that moment in the symposium she did not feel disabled: she was in an accessible space with technologies and human assistants for support and she was speaking with people interested in her ideas and aesthetics. Snow, who was adamant in stating her dislike of the term disability and preference for thinking in terms of inclusion, likewise pointed to the specific contexts and relations that determine her strategic use or non-use of the term. Although she worked more often in visual art, after years of international inclusion activism, Snow's collaborative theatre work led her to argue that "Theatre has proven to be a more powerful venue than advocacy for having ordinary people understand, experience and choose to be inclusive – to welcome diversity into their own lives."[29]

Interest in this aspect of theatre's potential was a key focus of the conference and among the attendees was celebrated disability playwright and actor Alan Shain, also the second person to hold the relatively new position of Disability Arts Officer at the Canada Council for the Arts. Elizabeth Sweeney, the first such officer from 2010 to 2012, was also in attendance. On tables at the event were copies of the 2012 Canada Council for the Arts publication *Expanding the Arts: Deaf and Disability Arts Access Equality*. A follow-up to the Council's 2008–11 strategic plan entitled *Moving Forward*, it introduces the Council's "understanding of deaf and disability arts" and includes observations from focus groups. It also outlines the Council's current tripartite strategy built around three areas of focus: increasing access, support, and participation in Canada Council programs; recognizing, supporting, and promoting Deaf and disability arts practices; and encouraging public engagement in the arts for Canadians who are Deaf or who have disabilities.[30] A similarly tiered approach shapes the document's definition of access, included among other definitions at the end of the document:

> *Access* is a broadly used term that has significant history and relevance to any conversation about ensuring the equality of Deaf Canadians and Canadians with disabilities. The Canada Council's understanding of access and the arts is best described in tiers that build and expand upon each other.[31]

The document moves on to outline these five tiers and offers illustrative examples. The first tier concerns "Access to physical spaces" while the second considers "Intellectual and sensory access." The third addresses "Aesthetics of access," a category which they note "refers to art practices which take into account accessibility in the creation process, which may include the artists' own access requirements and those of diverse audiences."[32] The final two categories concern "Access to the creative process, decision-making and artistic direction" as well as "Access to Deaf or disability arts." The document further explains that the phrase "providing access" means tackling power imbalances or barriers (in one or more interconnected tiers) that prevent Deaf people and disabled people from engaging with the full complement of opportunities.[33]

In an effort to uncover and share strategies and best practices for tackling barriers, a later conference panel entitled "Being All Right with Getting it Wrong," gathered

> producers, playwrights and educators who have pursued greater inclusion of different stories, experiences and ways of navigating this world in their creation and teaching practices. By sharing their experiences, the pitfalls and greatest strengths of this model of creation, they serve to remind us that moving forward an inclusive and accessible arts community means a change in practice being all right with sometimes getting it wrong along the way. What do we need to be doing in the performing arts scene to be more inclusive to diverse artists and audiences?[34]

In this context Brendan Healy, Artistic Director of Buddies in Bad Times Theatre, Canada's leading LGBTQ theatre, noted that the downtown, centrally located theatre had long been a favored performance site for disabled artists because it was one of the few in the city with physically accessible performance and audience spaces. Further, the company's broader interest in queer theatre meant that they were already focused on bodies and how they experience pleasure; themes he connected to their programming of the Queer and Able series. Another panelist, Lynda Hill from Theatre Direct, a thirty-nine-year-old theatre for young audiences, talked about the company's periods of success and drought with ASL assistance and also provided details about how it has responded to physical, financial, and geographical barriers preventing disabled youths' participation in theatre. A further panelist, Leslie Lester, producer and executive director from Toronto's Soulpepper Theatre, explained that because of the newness of their theatre facilities, they had strong access for people in wheelchairs as they had to follow Ontario accessibility policies and building codes. As evidence of their site's accessibility, she pointed to multi-award-winning playwright Judith Thompson's June production of *Borne*, a new play featuring nine performers in wheelchairs. Speaking candidly about challenges and errors along the way, the panelists cited the significant gains made through their efforts at inclusion and pressed for theatre producers and artists who currently work in more mainstream ways to risk change.

In marked contrast to the positive attitude toward theatre shared in Whitby, disabled performance artists at London's 2011 "Access All Areas: Live Art and Disability" event emphasized theatre's comparative limits for disabled artists in contrast with live art.[35] In her "Reflections on *Access All Areas*," former General Manager of the UK's Extant Theatre Mary Paterson explains that the two-day event sponsored by the Live Art Development Agency (LADA) was a "public symposium of papers and performances at the intersection of Live Art and Disability Arts" whose program reflected "the ways in which artists working with Live Art have engaged with and represented issues of disability in innovative and radical ways."[36] Many involved in the event argued that Live Art is, in the words of *Guardian* reviewer Lyn Gardner, "at the forefront of disability art practice, thinking and theory."[37] It has been a booming ground for many of the disability performance artists discussed in this book and elsewhere. As well-known multidisciplinary artist Mat Fraser has explained on his website, "I realized quickly that Live Art can offer performance opportunities you just can't get to in theatre, and for me the more brutal and confrontational aspect of my investigation into disability's difficult interface with mainstream cultural concerns was made possible by utilizing this great medium."[38] Later in the book which came out of the Access All Areas event, Aaron Williamson also argued for the greater possibilities for accessibility in the form by citing his own practice:

> We do ask the artists not to come with verbal pieces, because we can't afford interpreters. This is all done on zero budget, and we ask for it to be as low-tech as possible, since we only have one plug, nearby at the newsagents. So what I'm getting at is that it's intrinsic to Performance to work with those kind of low-fi, low-tec [*sic*], short actions, primal forms of communication that by happenstance solve the kind of access problems that you'd normally encounter when trying to get into a theatre. And often it's very easily documented and distributed on YouTube, which is a very accessible format.[39]

Artist and scholar Brian Lobel explained that the *Access All Areas* event included a provocation by Williamson and collaborator Katherine Araniello under the title of their performance group the Disabled Avant-Garde (DAG). Akin to the chance poetry associated with Dada manifesto author Tristan Tzara nearly 100 years earlier, in "Sicknotes" they drew notes from a hat, each beginning with "I am sick of" and attacking what Lobel described as the "sacred cows of both the Live Art world and the Disability Arts world."[40] Among these notes were several that pertained to the kinds of access questions we are considering here: "I am sick of missing art events because of fucking steps or because the soundtrack is so fucking great I can't actually understand it"; "I am sick of inaccessible arts funding application forms that are designed to give money to organisations that employ professional administrators"; "I am sick of there being no subtitles & I am sick of the sign-interpreters wandering off"; "I am sick of inclusivity, diversity and delivering pissing excellence"; "I am sick of being tickboxed & then the funders not bothering to turn up"; "I am sick of hearing about 'the body' when disability relates to attitudes and states of mind."[41]

The examples of Williamson's reflections and the "Sicknotes" provocations point to barriers at the levels of the built environment, funding policies, financial resources, adaptive technologies and support personnel, media engagement and, perhaps most of all, attitudes. Both support Lewis's aforementioned claim that "gaining access is a complex process, precisely because it is social, civic and aesthetic." Although there are countless further illustrative examples in many other contexts that could also be considered here, hopefully the various examples of access debates and negotiations noted above adequately suggest the many factors at play in "gaining access" through government policies, granting policies, aesthetics, access to work programs, community partnerships, accessible communication technologies, accessible spaces, and public interest. As Titchkosky has argued, "The fight for the rights to access may get people in—but that is only half the issue. Developing critical relations to access that are committed to recognizing how it already interprets embodied difference is the other half."[42] In other words, as Titchkosky insists, each time the question of access arises in the examples above it also demands critical engagement with what exactly access means and how this meaning rests on how disability is itself perceived, interpreted, and valued. Moreover, as each of the examples above also shows, not least among the means for interpreting and interpellating embodied difference are issues of design and the built environment.

In their 2012 book *Universal Design*, Edward Steinfeld and Jordana Maisel explain that the concept emerged largely out of the disability rights movement and note that a primary "activity in reaching the goal of equal rights for people with disabilities is removing barriers to access and use in the built and virtual (digital information) environment."[43] The authors are careful to distinguish the term's key features from other approaches:

> Today, many writers use the term "universal design" as a substitute for "accessible design" without understanding its significance or how the terms differ. The goal of universal design extends beyond eliminating discrimination toward people with disabilities. A universal design benefits everyone or, at least, a large majority. Moreover, to avoid stigma, it engages the aesthetic realm as well as the pragmatic because it has to appeal to everyone. Universal design is about dealing with barriers as artists or scientists would. It demands creative thinking and a change in perspective. It is not sufficient merely to apply design criteria in accessibility regulations in a mechanistic way. Often a change in perspective is needed.[44]

Emphasizing how, in principle, the designer's primary interest is in tackling barriers to create enabling environments, the authors underline how universal design's precepts, while drawn from disability rights advocacy, also aim to serve the broad scope of humanity. As such, they place universal design alongside such similarly creative and ethically motivated challenges as sustainability and affordability, suggesting that universal design is "perhaps one of the most profound ideas in the contemporary history of design."[45] The idea resonates with Tobin Siebers' earlier noted recognition of disability as fundamentally an aesthetic value. As he argues further, "Aesthetic judgments about the built environment remain unquestioned when architects make the case against accessible designs on the grounds that access produces ugly buildings, even though the buildings called beautiful are fashioned to suppress the disabled body from public view."[46] With regard to theatres' built environments, we can likewise ask, how are designs that suppress the disabled body from public inclusion and view beautiful?

Jos Boys has recently written critically about the place of disability in current design practice, including the principles of universal design, by arguing that a fundamental rethinking of the disability/ability binary and a fuller engagement with disabled peoples' experiences and spatial understandings will generate a messier but ultimately more creative and generative approach. In her 2014 book *Doing Disability Differently: An Alternative Handbook on Architecture, Dis/ability and Designing for Everyday*

Life, she argues that "*starting* from disability—rather than treating it as an afterthought to building design—does have the potential to generate some truly radical, avant-garde and creative architectural practices."[47] Like Lobel above, to illustrate her arguments, Boys begins by citing the artistic works of The Disabled Avant-Garde (DAG).[48] The ongoing collaborative works in the UK by artists Katherine Araniello and Aaron Williamson have garnered significant international attention and, on her website, Araniello describes DAG as "a satirical arts organisation, creating pitch-black and self-knowing performances, videos and interventions."[49] For Boys, DAG's satirical re-makings of past artworks (such as those by Simon and Garfunkel or Busby Berkeley) and other artistic performances, while often humorous, belie a fierce social critique inspired by popular incredulity in face of the idea that "disabled people could actually form a creative and artistic avant-garde."[50] Like Sandahl and Lewis's invocation of manifestos in the vein of the historical avant-garde cited earlier, the work of the DAG draws from the artists' understandings of what Lyon described earlier as "the exclusions and deferrals experienced by those outside the 'legitimate' bourgeois spheres of public exchange."[51] Boys invites architects and other designers to engage precisely with this knowledge derived from lived disability experience. Seeking greater engagement with disabled people's perspectives, creative impulses, and talents, she presses architects and other designers to recognize the centrality of the philosophical problems generated by the misleading binary of "dis/ability" for architectural practice. Through such work, she imagines a revived architectural avant-garde.

Thinking in terms of theatre, it is important to remember that the revival and avant-garde intervention Boys seeks involves more than stages and auditoria. Performance scholars and artists have likewise drawn attention to the spaces beyond the stage and auditorium. In 2001, for example, disability scholars and performers Petra Kuppers, Kanta Kochar-Lindgren, and geographer Derek McCormack undertook a residency and performance exploration at London's Chisenhale Dance Space under the name of The Olimpias to highlight a further salient site for architectural revival: "The blueprinting of behavior and values through environmental practices is particularly noticeable in 'service' areas of buildings: the secondary spaces that provide access to primary spaces."[52] *Landscaping*, a performance experiment by The Olimpias, emphasized these service areas; their exclusions and stories became the focal point of a performative investigation into communication, flow, and personal space.[53] Kuppers notes that although Chisenhale has been an influential, active, artist-run space that is open to disabled artists and which has fostered international experimentation and development in new dance techniques, it has also "traditionally been inaccessible for wheelchair users: six flights of narrow staircases need to be overcome before one can see a show in the performance spaces or attend a workshop on the top floor."[54] Kuppers notes that a primary challenge of the project was that the space of the inaccessible stairwell signified differently for each contributor:

> The narrowness of the corridor meant that Kanta, a hearing impaired woman, had to deal with echo and diminished availability of lines of sight during the performance work. No ground level storage, comfortable places, or toilet facilities meant a clear physical challenge to me, as a mobility impaired person, for whom the stairs at the end of the corridor became an open knife, a harrowing reminder of pain. All of us had to deal with the cold and dampness, and the lack of natural light and privacy.[55]

Although they are typically considered as secondary, transitional, and directional, in *Landscaping* these spaces were brought forward to question their potentially central place in a revived set of principles for built environments that hail rather than hide the hitherto suppressed disabled body.

A further example of the importance of such spaces can be found in Vancouver's Fei and Milton Wong Experimental Theatre, officially opened in 2010. I cite it here chiefly because Canadian disability theatre performer James Sanders, an artist whose technically innovative performances have toured widely and who has been critical of facilities that do not provide adequate access to "secondary spaces," has publicly touted it as an exceptionally accessible space. In advance of the opening of his company's co-production of *Spine* that ran alongside the 2010 Paralympic Games, Sanders contrasted his experiences navigating other theatres in his wheelchair to those at "the Wong":

> I need an accessible rehearsal space and dressing room, I need a bed to get on and off of when I change in and out of my costumes, and I need the schedule to allow for the extra time that it takes me to get to and from the theatre ... The Wong is extremely accessible. It's been built with the mandate that any person with a disability can do any job— including hanging a light.[56]

The aim here is not to cast The Fei and Milton Wong Experimental Theatre as somehow perfect but, rather, to draw attention to Sanders' emphasis on the disabled performer, technician and patron in the planning and execution of the built environment.

Professional theatres in the UK that have received public praise for their improvements along these lines include those cited by the Adapt Trust. Initiated in 1989, the Adapt Trust sought to "achieve access to all major arts and heritage premises by the year 2001" and took its name as an acronym for Access for Disabled People to Arts Premises Today.[57] A founding trustee for the group, architect C. Wycliffe Noble, is the creator of "The Journey Sequence," an assessment tool concerned with building for disabled people, which also emphasizes secondary spaces in the built environment. In the first pages of their 2004 book, *Access for Disabled People to Arts Premises*, C. Wycliffe Noble and Geoffrey Lord outline the entries of Noble's award-winning and copyrighted sequence:

Place to Park

Place to be Set Down

Approach to the Building

The Building Entrance

Lateral Circulation

Vertical Circulation – Stairs and Lifts

Reception and Box Office

Auditoria

Backstage Facilities

Rehearsal Rooms

Performer Dressing Rooms and Facilities

Bars and Restaurants

Bookshop

Offices

Conference/Meeting Rooms

Unisex WCs

Staff Rooms

Technical Aids

Communication System for the Hearing Impaired

Systems for the Visually Impaired

Signage[58]

Noble and Lord, inspiration, founder and vice president of the Adapt Trust, explain that the sequence has now been adopted by many European and international policies as the standard means for assessing, validating, or critiquing the built environment. The authors explain that for purpose-built environments, theatres for example, further "zones of use" can be imagined and imbricated into the sequence. The authors go on to provide a list of considerations under the title "Designing for people with disabilities," dividing these concerns along impairment distinctions:

People with Sight Impairments

People with Hearing Impairments

People able to Walk using Sticks or Crutches

People in Wheelchairs

People with Hand or Arm Impairments

People with an Attendant for Assistance

People with Cognitive Impairments

Criteria used in Providing Egress for People with Disabilities in an Emergency.[59]

Beyond providing alternatives to stairs and wide entryways to accommodate wheelchairs and guide dogs, among the points enumerated in this section, the authors highlight the need to minimize the built environment's shadows, echoes, and background noise while also taking care to offer uncluttered, tactile, acoustic, and aromal information and wayfinding cues. The book offers descriptive rather than technical accounts of buildings selected to showcase "the achievements and the solutions that have been incorporated into a variety of buildings within the purpose group of arts premises, galleries, museums, libraries and heritage buildings."[60] Among those they explore, and of chief interest for our thinking about disability theatre here, are the Royal Academy of Dramatic Art, London, the Royal Shakespeare Company, Stratford-upon-Avon and, under examples of good practice, the Royal National Theatre, London.

Although the book emphasizes architecture, Noble and Lord recognize that accessibility concerns more than the built environment, relying as it does on a range of communication techniques that are now used widely in the UK and elsewhere. They outline such techniques as VocalEyes, audio-description, audio introduction, advance information, touch tours, Stagetext, Lipspeakers, sign language interpreters, speech to text reporters (STT)—Palantype, induction loop systems, infra-red systems, text phones, and intellectual assistance in the form of escorts and interpreters for people with learning disabilities. Their efforts of enumerating such techniques are in line with those of other organizations that also seek to make publicly available descriptions and "tipsheets" for best accessibility practice. There are many rich online resources for artists, administrators, and patrons concerning how to plan for and implement technologies to make theatre auditions, rehearsals, advertisements, performances, and related events accessible for a diverse complement of disabled people. These include those found on the national Arts Council websites of the UK, Canada, and Australia, the National Endowment for the Arts Accessibility Office, and the Leadership Exchange in Arts and Disability affiliated with the John F. Kennedy Center for the Performing Arts as well as Inclusion in the Arts in the USA. Further, many, like the Leadership Exchange in Arts and Disability, run regular conferences and workshops that train and support artists, administrators, and producers as they pursue the goal of greater inclusion in their works and environments. As so many of these organizations have labored intensively to prepare these resources for public use, I will not duplicate those efforts here. Rather, my final focus will be on their relevance for the questions of access we have raised, particularly as they pertain to theatre audiences.

In the last chapter we focused on the importance of expanding theatre training, auditioning, casting, and performance opportunities for disabled artists. In the next chapter, we will explore in more depth how inclusion practices informed artistic processes and choices in specific contemporary disability theatre productions of modern drama. Here we will close by focusing on access, audiences, and critics.

Many theatres and festivals are moving toward greater audience inclusion practices. This can be seen, for example, in the growing international number of theatre companies that schedule and advertise "relaxed" or autism-friendly performances. As New York's Theatre Development Fund explains on their website, their Accessibility Program launched the Autism Theatre Initiative (ATI) in 2011, offering an autism-friendly performance of *The Lion King* on Broadway. Journalist Erik Piepenburg of the *New York Times* described the process behind the performance and its choices:

> The company of "The Lion King" and a panel of autism experts collaborated on ways to slightly modify the show to make sure autistic

children did not have negative reactions to loud or sudden sound or light cues. The volume in the opening number and other scenes, including the sound of a roar, was turned down. All strobe lights and lighting that panned into the house were cut. The sound and light reductions were done electronically so that neither the actors nor the orchestra had to tone down their performances. [Victoria Bailey, the fund's executive director], who attended the performance, said she noticed there were more than the usual number of people getting up during the show to go to the lobby, but the audience didn't seem frazzled.

Off stage, there were small activity and quiet areas set up in the lobby for children who needed a break from the show. Volunteers from local autism organizations were on hand to offer assistance. Victor Irving, the Minskoff's house manager, said he asked the pedicab drivers who park outside the Minskoff to refrain from ringing their bike bells.[61]

On the Theatre Development Fund (TDF) website, the ATI explains the choices involved in autism-friendly performances:

Each show is performed in a friendly, supportive environment for an audience of families and friends with children or adults who are diagnosed with an autism spectrum disorder or other sensitivity issues. Slight adjustments to the production are made, including the reduction of any jarring sounds or strobe lights focused into the audience. Plus, in the theatre lobby there are quiet and activity areas, staffed with autism specialists, for those who need to leave their seats during the performance.

Downloadable social narratives (in Word format), with pictures of the theatres and productions, are available several months in advance of the performances. These are designed to personalize the experience for each attendee with autism spectrum disorders. TDF also produced a video social narrative that describes how best to navigate Times Square.[62]

Other kinds of pre-show inclusion tactics that are becoming more commonplace are touch tours for vision-impaired or blind audience members. These allow participants to visit the stage and feel the textures and shape of the properties, set pieces, and costumes; all are opportunities that enhance the audience member's experience and facilitate his or her further engagement through audio-description or vocal-eye supports. Thus, attending theatre today, individual audience members might be or be seated among some who have visited the stage for a touch-tour in advance, some who have elected to attend a "relaxed" performance, some who may have read materials well in advance of the production, some who might be wearing earpieces for audio-descriptions, some who might be following the open-captioning or sign language performance alongside the stage, some who require flexible viewing spaces, some who cannot sit, and others who cannot stand. The sheer diversity in scale and scope of possible responses to questions of access, interpretation, perception, and critique reminds us of Carrie Sandahl's question, or *the* question as Lewis framed it earlier in this chapter: "How might consideration of disability transform the aesthetics and use of theatrical space altogether?"[63] While in the next chapter we will seek answers from specific disability theatre artists, it is well here to note the rich possibility this question holds for reception studies.

In her 2015 article "Participation, politics and provocations: People with disabilities as non-conciliatory audiences," disability performance scholar Bree Hadley notes the surprising lack of engagement between the lively fields of research concerning, on the one hand, theatre audiences and, on the other, "disabled people as theatre makers."[64] The paucity of engagement between the literatures is striking, argues Hadley, given that the trends in both point to many generative opportunities for exchange. Outlining different modes of disabled spectatorship, modes that can occur both simultaneously and in competition, Hadley asserts their value not only for theorizing about spectator and performer relations but also relations between spectators:

They emphasise the meta-conscious, meta-reflective dimension in which a spectator necessarily becomes aware of how their fellow spectators are perceiving, interpreting and making meaning of the work. The negotiations that occur in a disability-inclusive space mean that spectators are conscious of other spectators' approach to perceiving, interpreting and meaning-making, along with the fact that these may or may not match up with their own. They are aware of this in a way that may be less possible in a silent, dark [and, I would argue, following Siebers, disability-suppressed] space designed to create the illusion of being alone in thought. There is an engagement with each other's potentially non-compliant perspectives that comes from personal pain, suffering, pleasure, political positioning or any other baggage they bring to the encounter, and that is almost taken for granted amongst disabled audiences.[65]

Noting a strong current in more mainstream studies of spectatorship to challenge the idea of audience homogeneity and recognize individual audience members or groups, Hadley offers the commonplaces of disabled spectatorship as rich means for rethinking audiences in theatrical spaces altogether. For Hadley, this rethinking also extends to theatre critics who, likewise, gain from imagining disabled readerships, in all their diversity, for their artistic assessments. Drawing on her own experience as a theatre critic, Hadley helps us to imagine a different kind of regular theatre criticism that raises accessibility questions not just in relation to shows explicitly engaged with disability but rather, all theatre enterprise. How might imagining disabled spectatorship within the primary readership press critics to question how access functioned as part of the whole aesthetic?

Pressing for a politics of wonder above all else, Titchkosky favors the question "how" in relation to access: how is access perceived here? In the above discussions we have considered how inclusion strategies have emerged, operated, and held meaning at the levels of policy, institutional implementation, built environments, adaptive technologies, and artistic creation. It is worthwhile bearing in mind, however, that in each of these cases, Titchkosky reminds us, "[d]isability is not merely a word to be added into the chain of our existence; it is not the et cetera clause of identity politics. Instead, disability and questions of access are normatively ordered, ongoing forms of recognition and communication accomplished between people."[66] As a longstanding form of recognition and communication accomplished between people, theatre gains from querying the place of disability in its past, present, and future.

In his 2014 book, *How Theatre Means*, Ric Knowles explains, "To mean is not the only thing theatre does—it also entertains, and moves—but it is one of the most important things. This is so because one of theatre's primary functions is to serve as a live forum for the negotiation of values within and between cultures."[67] Elsewhere Knowles has also asserted the primacy of space in these negotiations, arguing in *Reading the Material Theatre*, for example, that "the geographical and architectural spaces of theatrical production are never empty. These are spaces full of histories, ghosts, pressures, opportunities, and constraints, of course, but most frequently they are full of ideology—the taken-for-granteds of a culture, that don't need to be remarked upon but which are all the more powerful and pervasive for being invisible."[68] As we note throughout this book, Western theatre has a long connection to the ideology of ability, an ideology that rests, as Titchkosky explains, on a neglected question of perception. Attending to that question, and following Siebers, we can look for ways in which theatre's built environments have shaped perception, upholding or challenging aesthetic judgments that suppress the disabled body. Theatre inclusion, in this framing, cannot be understood only through minor adjustments or last-step additions to theatre's production and reception processes but rather as a fundamental querying of how denials of access have or have not informed the whole. As we saw above, some disabled artists reject the space of theatre entirely in their practice while others value it precisely for its "histories, ghosts, pressures and constraints" as a live forum for renegotiating disability's aesthetic value between the infinitely diverse complement of bodies affected by this evaluation themselves.

CHAPTER 4
INHERITED PLAYS AND NEW APPROACHES

In June 2014, London's Secret Theatre produced Tennessee Williams' *A Streetcar Named Desire* starring disabled actor Nadia Albina as Blanche DuBois. Lyn Gardner's review in *The Guardian* focused on this choice, citing Albina's concern that her disability "would be a lens through which everything would be seen." Ultimately, Gardner argued,

> one of the things that this Streetcar proved (alongside the fact that you don't have to play Williams in southern accents) is that visible disability can enhance and layer a classic text in fascinating ways, both emotional and political. [*Guardian* reviewer] Matt Trueman remarked that "Albina's disability makes every mention of beauty ping out of the text". Albina says that, as a disabled woman, she is used to feeling "isolated, not belonging, an alien in your surroundings" and all those feelings are heartbreakingly apparent in her Blanche, a woman who also feels like an alien in her surroundings.[1]

In this passage, Albina, Gardner, and Trueman articulate ways in which disability makes a difference to interpretation. Albina worries that her disability will become the production's sole interpretive angle but also argues that she draws on her disability experience to understand Blanche's social isolation and alienation. Gardner does find enhanced emotional and political meanings through Albina's visible disability while Trueman argues that disability presses the textual aesthetics in new ways, defamiliarizing their references to beauty. Neither Gardner nor Trueman focus solely on disability in their reviews but in each case Albina's casting was a notable feature in their interpretation of the whole, whether cited through the language of textual enhancement, layering or "pings."

With its motto "For the love of the art," and interest in promoting emerging artists, the Secret Theatre is a young company that does not cite disability in its mandate or aims. Nonetheless, the company's casting of Albina connects it to the spadework of many disability theatres that have been experimenting with new approaches to modern plays over the past few decades. Indeed, prior to joining the Secret Theatre in *Streetcar*, Gardner notes that Albina was perhaps best known for her "zinging performance as the mouthy Janine in Graeae's riotous Ian Dury musical, *Reasons to be Cheerful*."[2] In addition to devising and producing newer works, Graeae Theatre Company and other disability theatres have been exploring modern and other extant plays for decades.

While it will not be possible in this chapter to look at all instances of modern drama produced by disability theatres, it is possible to explore key examples that have prompted artistic reflection and critical responses about the place of disability in contemporary modern drama production. As in the example of *A Streetcar Named Desire* noted above, critics and artists often express a sense of difference in approach and interpretation. As we shall see, many find the experience defamiliarizes the text or, in the words of Brecht, invites more "complex seeing."[3]

As we noted in the introduction, theorists of modernism and disability anticipate this critical turn. Throughout his book *Concerto for the Left Hand: Disability and the Defamiliar Body*, for example, Michael Davidson argues that disability is itself a defamiliarization, in the modernist, formalist, avant-garde sense of the term as a means for rescuing the quotidian, assumed, or unnoticed from oblivion to render it strange and engaging. Indeed, he argues, "the defamiliarisation of the normate body is also the generative force in new cultural production."[4] In this volume's next chapter, Davidson explores this idea further in relation to Beckett's *Endgame* and other works. Here, however, we will explore how specific disability theatre companies have interrupted longstanding traditions for casting and interpreting modern drama to involve disabled artists in such generative new cultural production.

It is well to begin this survey of how some such companies have interpreted modern drama with Graeae for it is widely recognized as the flagship disabled-led theatre company in the UK and has demonstrated leadership internationally. Although the company has a diverse program and mandate and has changed a great deal since its founding in 1980, examining how it has woven modern plays into its artistic ambitions helps us to answer the questions that drive this chapter: that is, why modern drama; and how has it been approached by disabled artists?

Like many of the disability-focused companies mentioned in Chapter 1, Graeae has helped to develop and produce the new drama of disabled playwrights.[5] Importantly, however, it has also co-produced and toured large-scale productions of major modern plays including, most recently, Brecht's *The Threepenny Opera* in 2014 and Lorca's *Blood Wedding* in 2015. Focusing on these productions and some other salient examples from other disability theatre companies, we will query the difference that disability makes in these productions. What is the historical context for particular disability theatre companies taking up these texts? Why these plays? How have they wrestled with the issues of casting and accessibility noted in the previous chapters? When disabled actors have taken up leading roles in Brecht, Beckett, Lorca, and Williams' plays, what kinds of interpretations and critical responses have followed? Beginning with and centering our analysis largely on Graeae, we must ground ourselves first in their history to give context for their more specific artistic choices.

Graeae Theatre Company: Origins

Graeae Theatre Company was founded in 1980 by Nabil Shaban and Richard Tomlinson, the first a pioneering disabled actor, the second a non-disabled advocate and leader in education and disability. Aiming to redress the absence of disabled artists in British theatre, Graeae developed plays about disability to educate audiences and to upend through talent and theatrical innovation the pitying comment "didn't they do well, considering?"[6] As Shaban puts it in a retrospective history of Graeae's early days, he and Tomlinson aimed

> [t]o create opportunities for people like me to actively participate in the performing arts, but not on the basis of drama therapy. Graeae was not for occupational therapists or able-bodied careerist "do-gooders" who were looking for an alternative to basket making. No, we created Graeae to be a professional theatre of the highest artistic excellence. Secondly, we saw the need to change and subvert public attitudes, misconceptions, disrupt myths about disability and disabled people.[7]

The company emerged out of a long-running and episodic collaboration between Tomlinson and Shaban which began when the two met at Hereward College in Coventry where Tomlinson taught and ran a drama group and Shaban attended as a student. Over the years, the two organized several shows on a shoestring, but only coalesced as a company with a name after an invitation to present to a special conference on disability and rehabilitation in

Winnipeg, Canada in 1981, as part of the International Year of Disability. Their production, *Sideshow*, was an original script "lampooning stereotypes" and "confronting audiences."[8] In these early stages, Shaban and Tomlinson also experimented with "conventionally scripted plays" including a production of the medieval *Everyman* and a production of Harold Pinter's two-person play, *The Dumb Waiter* in 1975.[9] As Shaban later recalled, *The Dumb Waiter* "was a deliberate choice to do something from the mainstream."[10] After formally establishing Graeae, Shaban and Tomlinson also considered staging Ionesco's *The Chairs* and Beckett's *Endgame*, but both artists had left the company before realizing these plans.[11]

The use of "conventionally scripted plays" introduced the challenge of how to deal with disability on stage when the play had not been explicitly written for disabled actors or highlighted disability as a theme. Graeae determined that, in these situations, disability "was to be a positive force, a complement to the characterisation, and not a detraction."[12] Tomlinson explained this process with respect to Pinter's *The Dumb Waiter*, a play about two killers waiting for instructions in a restaurant kitchen, who eventually learn that one of the two is the intended victim. The play, Tomlinson suggested

> allowed us to pursue a little further the notion that disability should be used as an integral and complementary part of the production . . . The fact that the play's setting is pretty absurd and the characters themselves somewhat bizarre was a great help in deliberately playing up disability. In effect this only served to heighten the absurdity . . . In our production the actor playing Gus was in a wheelchair and the actor playing Ben was on crutches. The motivation for their actions is not immediately clear, and interpretation is in the hands of the director and the actors. We followed Pinter's stage instructions to the letter, except that instead of walking across, Gus wheeled across. He still stopped, took off his shoe, etc. The effect was arresting, and not, I would argue, in any way out of keeping with Pinter's intentions when writing the piece.[13]

Indeed, in the final scene of the production, Gus enters not only without his jacket, as the stage instructions demand, but also crawling, without his wheelchair. Tomlinson argues that this choice positively reinforced Pinter's portrayal of Gus as "totally vulnerable" in that final instant, a "sacrificial offering."[14]

Although the incorporation of disabled actors into productions using scripts that did not explicitly envision the possibility proved fruitful for

Shaban and Tomlinson, Graeae's early work built largely on original scripts, devised in the context of a given cast, exploring some dimension of disability. Partly this was the result of happenstance and opportunity and the need to tour works with an educational purpose. Tomlinson also reflected, however, that early attempts to take on established scripts challenged the company's actors and revealed the gaps in their training, which for most was limited—a fact he put down to the inaccessibility of mainstream actor training options.[15] The problem, then, became to work out a training system for actors with disabilities, which remains an enduring feature of Graeae Theatre Company's mission and practice.

After the establishment of Graeae, Shaban and Tomlinson went their separate ways, but the company continued to exist, develop and grow, despite several periods of furlough. By the mid-1990s, the company had an international reputation and an established body of work. Under the artistic directorship of Ewan Marshall, Graeae gained funding to support playwright and script development. This led to a series of highly innovative, challenging plays and productions, developed in a collaborative environment that took up disability themes, but aimed not to produce didactic "message" pieces. The aim, rather, was to approach difficult subjects and "tell the hidden stories of disabled people."[16] Plays such as April De Angelis and Albie Sachs' *Soft Vengeance*, about the aftermath of a political bombing in South Africa, and Ray Harrison Graham's *Sympathy for the Devil*, which addressed the complex intersections of race and disability, continued to explore disability perspectives on stage, but extended the conversation into new domains.

Under Artistic Director Jenny Sealey, who succeeded Marshall in 1997, Graeae continued to commission new works, but with an additional emphasis on questions of access. In addition to generating scripts, the collaborative process adopted by the company began to address the question of how different audiences and actors might require different inclusion tactics to perceive the work and perform in it. In Sealey's words, this led the company to "encompass an aesthetic as well as a practical and political vision."[17] As a result, new attention was paid to incorporating live audio-description into plays for blind audience members, and sign language for Deaf audiences. This attention to audience needs had a corollary effect on stage. New works, such as *Fittings: The Last Freak Show*, developed by Mike Kenny in collaboration with Garry Robson, Jenny Sealey and the show's actors, incorporated Sign Supported English in such a way that "the structure of the text worked with the actors' particular delivery of speech."[18] Later works, such as Kaite O'Reilly's *peeling*, similarly incorporated audio-description and sign language with a view to providing all members of the audience "the same information, but not necessarily at the same time."[19]

While the commissioning of new works has had and continues to have a crucial and central function for Graeae, in the late 1990s the company also began to reinterpret modern drama. A year after Jenny Sealey assumed the artistic directorship, the company produced Tennessee Williams' 1978 *A Lovely Sunday for Creve Coeur*, a one-act play with two scenes which focuses on the lives of four women in St. Louis in the 1930s, their loves, concerns, and disappointments. Williams' script describes one of the four characters, Bodey, as hard of hearing. The Graeae production cast Deaf actress Caroline Parker as Bodey alongside Sarah Howard, who has a mobility impairment, as Dorothea. Ailsa Fairley, who is blind, played Helena and Ali Briggs, also a Deaf actor, played Sophie. In the staging of the production, the sign language interpreter was, at times, also incorporated into the scene. As Maeve Walsh noted in a review of the production in *The Independent*, "under Sealey's direction [the sign interpreter] frantically signs Dottie's tale of seduction while pulling a disgusted grimace."[20] Overall, Walsh suggested, Graeae managed to make the performance "drip with unforced pathos while skillfully milking its potential for farce."[21] Interestingly, while Walsh's review mentions Caroline Parker's disability with respect to Bodey, and flags the role of sign interpreter, she does not mention that Helena, a non-disabled role, was performed by a blind actor. In fact, only Bodey's disability is specifically named. Graeae's 2009 guide for actor training addresses the issue of assigning disabled characters to non-disabled roles, using the example of Helena in *A Lovely Sunday for Creve Coeur* to make the point that an actor's impairment will "**inform** the playing of the character (because you cannot disguise most sensory and physical impairments) e.g. A blind actor playing Helena ... will use their particular spatial awareness [and] style of movement to enhance the stiff upper lip of the character."[22]

A year after *A Lovely Sunday for Creve Coeur*, Graeae produced Georg Büchner's *Woyzeck*, directed by Philip Osment, and performed in London by graduates of The Missing Piece One Training Course, described by Graeae as "a four month training programme for disabled actors which ran for five years, the last three in partnership with London Metropolitan University."[23] The following year, they moved on to the foremost Spanish modern playwright's most famous play, Federico García Lorca's *Blood Wedding*, again directed by Philip Osment and again performed by graduates of The Missing Piece One Training Course, this time touring the English Northwest. The company would revisit this script again in 2015, in a co-production with Dundee Rep and Derby Theatre that toured across England and Scotland.

Graeae's *Blood Wedding*

Blood Wedding: A Tragedy in Three Acts and Seven Scenes was first performed in 1933 in Madrid in Spanish. Its famously spare and compelling narrative structure follows love triangles between a bride, her former lover (now unhappily married to her cousin), and her bridegroom. When the play opens, the bridegroom's mother has already lost another son and her husband through a family feud with the bride's former lover's family. She warns her son against the marriage but to no avail. Although the groom and bride do marry, before the marriage is consummated, the bride runs away with her former lover. The groom finds and confronts them. Mingling prose and verse, magic realism, and symbolism, the play concludes with the deaths of the groom and former lover in a duel and the bride moving in with her mother-in-law. Although the play was famously based on a real incident, Dennis A. Klein has argued that the play shows the heavy influence of stage symbolism, especially in Lorca's "use of allegorical characters, the Moon and the Beggar-Woman, who represent Death."[24]

Explaining Graeae's choice of *Blood Wedding* for production in 2015, Jenny Sealey notes that it was the favorite among a few that she and Jemima Levick, joint Artistic Director at Dundee Rep, considered following a development week aimed at finding a co-production opportunity that involved actors from both companies.[25] The experimentation of that week convinced Sealey that the character of the mother would be Deaf and she says that was the only note she gave David Ireland as he developed his adaptation for the co-production. Elsewhere Sealey also explained the play choice as defiant: "Someone once said to me, 'Lorca did not write *Blood Wedding* for people like you (Deaf and disabled actors) to be in it': Graeae, Dundee Rep and Derby Theatre beg to differ and challenge that statement with our adaptation by David Ireland, placing a glorious diversity of people centre stage, all of whom have a right to be there to claim their stake in the narrative."[26]

In a preview interview with Paul F. Cockburn for *Disability Arts Online*, Sealey described communication challenges in the development process as "the beautiful dilemma," and shared an example of the company's process for creating an aesthetics of access:

EJ Raymond, who's playing the mother, is fantastic. She has a really beautiful, profound deaf voice, but I know that for some hearing people ... they can't always hear what she is saying. So everything is captioned ... For blind audiences though, it's a whole other area of having to tune in to what it is she's saying. Making sure that deafness is accessible to blind people in the audience – that's quite an interesting one. I think it is one of those things that we'll "have to suck it and see" ... There's also the whole area of family signing, because it's not pure BSL (British Sign Language). It's casual, sometimes it's with just one hand, sometimes it's lipreading, it's very specific. That's another communications dilemma because, if the diehard BSL community are expecting this to be a fully-fledged BSL production, it's not—it can't be, because of the characters. During the wedding scene, they book an "interpreter" for the wedding to "help mum"—so there are moments when we have flashes of real interpretation on stage—but we can't have that interpreter throughout the whole of it, because that's not what the play is about ... I think the play is about what you see and hear, what you don't see and hear, and you, the audience, have to fill in the gaps. I think that's what Lorca does; most action in Lorca happens offstage. I'm still trying to follow that thematic desire of Lorca, but we are necessarily showing and saying more than he'd probably allow."[27]

Most critics noted the translator and production's interventions in the text, particularly in relation to the narrative's twenty-first-century urban setting in contrast with Lorca's original early twentieth-century rural village in Andalusia. By contrast, critics responded in more varied ways to the place of disability in the production. For example, in her positive *Exeunt Magazine* review of the 2015 Graeae touring production, Alex Chisholm explained some of the ways disability shaped the performance:

I love the way that all aspects of "integration" and "access" add layers of meaning and nuance that just makes it better theatre. In this production, the Groom's Mother is Deaf (a very brilliant EJ Raymond), she communicates with her son, Edward (equally brilliant Ricci McLeod) in BSL. He interprets for her. Their co-dependent relationship, the pain and embarrassment they cause each other is clear in the language they speak and the language they sign (there are a couple of pointed moments using very un-PC signs for "Chinese" and "cripple"). When at the end they fight and he stops signing and just shouts in her face—it is shocking, heartbreaking. I loved the way the audio description functioned as the other characters/performers describing and commenting on the action, so took me further into not away from the performance. In the final scenes in particular, where the tone shifts towards the poetic and tragic (though still thank goodness with a leveling dose of sarcasm), I noticed how I took in the text both hearing and reading it. It gave me both a dramatic and literary appreciation at the same time, both more into the scene and into the language which I wanted to hold, savour and commit to memory for further use.[28]

Like Chisolm, theatre blogger Andrew Haydon saw the production at Liverpool's Everyman Theatre. He was also struck by the layering of language and his review offers further perspective on the differences disability made in interpretation:

Watching this version of *Blood Wedding*—and *version* it most definitely is—I was struck by the realisation that Graeae are pretty much *the* blueprint for what I wish Mainstream British Theatre was like ... Jenny Sealey's production—inextricably linked to Lisa Sangster's design—offers a way of playing the text which nimbly hops between demotic naturalism and a kind of post-Brechtian European arthouse style without ever feeling like it's doing anything even remotely so wanky. At the same time, the company offers more British national and regional voices than you hear over a whole season at the National, is effortlessly mixed race (but emphatically *not* colour-"blind"), and, oh yes, several of the actors are disabled too ... What we get here is: the plot of the original; an updating of it, a stage picture of the multicultural (and multi-national – Graeae co-produce with Dundee Rep) society we actually live in; and a kind of deconstruction of what the hell Lorca was up to in the first place. After all, the plot is the stuff of Eastenders: man with murdered brother and father is marrying a woman who is having an affair with the nephew of their murderer ... Apart from the obviously updated script and the nicely abstract (if a bit too *clean* for my money) set, I think part of what makes this production so brilliantly contemporary is the way that Graeae use language. Because of their status as "a disabled company", their default way of treating a stage—incorporating surtitles and signing for the deaf and plentiful audio-description for the blind *as a matter of course*—means that at any given moment about three languages are being used simultaneously. As an approach it simply makes all of us *read* the stage more carefully. As a result, it effortlessly aces the kind of stage semiotics that some "visual theatre" companies are still struggling with after more than a decade.[29]

Both Chisolm and Haydon referenced disabled actors' roles onstage and found pleasure in David Ireland's adaptation of the script and Sealey's casting and design choices. Mark Fisher, by contrast, reviewing the production for *The Guardian*, did not acknowledge the presence of disabled actors on stage. Rather, he focused first on Ireland's translation, something he described as "lightweight" and insufficiently connected with the original play's mythic, tragic core, criticisms he extended to the production as a whole:

> But by moving the play into a 21st-century world of knife crime, neon lights and Elvis-themed wedding discos, Jenny Sealey's production works against these mythic dimensions. At the heart of the story are Leonardo, Olivia, Vicky and Edward—their initials ironically spelling out LOVE—caught up in a sorry tale of adultery. But for all the spirited performances of the cast, in the absence of Lorca's cloying sense of inevitability, this is a story of soap-opera banality not tragic weight.
>
> It is, though, a lively production. The integrated surtitles, signing and audio description lend it a Brechtian theatricality, which is matched by the unexpected irreverence of Ireland's translation. Likewise, the actors establish a mood of informality and a cheerful connection with the audience. But even with a play that's all about the power of community, it takes more than a strong ensemble to do this tragedy justice.[30]

Strikingly, this more negative view does not touch on the mother's deafness. Rather, Fisher argues, the production's twenty-first-century, sensational qualities get in the way of the sense of tragic fate and, arguably, Lorca's famous sense of *duende*. The aesthetics of access are once again described as Brechtian, an interpretation that, as we shall see, returns again and again in relation to Graeae and other disability theatre interpretations of modern plays. Brecht's aesthetics famously sought to interrupt the inevitability associated with tragic form, challenging the clear causal links in the narrative and the integrity of the fused artistic whole to bear witness to and resonate with the choices historical subjects must make in difficult historical contexts. While "Brechtian theatricality" seemed at odds with Lorca's original text for Fisher, it arguably also opens up the text to precisely the kind of questioning

Brecht would have valued. As Sealey notes in her interview later in this book, however, references to Brecht seem most appropriate to the company's spring 2014 touring co-production of Brecht, Hauptmann and Weill's *The Threepenny Opera*. The production affords an opportunity to think about how casting disabled actors and approaching the text from an aesthetics of access aligned with Brechtian staging ideals, ideals frustrated since the earliest examples of its production.

Graeae's *The Threepenny Opera*

Co-directed by New Wolsey Theatre's Peter Rowe and Graeae Theatre Company's Jenny Sealey, *The Threepenny Opera* toured to Nottingham Playhouse, New Wolsey Theatre in Ipswich, Birmingham Repertory Theatre and West Yorkshire Playhouse from 21 February to 10 May 2014. New Wolsey and Graeae had collaborated before but, in this case, Rowe explained,

> We were looking for a piece that would take exposure for disabled actors to another level ... *The Threepenny Opera* is a satire of the gross inequalities in society, and our inspiration came from the Occupy movement. Our beggars are a group of contemporary activists who take over the theatre and put on a version of *The Threepenny Opera* that reflects their own diversity."[31]

The company used an English translation of the dialogue by Robert David MacDonald and an English translation of the lyrics by Jeremy Sams.[32] The eighteen-member cast included both seasoned and emerging Deaf, disabled and non-disabled actor-musicians who were complemented in their efforts by an audio-describer/access support worker, a sign language interpreter, and a further access support worker. In contrast to the spare formal structure of Lorca's original *Blood Wedding*, *The Threepenny Opera*'s large cast, episodic formal structure, and more complex narrative posed different challenges for Graeae and New Wolsey Theatre.

Brecht and collaborator Elisabeth Hauptmann rewrote John Gay's 1728 socially provocative *Beggar's Opera* in collaboration with avant-garde musician Kurt Weill to open in 1928 and emphasize crime's interconnectedness with capitalism.[33] The result was the most commercially successful work associated with Brecht. In notes published three years after the play's first production, Brecht explains that the whole weight of this kind of drama comes from the piling up of resistances. The material is not yet arranged in accordance with any wish for an easy ideal formula. ... Today, when the human being has to be seen as the "sum of all social circumstances" the epic form is the only one that can embrace those processes which serve the drama as matter for a comprehensive picture of the world.[34]

In contrast with the sense of tragic fate and inevitability that critics associated with Lorca, Brecht's epic theatre champions what he calls epic form, or more episodic, dialectical form that highlights conflict between equally compelling ideals but resists pat resolution within the theatrical event itself. *The Threepenny Opera*'s primary resistance is between criminal figures Macheath and Jonathan Jeremiah Peachum, with Macheath's old friend and army comrade Police Chief "Tiger" Brown complicating matters between them. Where Macheath, "Mack the Knife," is a notorious thief and criminal, Peachum is the proprietor of the Beggar's Friend Ltd., a business through which he directs and costumes London's street beggars, taking half their profits and charging for their outfits. His costuming choices share much in common with the idea of "cripping up" we explored in Chapter 2. For example, consider Act One Scene One in which Peachum negotiates with Filch, a prospective new beggar for his company:

Peachum   Your name?

Filch   Charles Filch.

Peachum   Right (*shouts*) Mrs. Peachum! (*Mrs Peachum enters*) This is Filch. Number 314. Baker Street district. I'll do his entry myself. Trust you to pick this moment to apply, just before the Coronation, when for once in a lifetime there's a chance of making a little something. Outfit C.

He opens a linen curtain before a showcase in which there are five wax dummies.

Filch   What's that?

Peachum   Those are the five basic types of misery, those most likely to touch the human heart. The sight of such types puts a man into the unnatural state where he is willing to part with money. Outfit A: Victim of vehicular progress. The merry paraplegic, always cheerful (*He acts it out*) – always carefree, emphasised by arm-stump. Outfit B: Victim of the Higher Strategy. The Tiresome Trembler, molests passers-by, operates by inspiring nausea – (*He acts it out*) – attenuated by medals. Outfit C: Victim of advanced Technology. The Pitiful Blind Man, the Cordon Bleu of Beggary.[35]

The scene itself uses the performance of "cripping up" to highlight the conflict between appearance and reality, Filch and Peachum, those who have and those who do not. Peachum's daughter Polly and Brown's daughter Lucy also play pivotal roles and likewise add to the pile of resistances Brecht described. Polly, in defiance of her father, who fears her marriage will impede his business, marries Macheath in a secret ceremony attended by Brown. When Polly reveals the marriage to her parents, they determine to involve the police. Macheath's notoriety and past crimes force him to flee, landing him at his favorite brothel. Betrayed there, however, he is arrested, placing Brown in an awkward position with his friend. In prison, Macheath is visited by Brown's daughter Lucy, whereupon Polly arrives, allowing for the play's famous fight between the women over whom Macheath really loves and to whom he is married. Brown faces a dilemma after Lucy helps Macheath escape: if he does not return Macheath to prison, Peachum promises to marshal all the beggars under his sway to scatter strategically throughout London in order to disrupt the upcoming Queen's Coronation. Betrayed again after returning to the brothel, Macheath is sentenced to hang. Joined by their sorrow, Polly and Lucy watch over Macheath, a doomed man with no further options, who sings a ballad asking all men for forgiveness. In a striking reversal, however, one that mocks the very possibility of such an ending outside the theatre, a mounted messenger arrives, explaining, "I bring a special order from our beloved Queen to have Captain Macheath set at liberty forthwith (*All cheer*) – as it's the Coronation, and raised to the hereditary peerage. (*Cheers*) The castle of Marmarel, likewise a pension of ten thousand pounds, to be his in usufruct until his death."[36]

The musical drama famously opens with a moritat singer and his street organ singing "Mack the Knife," a murder ballad in the tradition of medieval strolling minstrels that in this case details the many crimes associated with Macheath: thieving, rape, murder, and committing arson. As the many famous standalone recordings (Bobby Darin, Frank Sinatra, Ella Fitzgerald, etc.) of this narratively harrowing but undeniably catchy song suggest, this ballad and Kurt Weill's now iconic music throughout *The Threepenny Opera* have led many critics to argue that the play can too easily be absorbed by audiences without the political edge and intellectual questioning demanded by Brecht's broader aesthetics of defamiliarization. Through such notes as those cited above and his involvement in subsequent productions of *The Threepenny Opera*, Brecht was interested in trying to shift emphasis away from what he felt were the main sources for popularity but, in his view, unimportant aspects of the play: "the romantic plot, the love story, the music."[37] More important, in his view, were the means for production:

> *The Threepenny Opera* is concerned with bourgeois conceptions not only as content, by representing them, but also through the manner in which it does so ... The screens on which the titles of each scene are projected are a primitive attempt at literarizing the theatre. The literarization of the theatre needs to be developed to the utmost degree, as in general does the literarizing of all public occasions ... Literarizing entails punctuating "representation" with "formulation"; gives the theatre the possibility of making contact with other institutions for intellectual activities; but it is bound to remain one-sided so long as the audience is taking no part in it and using it as a means of obtaining access to "higher things" ... Some exercise in complex seeing is needed—though it is perhaps more important to be able to think above the stream than to think in the stream. Moreover, the use of screens imposes and facilitates a new style of acting. This style is the *epic style*."[38]

Organized in part to serve artists and patrons with visual impairments as well as hearing-impaired and Deaf audiences, the Graeae production mingled film, audio-description, captioning, and live onstage signing, the combination of which onstage certainly created an exercise in complex seeing as well as complex hearing. Given how often critics have connected disability with defamiliarization, Brechtian or otherwise, it is therefore particularly interesting to consider how this disability theatre-led production was reviewed on this count.

Although he did not care for Jeremy Sams' updated lyrics, finding their more topical, contemporary references "superficial," Matt Trueman's review for *The Guardian* praised the production overall:

> Theatrically speaking, however, it's super-smart. Disabled actors make natural Brechtians. How can you lose sight of the actor behind the character when their physicality or vocal quality is a constant reminder

of their reality? Various approaches to accessibility—surtitles and BSL interpretation—add extra disruptive layers without the usual contrivances. Jude Mahon's expressive signing carries the music's tone and rhythms as well as nailing its images.[39]

Trueman's idea of disabled actors being "natural Brechtians" is remarkable in view of Sealey's interview remarks to Alfred Hickling in *The Guardian* a few weeks earlier in his preview for the production:

> People frequently tell me that I have a Brechtian directing style, but I don't pretend to know what that means ... I'm no great Brecht expert—I just follow my instincts. But whenever you put a group of talented and empowered disabled actors on stage it demands that an audience think twice about what they are seeing.[40]

As we shall see in her interview later in this volume, Sealey recognizes that some audiences experience her directorial choices as akin to Brechtian alienation. For her, however, they emerge more directly from a process that aims to serve the access needs of an audience conceived as fundamentally inclusive, a process she has preferred to describe elsewhere as "cluttering," "a cross-fertilization of forms, enabling the recognition and appreciation of access requirements between artists, designers, actors and audience and, moreover, between communities ... At the heart of every creative decision is the audience's ability to access the story through a collective experience of play watching."[41] Practically, this cluttering process demands that access be

> embedded in every production to enable accessible performing and spectating. Graeae's live performance is layered with spoken/signed languages and visual/aural technology, weaving a multi-sensory narrative that engages and communicates with audiences in diverse ways. The use of headphones and projections specifically aims to facilitate connection, highlighting a relationship between performer and audience. With technological support and the presence of integrated access conventions, each Graeae production connects identity, story and access and appeals to audiences who have diverse learning and engagement styles.[42]

Writing for the Graeae Theatre Company blog, renowned disablility performer, Graeae alumnus and now patron Mat Fraser explained that cluttering in the case of *The Threepenny Opera* involved a combination of "photos, pictures, scrawls and graffiti images nestling next to the vicious words of Brecht, the stage text, sign language interpretation, and onstage audio description provided by cast members."[43] Beyond the design elements, casting choices proved pivotal for the production and Sealey described the ensemble as "a wonderful, highly-skilled motley crew of Deaf, physically impaired, blind and visually impaired people, people with hidden impairments and non-disabled people."[44] A primary example of the production's aesthetics of access through casting decisions was the choice to have the Narrator act as an audio-describer. Peter Kirwan's review of the Nottingham production for *Exeunt Magazine* emphasized the centrality of this role from the top of the production:

> John Kelly's Narrator introduces *The Threepenny Opera* by barking obscenities at the audience from before a tattered red curtain while mocking his fellow company members. Buzzing around the stage in his electric wheelchair, Kelly's voluble and volatile presence whips up a level of energy which this Graeae co-production manages to maintain for almost three hours, during which time the company unleash a charged, hysterical, non-stop onslaught of political commentary combined with riotous entertainment.[45]

Emphasizing the Narrator's role in pacing and creating anti-illusionistic moments throughout by "whizz[ing] about, screaming for scene changes," Kirwan did not mention the Narrator's role in audio-description.[46] This omission stands in contrast to Liz Porter's review of first the Ipswich and then the Birmingham production for *Disability Arts Online*.

Explaining that she wrote from a visually impaired perspective and describing the play choice as "timely and well-considered," Porter's arguments centered largely on the strengths and weaknesses of the production in relation to developing "an inclusive aesthetic around creative access."[47] Her review noted how John Kelly acted as both Narrator and audio-describer, a choice she felt was clever in that his descriptions "did help set up the scenes."[48] She was frustrated, however, that his basic description "was not always consistent."[49] She appreciated that other ensemble members also delivered audio-descriptions that visually impaired audience members received "through headsets as scenes unfolded" (in her estimation with varying success) but wished that they had done so in character.[50] In contrast with her critiques of the show's uneven use of the film captioning and audio-description, she praised the pre-show access information she found in Ipswich. Here, she notes, "[i]t included programme notes and character descriptions (described by the actors), which were also available on headsets. There was a show synopsis in alternative formats, braille, LP easy read and BSL as well as swatches of costume fabrics to convey the look and feel of the show up close."[51] Overall, Porter concluded in Ipswich, "[t]his production grabs you way beyond the end of the show and I certainly want to catch it again."[52] A further passage in her review also suggests the degree to which the production as a whole accomplished Brechtian defamiliarization:

> The new English translation of the dialogue (Robert David McDonald) and lyrics (Jeremy Sams) creates a tension between the past, present and future. As the audience we question life for the oppressed through wicked political satire. This is a busy and often crowded experience with 21 actor/musicians on stage for the majority of the time. The degree of concentration needed made it difficult to emotionally engage and pull all the strands of the story together.[53]

Arguably, Brechtian defamiliarization seeks precisely such a response: building a greater awareness among audience members of their historical context, pressing them to question the causal links between narrative strands, and pulling audiences in and out of emotional engagement in dynamic ways that alternately delight, frustrate, and prompt further critical reflection.

Perhaps the most obvious disability content in the play's narrative concerns Peachum's aforementioned coaching of the beggars under his sway to use artificial limbs and disability as means for gaining greater sympathy and money from passers-by. In his review for *The Guardian*, Hickling focuses on this aspect, quoting Sealey in regard to how casting choices in this version offered a "further twist": "In this production, the character who complains that he has been given a defective stump is played by a non-disabled actor . . . though Peachum himself is in a wheelchair. And Mrs Peachum is played by a blind opera singer, though she is the one character in the piece who sees everything."[54] Thus, Sealey and Rowe cast roles in ways that ran against the grain of each actor's lived experience of disability.

Kirwan's *Exeunt Magazine* review also highlighted the ways in which Peachum and other disabled actors' bodies recast lines in ways akin to the defamiliarizing "pings" surrounding mention of beauty that Matt Trueman noted in relation to Nadia Albina's performance in *A Streetcar Named Desire*. From his wheelchair, Kirwan notes, Peachum jokes in one scene that "someone would steal his legs out from under him" and screams in another at "his wife (the blind Victoria Oruwari) about her failure to see what's going on in front of her."[55] Leading UK disabled artist and actor Garry Robson, who played Peachum, explained to Colin Hambrook in a preview for *Disability Arts Online* that it is striking how much disability is in the play: "My character talks about 'the happy cripple; always free, always carefree.' There is a lot of satirical use of language—and because we are an integrated cast that in itself speaks volumes."[56] Indeed, it was not the first time Robson had performed in the play among other disabled actors. In 2004 he performed in it alongside Nabil Shaban in Theatre Workshop Scotland's production.[57] In that case director Robert Rae also made a case for disability's central place in the text:

> *Threepenny Opera's* not often put in that sort of historical context, but it's a play about beggars, it's about prostitutes, it's about the disabled. It was written by a communist and composed by a Jew, so many of whom were about to be annihilated. So the play seems to scream to the audience, "who are you to judge?"[58]

Taken up by two different disability theatre companies that each lay claim to the centrality of disability in the text, the play might also serve as a historical document for those seeking evidence of disability's changing place over time. In her chapter later in this volume, Ann M. Fox encourages disability scholars to revisit rather than dismiss *The Glass Menagerie* for its potential value as a source of disability history and evidence that "disability has been an integral subject and part of social protest for longer than we might suspect." Fox's arguments extend well to the analysis of *The Threepenny Opera*, particularly in view of Carol Poore's notes concerning the play in her recent book *Disability in Twentieth-Century German Culture*:

> Immediately after the war, the press was full of articles about the "plague of beggars." Journalists often criticized these veterans from an aesthetic standpoint for offensively confronting the postwar public. On November 26, 1919, for example, the *Deutsche Tageszeitung* took men to task "who take to begging while insistently emphasizing their suffering and present an ugly sight in the streets and squares of the big cities." This entire phenomenon, however, was more complex than it appeared on the surface. For, when welfare officials investigated the "mass epidemic" of military beggars in 1919–20, they found that many were either disabled

civilians or nondisabled people feigning ailments who found that they received larger handouts when they put on a uniform. In turn, this "comedy of misery" fueled major ongoing controversies over malingering (*Simulantentum*) and pension psychosis (*Rentenpsychose*) throughout the Weimar era, particularly with regard to psychiatrists' doubts about veterans' claims of mental illness—the so-called war neurotics or *Kriegszitterer* (war shiverers). It also furnished plentiful material for a writer such as Bertolt Brecht, whose *Dreigroschenoper* (*Threepenny Opera*, 1928) took up the theme of begging to point out in an entertaining way how ludicrous it was to expect human sympathy in a capitalist society based solely on profit.[59]

As Poore and Fox assert, Brecht not only took up the theme of begging but also contemporary Germany's discourses about disability and its place in society. How does encountering these plays through disability theatre help to revitalize disability's integral place in the narrative and uncover new angles for disability history? Further, might pursuing these questions allow scholars to uncover further evidence in support of Tobin Siebers' claim that modern artistic movements form an aesthetic tradition increasingly preoccupied with disability?[60]

Our final example of disability theatre production of modern plays concerns a playwright whose *oeuvre* is unquestioningly preoccupied with disability, Samuel Beckett. In 2007 Theatre Workshop Scotland produced a notable version of *Endgame* that once again starred Garry Robson and Nabil Shaban. To understand what drew them and this company to these texts in particular, it is important to ground ourselves first in the company's origins and particular impulses for inclusive theatre practice.

Theatre Workshop Scotland and Beckett's *Endgame*

Theatre Workshop Scotland (TWS) originated in the mid-1960s as a drama center for children, then called Theatre Workshop Edinburgh. From the mid-1970s, the company worked with disabled people, but the sharp focus on processes of disability and inclusion emerged when Robert Rae assumed the TWS artistic directorship in 1996.[61] Rae's personal website underlines that "His diverse range of work for both adult and children's audiences reflects a passionate concern for outsider experience—placing their culture and history at the heart of the creative process."[62] Apart from his directorial work in theatre and film, Rae has written on the need to build inclusive practices into professional theatre. In 2000, under Rae's leadership, TWS introduced a new inclusion policy, making it "the first professional building based theatre in Europe to cast disabled actors in all its productions as a matter of policy."[63] In practical terms this led to over one hundred paid acting roles for actors with disabilities by the 2006–7 season and became a distinctive and valued dimension of TWS's artistic work.[64] Alongside devised work, Rae and TWS developed several modern drama productions, including *The Threepenny Opera* (2004) and Samuel Beckett's *Endgame* (2007), all of which showcased disabled actors. Nabil Shaban, the co-founder of Graeae, held starring roles in each of these and gained critical acclaim for his performances, including a Critics Awards for Theatre in Scotland nomination for Best Actor for his role as Macheath in the TWS production of *The Threepenny Opera*.[65] Finally, TWS hosted a series of "degenerate" disability arts festivals which brought Scottish and international disability artists together at the Theatre Workshop site in Edinburgh.[66] Although TWS lost its building in 2009 and shifted increasingly towards major collaborative community film productions, such as the *Happy Lands* documentary about the 1926 general strike in a Fife mining community, the company modeled a distinctive approach to disability theatre, adapting professional theatre models with inclusive policies and integrated casts.[67]

In 2007, TWS produced Samuel Beckett's *Endgame* with a cast that included disabled actors; casting and performance choices led to rich debates among critics and artists akin to those engendered by Graeae's *Blood Wedding* and *Threepenny Opera*. Like Lorca and Brecht, Beckett is well known for his formal innovation. Inside the bleak, isolated world he creates in *Endgame*, remarkably little action builds dramatic tension.

The narrative of this enduring play follows Hamm, a blind man who cannot stand, Nagg and Nell, his parents who lost their legs in a bicycle accident and now live in ashbins, and Clov, a man who limps and is losing his sight. In *Endgame*, as in Beckett's other works such as *Waiting for Godot* and *Happy Days*, the characters' impairments are critical for the play's conflicts and effects. Indeed, as theorist Michael Davidson explains later in this book, *Endgame* is perhaps the most obvious but far from the only example among Beckett's works of disabled figures who "form tenuous alliances for mutual aid" or, in the characters' oft-stated phrasing, simply "to go on."[68] Davidson further argues that "while critics have seen their impairments as metaphors for alienation and solitude in the modern world we might see that alienation as the condition of disability in a world of compulsory able-bodiedness."[69] Davidson's reading offers a rare disability studies approach amid what critic Ato Quayson has identified as an odd tradition in Beckett studies to assimilate physical disability "to a variety of philosophical categories in such a way as to obliterate the specificity of the body and to render it a marker of something else."[70] Davidson and Quayson both seek to redress this tendency. Davidson argues that if we read Hamm and Clov through a disability optic, we see them functioning "within an ableist ideology [rooted in liberal ideals of individualism] that views dependent relations as weakness."[71] Ato Quayson, by contrast, emphasizes instead how "critics have managed to anaesthetize the disabled body in Beckett by assimilating it much too rapidly to abstract philosophical categories."[72] Quayson's main line of redressive inquiry turns on the provocative question: "what happens to our interpretation when we examine the status of disability within a representational system in which *the discomfort of disability is* not *accounted for*?"[73] Quayson builds his arguments through a close reading of *Endgame*, an overview of Beckett's own experiences of pain and disability, as well as consideration of the celebrated London 2004 production of *Endgame* starring Michael Gambon as Hamm. Importantly for my purposes here, however, Quayson also briefly imagines a production which might turn the tide of reception, a production in which the hospital-like smells of antiseptic "would forcefully locate the audience and the reader in a place they most likely would not like either to be at or be reminded of, thus situating them in in a conceptual domain that directly subtends the condition of immobility and discomfort displayed on stage."[74]

Quayson imagines a production choice that would foreground bodily discomfort and pain. In a different but equally forceful attempt to turn the tide and foreground lived disability experience, Theatre Workshop Scotland's 2007 production cast disabled actors in the roles of disabled characters. Both examples, however, run counter to the play's production history since its 1957 premiere at the Royal Court Theatre, London, a history that is rich, sustained, and marked with controversy. For example, Beckett famously censured a 1984 American Repertory Theatre production that changed the play's setting from a bare room with two high windows to a derelict subway station and used music by Philip Glass when Beckett insisted that there should be none. Grove Press, Beckett's publishers, took legal action, and an out-of-court settlement was reached which generated a production program insert that included Beckett's now famous admonishment:

> Any production of *Endgame* which ignores my stage directions is completely unacceptable to me. My play requires an empty room and two small windows. The American Repertory Theater production which dismisses my directions is a complete parody of the play as conceived by me. Anybody who cares for the work couldn't fail to be disgusted by this.[75]

The Beckett estate has remained litigious in pursuit of the writer's directions, halting some productions and recently challenging but failing to prevent the casting of women in an Italian production of *Waiting for Godot*.

I recount these controversies and legal details because one of the main reviews of the 2007 Theatre Workshop *Endgame* raised the question of whether or not this production might not have been similarly censured by the Beckett estate but for recent experience. "Had the estate's wings not been so clipped," wrote Mark Brown in *The Telegraph*, "one fears that this bold adaptation ... would have ended up in the courts."[76] This review and others make clear that something disruptive and challenging was at play in the TWS production. The production reviews and further critical debates afford another opportunity to think about how disability performance reorients the meaning of the whole. How was this famous play that turns on disabled figures changed by casting disabled actors?

Although one critic described it as a "radical departure," no reviewer expressed surprise that TWS would stage *Endgame* with disabled actors, for a commitment to inclusion and a policy of casting disabled actors was central to the company's mandate—a point that several critics in fact underlined.[77] While Theatre Workshop's casting decisions were likely anticipated by critics and audiences, they did nevertheless challenge some expectations about how *Endgame* ought to be staged. Rather than place Hamm (Nabil Shaban) at center stage in "an armchair on castors,"[78] Theatre Workshop placed the actor inside an elevated metal cage. Because the man performing Clov (Garry Robson) uses a wheelchair, he did not climb the ladder to report on the weather as the stage directions suggest, but mimicked the sound of walking to deceive the blind Hamm and then looked out of a periscope from stage level. Furthermore, Hamm's parents, Nagg (Raymond Short) and Nell (Dolina Maclennan), were performed by disabled actors contained within metallic bins on wheels, not quite the same as the "ashbins" described in the script.[79] These production choices, aimed at accommodating the particular corporealities of the disabled actors playing disabled characters, therefore forced audiences and critics with expectations based on previous knowledge of the play to make sense of several innovations in design, script interpretation, and performance.

For some, the effects were remarkable. Writing in the *Scotsman*, Joyce McMillan described the production as "a slightly unusual version of *Endgame*, in that it inverts the usual staging to place the servant Clov in a wheelchair, Hamm in a high mobile cage that seems both throne and prison."[80] Mark Fisher found the reinterpretation of Hamm and Clov's relationship "a tad confusing" but felt that it added "a layer of tension to an already fractious relationship."[81] After noting TWS's commitment to inclusion, Mark Brown, writing in *The Telegraph*, argued that "The pathos and cruel humour of Clov's deception of Hamm, which Rae has introduced, are quite at odds with Beckett's drama. The balance of power between the two men is altered almost beyond recognition, shifting away from Hamm towards Clov."[82] Writing in *The List*, Steve Cramer suggested that "Rae's production amounts less to a rewriting of Beckett's original and much protected script, as a succession of minor changes of nuance, mainly through design."[83] While McMillan found this to be "a rich and memorable staging of a great play," one of the Scottish Arts Council's specialist advisors rated the production as "poor" in a publicly available artistic evaluation, drawing particular attention to the failure of the stage design and the direction. Rae, argued advisor Sita Ramamurthy, "tried too hard to convey his interpretation of the text as opposed to allowing the text to be revealed."[84]

The Scottish Arts Council allows theatre companies to respond to advisors' reports and Robert Rae took the opportunity to do so in this case. His response noted that, rather than depart from the script as Ramamurthy and some critics had claimed, he had worked hard to remain faithful to

> Beckett's own interpretation … as articulated in his published notebooks of three productions he was closely involved with. I religiously turned to them for guidance. Ms. Ramamurthy is wrong to say that I tried to place my own interpretation on his script. . . . Apart from the adaptations required because of the impairments of the actors—I was faithful to Beckett's own directions.[85]

This final line is key for thinking about the difference that disability makes. The changes made in staging and design to include disabled actors performing disabled characters unsettled expectations, and for many changed the nature and tone of the central angst-ridden relationship between Hamm and Clov. And yet, as Davidson will argue in the context of

Beckett's play and Siebers argues in the context of modern art more broadly, disability is an integral part of the narrative. Recalling Siebers' question from the introduction, "To what concept, other than the idea of disability, might be referred modern art's love affair with misshapen and twisted bodies, stunning variety of human forms, intense representation of traumatic injury and psychological alienation, and unyielding preoccupation with wounds and tormented flesh?"[86] Beckett's text demonstrates all these features: from a cast filled with non-normate bodies, to the unanswered calls for pain medication, to the intense sense of alienation from the world beyond the shared space. Siebers' question strikes at the core of *Endgame* and the TWS production suggests that casting disabled actors revitalizes the play of disability, a crucial rather than incidental feature in his work.

Conclusion

At the beginning of this chapter, we considered how Gardner, Trueman, and Albina's collective responses to Albina's casting as Blanche DuBois cited the power of Albina's performance to ground, enhance, layer or "ping" key aspects of the text. We investigated how the relatively recent productions of *Blood Wedding*, *The Threepenny Opera*, and *Endgame* by leading disability artists were likewise recognized by critics and artists as engaging their respective texts in new, challenging, and revealing ways that were frequently described as defamiliarizing or Brechtian. While critical response was both positive and negative, the language of layering and defamiliarization coursed throughout. Revisiting modern drama through the work of disability theatre artists affords an opportunity to rethink disability's place within them, and, as these examples have shown, the layers that critics cite might be best understood not as added by disabled artists but uncovered by them as important features of the text that have been there all along.

PART II
CRITICAL PERSPECTIVES

CHAPTER 5
"EVERY MAN HIS SPECIALTY": BECKETT, DISABILITY, AND DEPENDENCE
Michael Davidson

I "To decompose is to live, too"

In *Bending Over Backwards* Lennard Davis coins the term "dismodernism" to describe the ways that disability challenges ideas of liberal autonomy and able-bodied normalcy that underwrite contemporary identity politics. As a social model, dismodernism shares with theories of postmodernism a skepticism toward grand narratives of subjecthood and historical teleology, but Davis faults much postmodern theory for maintaining a social constructionist view of identity on the one hand while retaining a politics of multiculturalism and core group identity on the other. Reprising recent scientific discoveries in the field of genetics that disprove the biological basis of race, sexuality or ethnicity, he asks "how does it make sense to say there is a social construction of it?"[1] Discourses of race, gender, and sexuality are products of late nineteenth-century medical science—as is disability—but, unlike these other areas, disability crosses all such categories and is the one identity position destined, as we age, to include all of us. Its pervasiveness and instability permit Davis to see disability as a kind of *ur*-identity constructed within the technologies of bio-power yet one not bound by specific genetic, economic, or racial markers. The dismodernist ideal "aims to create a new category based on the partial, incomplete subject whose realization is not autonomy and independence but dependency and interdependence."[2]

Although Davis conflates a postmodern philosophical stance toward performativity with a historical, post-civil rights cultural politics, he does point to a key limitation of rights claims that presume a healthy, independent (probably white, probably heterosexual, male) ideal to the exclusion of those deemed "defective" or unable to make "rational choices." In this respect he joins a number of recent theorists—Albert Memmi, Martha Nussbaum, Michael Berubé, Eva Kittay, and Alasdair MacIntyre—for whom a consideration of dependency challenges the social contract as it has been conceived from Rousseau and Hume to Rawls and asks whether contractarian ideals can stand the test of differently abled bodies. Stated succinctly by Eva Kittay, dependency critique asserts that the idea of society as an association of equals "masks inequitable dependencies, those of infancy and childhood, old age, illness and disability. While we are dependent, we are not well positioned to enter a competition for the goods of social cooperation on equal terms."[3] Although liberal theories of social justice stress equal access to the public sphere, they do not account for individuals who, because of cognitive impairment or physical disability, cannot cooperate on "equal" and independent terms. Nor are dependent relations validated in the common weal. Citizens who need special accommodations are often stigmatized as narcissists, whiners, and drains on public funds. Their requests for "reasonable accommodations" under the Americans with Disabilities Act (ADA) have led to a series of court cases that have been, for the most part, decided against the plaintiffs. The need for interpreters, caregivers, therapists, and social services places persons with disabilities in conflict with liberal ideals of independence and self-reliance.[4] Can a model of independent living—the basis of the disability rights movement—coincide with what Alasdair MacIntyre calls the "virtues of acknowledged dependence" that implicate all of us?[5]

Martha Nussbaum's *Frontiers of Justice* answers these questions with a resounding "not yet" and in particular charges John Rawls' *Theory of Justice* with bracketing the rights of persons with disabilities, poor persons, and nonhuman animals as constituencies that cannot be included in Rawls' "original position"—those "normal conditions under which human cooperation is both possible and necessary."[6] Against contract models of human rights that stress cooperation for mutual benefit, Nussbaum argues for a rights discourse from the standpoint of what she calls, adapting Amartya Sen, "capabilities"—"what people are actually able to do and to be in a way informed by an intuitive idea of a life that is worthy of the dignity of the human being."[7] The contractarian model presumes a utilitarian theory of justice based on the nation state and a self-sufficient society of relative equals.[8] Nussbaum's critique of Rawls challenges the equality thesis that underwrites liberal ideals of social justice by pointing to a global economy dominated by unequal relationships of interdependence that benefit dominant nations and consign matters of social justice to charity and debt relief. By deferring social justice to those who either cannot afford access to the public sphere or who find it physically inaccessible, Rawls creates a social contract that is incomplete and partial. It becomes what Walter Lippmann, in another context, calls a "phantom public," an ideal of participatory democracy that cannot be realized in practice under current conditions.[9] As

Nussbaum says, "all the major social contract thinkers choose to imagine their parties as rationally competent adults who, as Locke says, are, in the state of nature, 'free, equal, and independent.'"[10] Not everyone who enters the state of nature is "free, equal, and independent," and although Rawls acknowledges the needs of such persons he withholds consideration of their "special needs" for some future just state. Nussbaum counters by saying that if a theory of justice is to be adequate it cannot be more adequate for some or deferred until the ethical infrastructure is in place.

I want to explore the dialectics of dependency—the interplay between a social contract based on free, equal agents and one that recognizes contingent interrelationships—by looking at one modernist writer, Samuel Beckett, whose work dismodernizes liberal theories of autonomy and independent agency by creating scenes of what we might call "abject dependency." Beckett's characters often exist in tragi-comic relations of co-dependence that seem to mock communitarian ideals of charity and mutual aid while laying bare the edifice of liberal individualism as a flawed document. Hamm and Clov, Mercier and Camier, Pozzo and Lucky, Winnie and Willie, Vladimir and Estragon—and, if we extend co-dependence more broadly, Molloy and Moran, Malone and his reader, old Krapp versus younger Krapp—all rely on each other to "go on." Their formulaic routines and dialogues often seem parodic versions of a rational discourse whose content has been evacuated, leaving interlocutors to exchange empty signs. It is less often observed that many of these characters are disabled and form tenuous alliances for mutual aid. In *Endgame*, to take the obvious example, Hamm is blind and lacks the use of his legs; Clov has a stiff leg and is losing his sight; Nagg and Nell have lost their limbs in a bicycling accident and have been relegated to trashcans.

Most critics, as Ato Quayson observes, see Beckett's disabled characters as metaphors for alienation and solitude in the modern world, but do so "in such a way as to obliterate the specificity of the body and to render it a marker of something else."[11] Quayson notes that the presence of disability produces a certain anxiety or nervousness around the issue of bodily contingency. Stated succinctly in his introduction, he asks: "[W]hat happens to our interpretation when we examine the status of disability within a representational system in which *the discomfort of disability is* not *accounted for*?"[12] Such an interpretive encounter represents a "hermeneutical impasse" in which the presence of pain and disability cannot be interpreted through strictly textual matters. This impasse is the aesthetic version of the nervousness that able-bodied persons experience when confronted by a person with a disability, but in his Beckett chapter he speaks more directly about how characters negotiate such anxieties within a text that provides no simple origin for such nervousness. His chapter coincides with my own in his observation that in the case of *Endgame* Hamm and Clov's co-dependence is a sign of "radical contingency that governs the entire play."[13] Where I locate this anxiety over contingency in relations of dependency that challenge liberal ideals of individualism, Quayson locates it in pain as "*a mode of intersubjective recognition and identity.*"[14]

Quayson recognizes the foundational importance of disability in Beckett against the critical tendency to see it as a sign of existential alienation in the modern world. We might understand such alienation, however, as the condition of disability in a world of compulsory able-bodiedness.[15] When disability is the norm—as it is in Beckett's work—the human condition must be revised in terms of nontraditional bodies and sensoria. We might also see characters' co-dependence as a means of survival, the social contract reduced to its most naked form. That Beckett chooses to represent his human comedy by disabled figures whose bodies have ceased to be "productive" according to modern imperatives of progress and improvement offers a parable about the limits of agency and community in a post-ableist era.

Beckett offers little in the way of Christian solace, preferring a darker wager that he identifies with early church fathers: "Do not despair, one of the thieves was saved; do not presume; one of the thieves was damned."[16] Beckett's often-quoted version of Augustine serves as a caution to those who read *Waiting for Godot* as a modern parable about the existence of belief in a Godless world. Vladimir (Didi) and Estragon (Gogo) themselves seem aware of the odds ("One of the thieves was saved," Didi says; "It's a reasonable percentage") and occasionally entertain the thought that, as Gogo says, "We always find something, eh Didi, to give us the impression we exist?"[17] The form that this "something" takes is a series of verbal pratfalls and vaudeville routines that, in Godot's absence, fill time and keep them together.

Estragon   That's the idea, let's abuse each other.

They turn, move apart, turn again and face each other.

Vladimir   Moron!
Estragon   Vermin!
Vladimir   Abortion!
Estragon   Morpion!
Vladimir   Sewer-rat!
Estragon   Curate!

Vladimir   Cretin!
Estragon   (*with finality*) Crritic!
Vladimir   Oh!

He wilts, vanquished and turns away.[18]

Although such rituals offer a hilarious riposte to the idea of reasonable discourse, they expose the pragmatics of communication as a contract among participants to further the language game. They also cement relationships around interdependency that, as current vernacular performances (dozens, rap, verbal contests) demonstrate, create community and forge alliances. The "Crritic!" whom Gogo invokes to trump Didi needs to see such routines as socially significant speech acts that "create the illusion that we exist."

Persons with disabilities depend on others in ways that challenge post-Enlightenment ideals of autonomy and independence, and it is here that Beckett's work offers an important challenge to ideas of embodied normalcy.[19] His novels and plays depict characters that are thrown into a state of nature without ontological supports or metaphysical assurances. They depend on objects (stones, sticks, bicycles) as prostheses for limited mobility and agency, and their personal interrelationships seem based less on love and affection than on contingency and survival. Although their bodies are in states of increasing decay, with limbs becoming unusable and memories unreliable, they acknowledge the fact that, as Molloy ruefully says, "To decompose is to live, too."[20] Although we often think of Beckett's characters as solitary Bartlebies, they are more often locked in complicated interrelationships, bound by ties whose necessity has long since turned into routine. Even when characters are alone, they are haunted by specters from the past with whom they commune in paranoid, guilt-ridden monologues. *Eh Joe, Ghost Trio, Krapp's Last Tape,* and *Ohio Impromptu* utilize monologue and mime to converse with an absent interlocutor from whom the character is unable to separate himself. Krapp's futile endeavor to control the tape on which an earlier version of his life is recorded represents an attempt to revise a narrative whose present failures are all too apparent. In *Ohio Impromptu,* the silent Listener knocks on a table to indicate when his virtually identical Reader may read aloud what appears to be the former's story of lost love and growing isolation. In such plays, the Subject is split in two, permitted to visit himself as Other through a dialogic encounter.

Dependent relationships in Beckett are never symmetrical, and power imbalances between characters are often mediated through parodies of Christian charity, on the one hand, or the master–slave dialectic on the other.

Neither scenario—charity or force—is tenable, and characters are left to act out rituals of deference and leadership, support and authority, without knowing why. In Part I of *Waiting for Godot*, Pozzo and Lucky perform a theatrical parody of master and slave with Pozzo as the pompous landowner/ impresario who expects dog-like fidelity from his servant and lackey, Lucky. When the two characters return in Part II, Pozzo's authority is diminished, his eyesight lost, his impresario status reduced to helpless appeals for aid. Didi and Gogo, who in Part I deferred to Pozzo's authority, now imitate it by refusing help while subjecting Lucky to cruel punishment. Not only are dependent relations between master and slave reversed, a reciprocal inversion occurs between disabled and able-bodied characters in the play. Far from reversing the polarities of the master–slave dialectic, Beckett shows its tenacity and adaptability, even when the master's authority has been lost.

The basic formula for Beckett's treatment of abject dependence can be stated thus: individuals cannot realize themselves as independent agents without first recognizing their dependent and contingent relations with others and with their own animal bodies. In a world that valorizes independence and able-bodied normalcy, dependent relations are regarded as signs of weakness, usually gendered as "women's work" or that of ill-paid menials. When individuals find themselves in situations of dependence they act out their ambivalent relations to others and to their frangible bodies through narratives of beset embodiment that mimic social attitudes in the larger "rational" world. As their bodies decline, they become dependent on certain objects as extensions of their atrophied limbs, sight, and hearing. These objects replicate materially the stories they tell that extend their lives aesthetically. Sucking stones and narratives stave off cosmic boredom. Mobility, rather than a descriptor of agency, becomes a curse. As Malone says, "If I had the use of my body I would throw it out of the window. But perhaps it is the knowledge of impotence that emboldens me to that thought. All hangs together, I am in chains."[21]

The formula I have outlined can be seen in *Rough for Theatre I*, a little-known work written in French (*Fragment pour theatre*) in the 1950s that could serve as a prologue for *Endgame*.[22] Two old men, A and B, inhabit a deserted corner of a post-apocalypse urban ruin. A is blind and sits on a folding stool, occasionally playing a violin "scratching an old jangle to the four winds."[23] B has lost one of his legs and wheels himself around in a wheelchair that he propels by means of a pole. When B first encounters A, he retreats until he realizes they might "join together, and live together, till death ensue."[24] This recognition scene marks the moment in which dependency is acknowledged as mutually beneficial to both parties rather than being seen as a tragic loss of autonomy. As in other Beckett plays, a character's acquiescence to dependence is figured as a marriage contract, a bond "till death ensue." As B observes, prior to their joining forces, he would "sit there, in my lair, in my chair, in the dark, twenty-three hours out of the twenty-four."[25] Now there seems the possibility for a kind of communion. B performs certain functions for A such as describing the scenery and the quality of light while A pushes B's wheelchair. Soon, however, A fails to accede to B's wishes, and B strikes him with his pole. Feeling guilty over his action, B despairs,

> Now I've lost him. He was beginning to like me and I struck him. He'll leave me and I'll never see him again. I'll never see anyone again. We'll never hear the human voice again.[26]

The blind A threatens to leave the crippled B, but finds himself unable to depart without his "things"—the few material objects: his violin and alms bowl—that represent his tentative hold on reality. Such objects, as we know from the rest of Beckett's *oeuvre*, are both prosthetic and aesthetic, extending and articulating an existence whose ontological supports have been withdrawn. B plays upon A's ambivalence by reinstating him into regimes of pity and obligation. B pleads with A to

> Straighten my rug, I feel the cold air on my foot. (*A halts.*) I'd do it myself, but it would take too long. (*Pause.*) Do that for me, Billy. Then I may go back, settle in the old nook again and say, I have seen man for the last time, I struck him and he succored me. (*Pause.*) Find a few rags of love in my heart and die reconciled, with my species.[27]

In this passage, expressions of forgiveness and pity are revealed as speech acts whose exchange allows characters to live in the illusion of a moral universe. At different points in the play, each character calls the other "poor wretch," not to express piety but to reinforce the value of expressing it. *Rough for Theatre I* is less a parable about the virtues of mutual aid than a comedic display of human intercourse when relations are founded not on independent agency but on dependence. Beckett's post-lapsarian world of itinerant tramps, clowns, and cripples may simply be the bourgeois order's camera obscura on itself and on bodies it can't imagine or contain.

II "What a curse, mobility!"

The interdependence of A and B defines a post-human, prosthetic body in which acts and intentions in one individual are completed by the other.[28] Here, disability is not a metaphor for something else (blindness as a sign of weakness, immobility as a sign of castration) but a constitutive feature of the social contract. In an ableist, goal-driven world that treats dependency as hated subservience, non-contingent acts are deemed wasteful or expendable. At one point A extends his hand to B, who exclaims, "Wait, you're not going to do me a service for nothing? (*Pause*) I mean unconditionally? (*Pause*) Good God!"[29] Here the non-contingent act, performed out of empathy or generosity, becomes the anomaly. Beckett's favorite philosophical conundrums usually involve aporias of contingency, his favorite being Bishop Berkeley's *esse est percipi* (to be is to be perceived). Critics observe that many of Beckett's works could be summarized by this proposition, from Belacqua's solipsism to *What Where*'s dark vision of state surveillance. In Beckett's 1963 *Film* (for which Berkeley's phrase serves as epigraph) the solitary actor, played by Buster Keaton, spends the entire film evading the camera's scopic gaze. The camera (called "E" for "eye" in Beckett's notes) relentlessly pursues Keaton ("O" for object) through a ruined street, into a vestibule, up a flight of stairs and into a bare room, but he manages to avoid being seen frontally until the very end of the film. People who encounter him on the street inexplicably turn away in horror, but we are never told why. Not only does O evade the camera's gaze, he attempts to efface anything remotely resembling a pair of eyes. He conceals all optical images (a fish in a fishbowl, the eyes of a parrot, two decorative holes in a rocking chair, two circular fasteners on an envelope) that threaten, however obliquely, to hold him in their gaze. When he finally turns toward the camera, Keaton's famous deadpan face is shown with a patch over one eye, as though to indicate that, just as the cyclopean eye of the camera reifies its subject, so the subject is sight impaired. O refuses to be constituted by the Eye, seeking an autonomy that the camera refuses to grant. And while the film focuses on one individual, its entire production illustrates the dualism of all perceptual acts, or, as Winnie says in *Happy Days*, "because one sees the other the other sees the one."[30]

Disabled people have long recognized the power (and violence) of such scopic regimes and are now seeking to rearticulate their object status through activism and performance. The social model of disability asserts that a physical impairment becomes a disability when one encounters physical obstacles and environmental barriers, and the same holds true for negotiating the stares and gawking of an able-bodied public. One is not born disabled; one becomes disabled through the objectifying gaze of compulsory able-bodiedness. In Beckett's world, however, all characters are disabled, and their acts of looking and being seen tend to foreground the performative features—the theatricality—of such constitutive acts of sight. Their attempts to negotiate a landscape that is inaccessible (whether because of limited mobility or because of an absent God) frame "bare forked man" at his most vulnerable.

Or "bare forked" woman. The drama of *Happy Days* reinforces precisely this constitutive aspect of sight as Winnie, buried up to her waist in Act One and her neck in Act Two, seeks to maintain the illusion that she is still being seen—and thus that she still exists: "Strange feeling that someone is looking at me. I am clear, then dim, then gone, then dim again, then clear again, and so on, back and forth, in and out of someone's eye."[31] Her chipper response to each "happy day" belies her restricted condition, and she alleviates her tedium by pattern and routine. She is awakened by a bell; says a brief prayer; unloads objects from her "capacious black bag, shopping variety"; muses upon each item before returning it to its place in the bag; repeats formulaic phrases to her husband who is half hidden behind her; sings a song at twilight. Willie's terse responses to her questions satirize domestic bliss, but they sustain Winnie's view that the two of them are maintaining some fiction of conjugal relations. Despite the absurdity of her situation, her reduced mobility is never an issue, and a good deal of the play's humor is linked to her buoyant refusal of what would seem to be an intolerable situation. The more Winnie seeks verification that someone is watching, the more we realize that we, as audience, are sustaining the illusion that she takes for reality.

Winnie is a virtuoso performer in her ability to fill time with an endlessly improvised script (and reticent interlocutor). She "performs" normalcy, insofar as her lines are often based on clichéd phrases that are the staples of social parlance. On another level, and despite her bourgeois trappings, Winnie is surprisingly well read, quoting fragments from Shakespeare, Milton, Gray, Yeats, Keats, and Browning, often prefaced by the query, "What is that wonderful [or immortal] line?" These "classic" lines establish continuity with tradition—what she calls the "old style"—that like the objects in her reticule keep her afloat. They signal her commitment to affirmative culture, yet their decontextualized usage often effaces the darker themes— madness, chaos, and suicide—that these passages often signal (at one point, in looking for her glasses, she quotes Ophelia's lines from *Hamlet*, "woe woe is me—to see what I see"[32]).

As Beckett's fullest treatment of a female character, the gendered implications of Winnie's performance must also be acknowledged. She performs a specifically feminine version of embodied normalcy that Berkeley could hardly have anticipated. The objects in her purse—mirror, comb, toothbrush—reinforce her performance as a woman; a performance that she must maintain despite her restricted movement. Steven Connor notes that "Winnie allows the dramatisation of the gaze as both violation and necessity . . . Here, the female spectacle looks at itself, and watches the audience look at it."[33] Like Clov in *Endgame*, who, at several points, gestures toward the audience, Winnie is acutely aware of being watched, and when, in Act Two, she is no longer able to turn around and see Willie, her monologue expresses her desperation at being cut off from this last vestige of human contact. Not only is she being sucked down into that "great extinguisher" the earth, she is facing the horror that she might ultimately have to do it alone. The extent that Winnie's anxiety relates to her disability can be seen by a moment, late in the play, when she recounts a memory of an encounter with a Mr. and Mrs. "Shower" or "Cooker" who look at her in her hill of sand and ask, "What does it mean?. . . what's it meant to mean?"[34] Curiosity leads to prurience:

Does she feel her legs? he says. (*Pause.*) Is there any life in her legs? he says. (*Pause.*) Has she anything on underneath? he says. (*Pause*) Ask her, he says, I'm shy. (*Pause.*) Ask her what? she says. (*Pause.*) Is there any life in her legs.[35]

Instead of helping her out of her predicament, the couple speculate on her disabled condition and in doing so participate in a common form of able-bodied voyeurism that sees the impairment for the whole person. Gendered and embodied otherness come together in Mr. Cooker's sexualized gaze.

It might be possible to see *Happy Days* as a comedy of modern solipsism, focused on woman as consumer, "buried" in the world and forced to recreate herself as spectacle. But if we were to see her immobile condition as an allegory of disability we might see the play as being more about dependence and vulnerability and the rhetorical strategies with which we negotiate between the two. There are two levels on which dependence is figured. The first involves Winnie's deictic construction of herself vis-à-vis an absent interlocutor, and the second includes her frustrated conversations with Willie. Both cases rely on Winnie's presumption that someone is hearing her speak, that she is "not merely talking to [her]self." In the absence of any confirmed listener, Winnie has recourse to a rhetorical surrogate, an imagined interlocutor who replaces Willie. In the following monologue, Winnie muses on the meaning of an advertising phrase on her toothbrush:

> Hog's setae. (*Puzzled expression.*) What exactly is a hog? (*Pause. Do.*) A sow of course I know, but a hog . . . (*Puzzled expression off.*) Oh well what does it matter, that is what I always say, it will come back, that is what I find so wonderful, all comes back. (*Pause.*) All? (*Pause.*) No, not all. (*Smile.*) No no. (*Smile off.*) Not quite. (*Pause.*) A part. (*Pause*) Floats up, one fine day, out of the blue. (*Pause.*) That is what I find so wonderful.[36]

Monologues such as this imagine an other whose response is anticipated but never fulfilled. In one sense her phrases are empty of content, their function to keep the dialogue moving. Her constant question, "What is that unforgettable line?" mocks its own answer, yet its pragmatic function in securing and sustaining her intersubjective fantasy gives form to an unimaginable situation.

As for Willie, he is an inadequate caregiver by any standard, spending most of his time reading his newspaper or else napping in his burrow behind Winnie's hill of sand. Throughout the play, he serves as a foil for Winnie's musings and a parody of husbandly detachment. Winnie strives to get him to respond, and her labors of beset communication produce much of the play's grim humor:

> **Winnie**   What would you say, Willie? (*Pause. Turning a little further.*) What would you say, Willie, speaking of the hair on your head, them or it? (*Long pause.*)
> **Willie**   It.
> **Winnie**   (*turning back front, joyful.*) Ooh you are going to talk to me today, this is going to be a happy day!

Willie's parsimonious response nevertheless excites Winnie to further conversation, just as his vulnerability under the blazing sun occasions her solicitous regard for his exposed skin. At times, Willie's perfunctory remarks seem to allude to his own restricted condition as Winnie's helpmate. Despite the inadequacy of Willie's conversation, at the end of the play he quite literally "comes around," leaving his perch behind her hill of sand and moving, stage front, to climb the hill—with great physical exertion—and stare into Winnie's eyes and pronounce the first syllable of her name, "Win." Since she is now buried up to her neck, she is obviously not "winning" the battle against decline. Nor is she able to turn her head, and Willie's act permits her to verify that not only does *he* exist but she also exists in his mirror. It is an ambiguous gesture. We are not sure whether he has come to court Winnie one last time (he is dressed in formal wear) or to pick up the gun that lies at her side and facilitate the suicide she is no longer able to perform. Winnie interprets his gesture as a romantic one, but her remark contains the darker possibility that, without his look, nothing of her remains:

> That's right, Willie, look at me. (*Pause.*) Feast your old eyes, Willie. (*Pause.*) Does anything remain?[37]

At one point in *Malone Dies* the titular narrator cries, "I wonder why I speak of all this. Ah yes, to relieve the tedium."[38] Later in the novel he ruminates, "the search for myself is ended. I am buried in the world."[39] This would seem to summarize Winnie's situation as well. She relieves the "tedium" of being-toward-death by talking-toward-being; she has stopped searching for a self beyond the world and acknowledges her immersion in it. Her most radical acknowledgment of this fact occurs toward the end of Act One as she tries to instruct Willie on how to enter his burrow:

> The hands and knees, love, try the hands and knees. (*Pause.*) The knees! The knees! (*Pause*) What a curse, mobility![40]

Far from despairing of her disabled condition, Winnie disparages the limits of compulsory able-bodiedness if its primary goal is, as in Willie's case, to return to a womb-like solitude. Willie may be more mobile, but his intellectual range is limited to monosyllabic grunts and "titbits from Reynolds' News." Winnie depends on Willie's presence but is not defined by it. Their shared twin initials hint at their interdependent natures, as though one is the complement of the other. If Willie is Winnie's on-stage audience, we become Willie, to some extent, by our triangulated relationship to Winnie's need to be seen. Hence the curse of Willie's mobility becomes our own; the cure of Winnie's solitude is the presence, imagined or literal, of the other.

III "No more nature"

The 2006 power-sharing agreement (the St. Andrews Agreement) in Northern Ireland between the Protestant Democratic Unionists and Sinn

Fein caps a century of struggle over Irish governance and national autonomy. Whatever success the new agreement may bring, the legacy of "the Troubles" will continue to haunt future relations between Britain and Northern Ireland. The endurance of residual social and historical conditions in emergent formations makes it difficult to impose a binary, master/slave model on works of Irish literature with characters like Pozzo or Hamm serving as thinly disguised representatives of Great Britain against their subaltern Irish vassals, Lucky and Clov. Speaking of *Endgame*, Nels Pearson points out that the play dramatizes

the lingering co-dependency between two leftover participants from an imperial/colonial (or at the very least ruler/subject) historical situation that no longer exists. The important thing is that Hamm and Clov maintain the respective roles of ruler and ruled as well as the assumption that there is no alternative to these roles, long after the external causes of specific historical circumstances of those roles have deteriorated.[41]

One might argue that the imperial/colonial situation has by no means gone away in Northern Ireland, but Pearson is right to observe that a strictly top-down model of colonial authority does not account for forms of reciprocal dependence. The co-dependency of Hamm and Clov marks *Endgame*'s reprise of *The Tempest* with Clov playing Caliban to Hamm's Prospero, but, as Albert Memmi argues, with regard to postcolonial societies, it would be wrong to assume that this form of dependency is the same as subjection.[42] There are reciprocal dependencies between colony and colonizer in which each sees itself through the mirror of the other. In *Endgame* Hamm holds the combination to the cupboard that feeds Clov. The latter can still walk and see, thus serving as Hamm's legs and eyes. Each resents the other's advantage, yet each recognizes the other's role in constituting himself.

Although other Beckett plays—*Not I*, *All That Fall*, or *Happy Days*—also deal with the interplay of disability and dependence, *Endgame* is the most operatic elaboration of the theme. The play is set in a post-apocalypse world in which all life has been destroyed—or perhaps more accurately, in which biological reproduction no longer organizes futurity. At the play's center is a relationship between two disabled characters, one who imitates a fallen king and one who imitates his son and servant. Hamm and Clov ritually interrogate the reasons for their interdependence. "What is there to keep me here?" asks Clov. "The dialogue," replies Hamm.[43] Elsewhere Clov asks, "There's one thing I'll never understand. Why I always obey you. Can you explain that to me?" to which Hamm responds, "No ... perhaps it's compassion. (*Pause*). A kind of great compassion."[44] Hamm knows how to manipulate his subaltern by providing moral justifications for living under oppression. At one point Hamm curses Clov's lack of compassion and compares it to his disability:

One day you'll be blind, like me. You'll be sitting there, a speck in the void, in the dark, forever, like me ... Infinite emptiness will be all around you, all the resurrected dead of all the ages wouldn't fill it, and there you'll be like a little bit of grit in the middle of the steppe. (*Pause*.) Yes, one day you'll know what it is, you'll be like me, except that you won't have anyone with you, because you won't have had pity on anyone and because there won't be anyone left to have pity on.[45]

Such maudlin rhetoric offers a variation on an all-too-familiar version of charity that maintains Hamm's control and validates Clov's continued subservience. It is also a warped variation on filial piety that visits the disability of the father on the vulnerability of the son. As Nagg heaps abuse on his disrespectful son, so Hamm complains about Clov's inattentiveness. As Stanley Cavell observes, "Like his father, powerless to walk, needing to tell stories, [Hamm] masks his dependence with bullying."[46]

Although Hamm postures and pontificates, he and Clov often acknowledge their impairments as a kind of reciprocity. Having pushed his legless father back into the ashbin, Hamm urges Clov to "Sit on him!" to which Clov responds, "I can't sit."

Hamm True. And I can't stand.
Clov So it is.
Hamm Every man his specialty.[47]

This brief interchange summarizes what Albert Memmi calls "reciprocal dependency," where "each partner counts on the other for survival or comfort, in which each is simultaneously the dependent of and provider for the other."[48] Although Hamm wields control over Clov's actions, his overblown rhetoric and grandiose theatrics show him to be less a tragic figure than, as his name implies, a ham actor with little power over his realm. The question of why Clov stays with Hamm—the subject of many of their dialogues—can be explained as the colonial acquiescence before subjection in the absence of alternative possibilities. Clov has become comfortable in his subjecthood, and because he knows the roles and rules, performs them faithfully, despite his underlying *ressentiment*.

Reading *Endgame* in postcolonial terms has helped to historicize the play's theatricalization of power; however, it does not specify the function of disability in maintaining those relations of power. Within a postcolonial reading, Hamm is a parody of imperial authority, barking commands and feigning sympathy for his colonial subject. Clov must throw off his false consciousness and expose Hamm's autocratic role. Read through a disability optic, however, Hamm and Clov function within an ableist ideology that views dependent relations as weakness. In a world where the blind man in a wheelchair is interpellated as doubly handicapped, his dependence on an assistant is regarded as tragically emasculating. Within the chess metaphor that organizes the play, Hamm is vulnerable to his opponent's pawns. As its title suggests, the world is coming to an end, but the game must continue to its conclusion. And in a world where the caregiver becomes socially and culturally disabled in the act of serving, reliance on the "patient" is no less disparaged. "We're not beginning to ... to ... mean something?" Hamm queries, at which Clov laughs: "Mean something! You and I, mean something! (*Brief laugh*). Ah that's a good one!"[49] The great fear that the formulaic routines and rituals that maintain their relations of interdependence might be evaporating is almost more than they can imagine. Hamm asks: "Imagine if a rational being came back to earth, wouldn't he be liable to get ideas into his head if he observed us long enough. (*Voice of rational being.*) Ah, good, now I see what it is, yes, now I understand what they're at!"[50] Theodor Adorno paraphrases these lines as saying "Not meaning anything becomes the only meaning," but this imposes a kind of negative theology on these lines, seemingly in violation of Adorno's critique of existentialist readings of the play.[51] I see these lines as showing Hamm's comedic response to the absurdity of his dependent relationship with Clov by ventriloquizing the voice of rationality and exposing it as a voice of power.

As in *Happy Days*, *Endgame* deploys a theatrical metaphor to reinforce the idea that dependent relations between patient and caregiver follow the pattern of dramatic role-playing. *Endgame* is full of theatrical references— audiences and performances, stage action, and memorized lines. As a ham actor, Hamm veers from pathos to music hall comedy, and seems perpetually caught in a vaudeville routine. Hamm and Clov often allude to their empty rituals as performances. At one point, Clov is looking out the window with a telescope. He turns it toward the audience, and Hamm asks him what he sees: "I see ... a multitude ... in transports ... of joy", to which he adds, "That's what I call a magnifier."[52] Hamm repeats Prospero's lines from *The Tempest*, "Our revels now are ended," as a marker of his kinglike status but also as the creator of the play in which he is both author and actor. Hamm, like Prospero, has given Clov language, which his Caliban-like subordinate now uses to challenge parental authority: "I use the words you taught me. If they don't mean anything any more, teach me others. Or let me be silent."[53] Hamm and Clov may resent their interdependence, but they construct their "revels" within recognizable theatrical roles.

Although in *Endgame* Beckett shows the abject character of dependency, he understands its function as a condition underwritten by attitudes about gender and class. Caregivers, as Kittay and Nussbaum demonstrate, are invariably women, responsible both for child rearing and care for the aged and infirm. Moreover, caregiving is unrewarded, if within the family, and, when a component of work, ill remunerated. Beckett builds Hamm and Clov's relationship upon such unequal, gendered divisions of labor with Hamm as a pitiful version of the breadwinner who sparingly doles out biscuits to his small fiefdom while Clov is relegated to the domestic kitchen to stare at the walls. We tend to think of Clov as Hamm's surrogate son, but we forget that he also occupies the position of wife and helpmate. If, as Eva Kittay says, dependency work is "labor that enhances the power and activity of another," then Clov is certainly a dependency worker, dispensing painkillers and moving wheelchairs but never given credit for his labors. The seeming symmetry of his dependency upon Hamm for survival reinforces the grim dialectic of unremunerated domestic service. Clov is not female, but by participating in dependency work he occupies the subject position often occupied by women as nurses, mothers, midwives, and caregivers.

Finally, there is the question of life after Hamm. The play's ending hinges on whether one believes that Clov will leave Hamm and eke out an independent life or remain perpetually bound to his master's service. This is a version of the more philosophical question of whether the play "means" anything beyond its own meaninglessness—whether it dramatizes a universal human essence or, as Georg Lukács complained, mirrors the chaos of modern life without taking a position on it.[54] The play leaves the question unanswered, not because Beckett wants to question Clov's willpower or Hamm's authority (or art's pedagogical potential) but because there is no post-diluvian life beyond dependence. The end game is not resolved by perpetuating another variant of Oedipal transgression, the son triumphing over the father by becoming independent of his reason. Rather the condition involves recognizing that independence and equality are bound to others, that, as Eva Kittay says, "interdependence begins with dependence."[55] The boy that Clov spies through his telescope offers a glimmer of hope for life outside the box, yet there is the equal possibility that Clov will re-establish on this newcomer the regime of dominance he has learned from Hamm. Their final dialogue reinforces this promise of repetition, now figured through the theatrical *mise en scène*:

> **Clov** This is what we call making an exit.
> **Hamm** I'm obliged to you, Clov. For your services.
> **Clov** (*turning sharply.*) Ah, pardon, it's I am obliged to you.
> **Hamm** It's we are obliged to each other.[56]

Whether this is simply a set of empty remarks made upon parting or a redemptive summary of their relationship in general, Beckett leaves the door (quite literally) open without showing Clov leaving the stage. The mutual obligation—what I have been calling reciprocal dependency—is the social contract viewed not as an alliance of separate individuals for a common good but a recognition of the labor such alliances entail. If Beckett presents a dystopic version of dependency, it is because the labor of love has yet to find an adequate narrative.

IV Dependent rational animals

"There is no more nature"— whose corollary, as Adorno has observed, is that there is nothing left that is not made by man. The catastrophe that *Endgame* survives could be an atomic holocaust with the play's characters depicting "the bombed out consciousness [that] no longer has any position from which it could reflect on that fact."[57] Although it is always dangerous to pin a specific historical allegory on Beckett's works, it is worth thinking of how plays like *Endgame* try to imagine a future when the grand narratives of Self, Soul, and Society no longer seem to hold. Rather than being a form of "writing after Auschwitz," which implies that something positive *could* survive, *Endgame* might better be seen as articulating what conditions still remain, what elements of the Enlightenment narrative of improvement and Darwinian survival still organize the way we understand bio-futurity. Nagg and Nell in their trashcans are the sad evidence of social attitudes about the aged and infirm that see human life, once past its prime, as disposable. That, as Adorno says, "is the true gerontology."[58] Expanded to my concern with disability, we might say that in Beckett's plays the old, the animal, the infirm, and the poor coincide, not as signs of what nature can't contain but of what society cannot afford to exclude.

And this returns me to Martha Nussbaum's critique of John Rawls' original position. A theory of social justice forged on equal access to "resources" rather than "capabilities" provides a constricted definition of participation in the social contract and limits human potential largely to economic considerations: "The main idea," Rawls claims, "is that when a number of persons engage in a mutually advantageous cooperative venture according to rules, and thus restrict their liberty in ways necessary to yield advantages for all, those who have submitted to these restrictions have a right to a similar acquiescence on the part of those who have benefitted from their submission."[59] This sounds good, Nussbaum says, if all individuals are independent actors, but when one of those persons is in a wheelchair or is engaged in dependent care for a child who is mentally ill, that "mutually advantageous" cooperation no longer applies. What does it mean for someone to "submit to restrictions" in a society that refuses to recognize her as fully human? Nussbaum argues for treating individuals not in terms of abstract personhood but in terms of what they are capable of, what anyone needs to live with dignity. And this includes taking into consideration physical and cognitive variability. Thinking about differently abled persons also means taking into account their varying levels of care, whether this is delivered by a family member or a paid employee. Finally, it means incorporating the caregiver into the dependent relationship as a full participant.

Beckett was obviously not thinking specifically of the claims of disability on social justice, but, by making his characters disabled and co-dependent, he counters the tendency to think of such conditions as belonging to "them" and not to "us." The human condition in Beckett's plays *is* living with disability and dependence, however abject their portrayal may be. In a liberal society, committed to liberating the healthy, independent individual, dependency must be bracketed (as it is in Rawls) or else subjected to various forms of paternalism. "Pity would be no more / If we did not make somebody Poor," Beckett's favorite poet, William Blake, observes in "The Human Abstract."[60] The disability rights movement and its challenge to celebrity telethon versions of pathetic impairment has gone a long way toward retrieving the disabled person from such patronizing myths, but in doing so has often made recourse to the same individualist or triumphalist ethos that it deplores in able-bodied society. Beckett's writings display the limits of liberal individualism as the telos, the endgame, of civilization. At the end of *Endgame*, Clov halts at the threshold of the room. He and Hamm stage their last dialogue, one that they have been repeating since the beginning of time: "It's we who are obliged to each other." We never know whether Clov can extricate himself from this play—or this room—but we do see the drama of their dependent relations as the "game" that keeps them alive. A society that brackets such relations from the social contract fatally ignores, as Alisdair MacIntyre says, the "virtues that we need, if we are to confront and respond to vulnerability and disability both in ourselves and in others."[61]

CHAPTER 6
RECLAIMING THE ORDINARY EXTRAORDINARY BODY: OR, THE IMPORTANCE OF *THE GLASS MENAGERIE* FOR LITERARY DISABILITY STUDIES

Ann M. Fox

In late 2010, I saw the movie *The King's Speech* with my mother. At the end of the movie, she turned to me in surprise and said, "That's not how I expected the movie to end!" What she meant was that the portrayal of the stuttering King George VI had not neatly solved the "problem" of the King's speech impairment or made it go away, but had shown instead how he lived *with* his stuttering. Even in the midst of the sentimental staging and music that are typical of how disability is represented in film, this movie attempted to understand the larger psychological and familial root causes for George's disability, questioned the attempts at cure, and disparaged those who stigmatized him. As a disability studies scholar, I had been prepared *not* to like the movie. Part of what disability studies has trained me to do is to recognize the limited range of tropes to which disabled people are assigned in representation, including the overcoming narrative. This scenario, in which a disabled person transcends their disability through sheer willpower (regardless of their physical or emotional realities, social supports, or economic circumstances, for example) is a cinematic favorite. And while *The King's Speech* certainly had its share of inspirational tropes, gave rise to a field day of sentimentalized news stories about stuttering, and continued the long tradition of films awarded Oscars for the performance of pluck, I could not forget my mother's reaction. For her, the non-disabled spectator, the film had complicated that typical overcoming narrative; in doing so, it had framed the king in terms of disability history for audiences who, like my mother, were not part of disability culture. Further, it introduced that history in a way that both linked to familiar touchstones and simultaneously swerved around them.

Disability history matters, for several reasons. Disability is an essential marker of human identity; after all, even currently non-disabled people could become disabled at any moment, or will become disabled if they live long enough. Contemporary society daily chooses to avoid that fact in a quest for perfection (and standardization), rather than embrace it as a representation of the amazing variability of human bodies. Ignoring disability means we ignore an important part of our cultural history: the activists and artists who created in and through disability, as well as those whose bodies were policed, rendered invisible, or erased altogether in hospitals, institutions, or concentration camps. Just as queer history, women's history, and the histories of people of color have modeled important challenges to the traditional ways we keep the historical record, so too does disability history. It renders visible the ways in which societies have used disabled people as that against which so-called normal bodies are then defined; importantly, it also shows how the tyranny of normalcy really works to regulate all bodies. Disability history, while acknowledging the reality of pain, also fosters pride in an experience that has too often been defined as isolated, joyless, and tragic; it also establishes disability community as a retort to individuation. Finally, and perhaps most significantly, it creates an understanding of what disability studies scholar Rosemarie Garland-Thomson has called "disability gain"—how we can appreciate the ways in which disability is a creative force, one from which we have real things to learn beyond simple inspiration or affective response.[1] Disability may be difference, but it does not follow that it is lack; it can be the conduit to radical innovation and insight.

Representation simultaneously reflects and creates a kind of history, which is why continually interrogating how disabled bodies are imagined in works of fiction, poetry, film, journalism, memoir, visual art, advertisement, popular culture, and drama matters. Disabled bodies can inspire, but if we limit our definition of their accomplishment to only overcoming or transcending disability, then we in actuality continue to make disability a monolithic identity, one we still dismiss as invalid. Indeed, we can most often begin our scrutiny of representation by simply asking: who is not there? Through the very conventions of mainstream theatre, with their emphasis on actorly virtuosity, and privileging of speech, sight, sound, and movement, drama has in the past lent itself to the exclusion of the disabled body from the stage. Disabled actor and activist for inclusive casting Christine Bruno describes the phenomenon:

Not only is the portrayal of disability by a non-disabled actor equivalent to blackface—what we in the disability community derisively call "cripping up" (pretending to have a disability)—and universally *accepted* as a technical skill tucked away in an actor's bag of tricks, it is always applauded and more often than not, rewarded. 16 percent of Academy Award winners have received the coveted statue for playing a character with a disability; just two of those were disabled actors.[2]

It is no wonder that, as is so often the case in the representation of disability in film, the disabled roles that do emerge in theatre almost always become a site for non-disabled actors to do a kind of disability minstrelsy, in which they approximate a representation of disability more reflective of stereotypes or tropes than lived realities.[3]

The study of dramatic literature already exists on the periphery of literary criticism, and familiar characters can feel more limited than radical or progressive. So often, the characters to which I must refer as familiar points of reference when responding to the question, "Well, who *are* the disabled characters in American drama?" are the ones who I have found the most frustrating and difficult to parse, at once iconic and infamous in equal measure—including Laura Wingfield, the ethereal, limping heroine of Tennessee Williams' *The Glass Menagerie* (1944). The play famously recounts the attempt of Laura's mother to find a husband for her disabled daughter. After a brief romantic encounter with the "Gentleman Caller" Jim O'Connor, who turns out to be engaged, Laura retreats back into anonymity and the memory of her brother, Tom, who has since abandoned the family and now serves as our narrator. This story is connected to a question that has nagged at me in regards to my own study of modern and contemporary drama, and one I think might be of equal value for readers of this book. What could a reconsideration of the most canonical images of disability in dramatic literature model do for directors, teachers, critics, and audiences? What could it do—if anything—to help us reconsider literature's role in portraying disability history and offering challenges to ableism? To study the representation of disability in drama, after all, seems on one level a *fait accompli*: certainly from melodrama on down, theatre, like other kinds of visual representation, has been guilty of recirculating disability stereotype; besides the heroic overcomer, there are also, to use theatre scholar Victoria Ann Lewis's phrase, a full host of "victims and villains" who have populated the stage.[4]

What if I have been overlooking an opportunity to understand disability history more fully through these iconic although seemingly problematic figures, an opportunity suggested by my engagement with *The King's Speech* through my mother's eyes? The history of disabled people is in part the history of their oppression by narratives of progress and overcoming. It is with no small irony, however, that literary disability studies scholars (including me, who once rather snarkily called Laura Wingfield "Myth Disability" in an essay earlier in my career) have, in a way, ourselves overcompensated: we have demanded a kind of overcoming narrative in art, to the extent that our examination of disability representation has attempted to demarcate a strict line between the subversive and the stereotypical, the positive and the problematic.[5] The implicit presumption here is, of course, that only with the rise of disability activism could art most fully embody activist images of disability. But I contend that disability theatre does not necessarily begin with contemporary playwrights like John Belluso or Lynn Manning, important as their disability-centric work may be. There's absolutely no denying that works like Doris Baizley and Victoria Ann Lewis's "P.H.reaks: The Hidden History of People with Disabilities," for example, are integral to activism and creating disability culture.[6] Yet we can find examples of disability representation that, when more carefully parsed, suggest that disability has been an integral subject for and part of social protest for longer than we might suspect, distracted by the superficial disability drag of characters who seem too untrue to be any good. That is important to critics like me *and* to readers new to disability studies: it encourages us to reclaim disability history in ways that, while acknowledging ableism and oppression, also fully appreciate its presence as generative, innovative, and creative. It suggests there are opportunities to explore disability *and* these plays anew, an exciting situation for both the critic and the artist.

It is not at all surprising that disability studies scholars have left such works largely unexamined within their social and historical contexts, doubly rejecting these characters—and the dramas for which they serve as the driving force—as immaterial, simultaneously constructing and condemning disability. As Michael Davidson points out, it is the consensus of many disability studies scholars (and admittedly all too true) that often, "metaphoric treatments of impairment seldom confront the material conditions of actual disabled persons, permitting dominant social norms to be written on the body of a person who is politely asked to step offstage once the metaphoric exchange is made."[7] Christine Bruno and Regan Linton, who have both played Laura (the experience of which I will discuss later in this essay), each noted that as disabled women, they had long resisted playing the seemingly one-dimensional "Blue Roses." Linton feared typecasting: "I felt [playing Laura] ... would be succumbing to a facile assumption of 'having the disabled girl play the disabled role,'" while Bruno initially, and vehemently, rejected any affinity with the character: "How could I possibly play Laura? I was nothing like her. She's a weak, shrinking violent paralysed by insecurity and trapped between her mother's disappointment, delusions, and unrealistic expectations for her children."[8] This chapter is not attempting a willful forgetting of the play's more problematic elements; there's no denying, for example, that Laura's disappointment over her lost love and retreat by the end of *The Glass Menagerie* is sad, or that, even long before that, there is ample opportunity to play her as a stock-in-trade disability stereotype, as "asexual, dependent, a perennial child."[9] Even the most recent biography of Williams by John Lahr refers to her as the "crippled dateless Laura" who "knows her disability debars her from a normal life."[10] Yet I wonder if we might engage in a reconsideration of Laura as a model for a more nuanced deployment of disability. In so doing, we can come to see that modern drama, particularly that which was popular and has become canonical, is another source of disability history to which we all might productively attend.

Besides more fully embodying disability history, as well as suggesting how disability can invigorate our understanding of cultural texts, there are other benefits to this approach. For one thing, it eschews critical paternalism of the kind evinced by Lahr; while fully acknowledging that there have been (and continue to be) oppressive representations, it rejects passivity and ahistoricity as default positions, refuting the notion that the disabled body in representation is simply a victimized one. It likewise disturbs a presumed disabled/non-disabled divide as we look to write disability history; authors outside disability culture can also reveal an understanding of the larger dangers of the normate and subsequent impulses that push back at ableism. In short, it is a way to confront the avoidance of the study of disability within drama studies.[11] What results is a fuller, more nuanced version of disability history, one where there is an important disability presence—even if it may not look like the overt activism to which we are accustomed—in the histories of all kinds of performing and visual arts.

We see models for this kind of movement toward complicating what it means for popular representation to be political among scholars of both theatre and disability studies. For example, Jill Dolan, a founding scholar of feminist theatre, wrote in 2008 of her own reconsideration of the feminist possibilities of popular theatre: "Perhaps it is now time to acknowledge the potential of looking inside [rather than on the political and artistic margins] as well, and to address feminism as a critique or value circulating within our most commercial theatres."[12] She worries that she and other critics may have been denying themselves the opportunity for a more nuanced understanding of canonical plays and playwrights:

> I now find tedious the somewhat facile pose of scholars always looking for the next new outlaw or the most outré performance examples to boast as aesthetically radical and politically subversive. While the work they uncover is often effective and important, in the rush to innovation, already-noted artists are too often dismissed.[13]

Davidson posits a similar concern, this time from a disability studies perspective:

> By framing disability in the arts exclusively in terms of social stigma, on the one hand, and advocacy, on the other, we may limit disability aesthetics largely to thematic matters, leaving formal questions untheorized. How might the aesthetic itself be a frame for engaging disability at levels beyond the mimetic?[14]

Scholars including Ato Quayson and Tobin Siebers have created work looking beyond simply identifying various disability representations as progressive or regressive; Siebers, in his 2010 book *Disability Aesthetics*, for example, argued that a disability presence is intimately interwoven into the rise of modern art, and that it is imperative for scholars to embrace a richer, more multivaried sense of that presence in order to discern disability history more fully:

> Disability is not . . . one subject of art among others. It is not merely a theme. It is not only a personal or autobiographical response embedded in an artwork. It is not solely a political act. It is all of these things, but it is more. It is more because disability is properly speaking an aesthetic value, which is to say, it participates in a system of knowledge that provides materials for and increases critical consciousness about the way that some bodies make other bodies feel.[15]

All these scholars call for reconsidering the performance of ideology in context, for understanding in a more complex manner the societal discussions circulating around either gender or disability in representation, and for re-examining how our own critical assumptions might well circulate through what we deem as the proper object of our study.

Laura Wingfield, limping girl of *The Glass Menagerie* whose disability is never specifically diagnosed for us as audience members, is unquestionably one of the most recognizable characters in American drama, if not one of the most iconic disabled figures in American literature. She is invariably cast as tragic, unable to fit in within a world that has become banal, mechanistic, and insensitive to the poetry and imagination she represents. As we hear often from critics and biographers, the figure of Laura had her genesis in Williams' sister Rose, who "at the age of thirty-three was given one of the first prefrontal lobotomies in America," a procedure that "transformed her literally into a ghost of her former self."[16] Critics have psychologized Williams, at least in part attributing Laura's depiction to an attempt by the author to exorcise his guilt over his lack of intervention. But while that genesis point may have been real, to define Williams' creation of Laura as simply a form of atonement seems limiting. C.W.E. Bigsby has pointed out that within the play "there is a powerful sense not merely that the animating myths of America have failed those who look for some structure to their lives, but that those myths are themselves the root of a destructive materialism or deceptive illusion."[17] Expanding on this assertion, I have argued elsewhere that in his later plays, particularly *Suddenly, Last Summer* and *Cat on a Hot Tin Roof*, Tennessee Williams is damning those myths of normalcy circulating at the time, ones that particularly singled out both disabled and queer bodies for persecution.[18] But what if *The Glass Menagerie* is an even earlier place where Williams begins to set up a critique of the "progressive" forces constraining disabled bodies? Furthermore, what if it is also a place where he creates for his audiences a kind of authentic disability experience, showing how that experience illuminates our understanding of the variation and contingency of human embodiment? This does not mean Laura becomes a proto-activist or the subversive poster child that we disability studies scholars, who see activism intertwined with our criticism, might prefer. But so many years before the widespread rise of the contemporary disability rights movement, that would be an anachronistic reading on our part: in the quieter elements of her depiction there is perhaps more that is significant for and through disability than we have given credence to in our search for literary role models.

The general, but often overlooked criticism the work makes of the normate frames and bolsters this disruptive read of disability, given the tyranny normalcy holds over both disabled and non-disabled bodies. Granger Babcock makes the most thorough and powerful argument from a materialist perspective that Williams scathingly exposes an "enforced conformity [that] resulted from a paranoia that threatened to eliminate the 'freaks'"; the "freaks," in this instance, are those who would resist their role in a democracy based on standardization and consumption.[19] Babcock underscores how Williams not only critiques the alienating effects of both technology and economics in the play, but links them to the tyranny of fascist movements on the rise in Europe at the time and in full flower in the year of its production. Babcock delineates in particular how Amanda and Jim serve as functionaries of value systems that, under the guise of promoting the extraordinary, instead reify the standardized:

> Both embody the prescriptions and values of organized society, and their identities cannot be separated from the conventionalized modes of behavior authorized by the Culture Industry. Amanda Wingfield's and Jim O'Connor's identification with organized society also expresses itself as consumption and surveillance. They consume and digest the narratives of the Culture Industry at the same time they police the identifications and desires of others. In fact, in *The Glass Menagerie*, they act as the instruments of organized society....[20]

As he details, all the narratives circulating in society work to promote adherence to a normate; bodies are as fiercely policed by the narratives of technology Jim takes in at the "Century of Progress" as the beauty myths featured in the women's magazines to which Amanda peddles subscriptions. Americans are content to let such narratives soothe and placate them, as Tom rages:

> You know what happens? People go to the *movies* instead of *moving!* Hollywood characters are supposed to have all the adventures for everybody in America, while everybody in America sits in a dark room and watches them have them! Yes, until there's a war. That's when the adventure becomes available to the masses! *Everyone's* dish, not only Gable's! Then the people in the dark room come out of the dark room to have some adventures themselves—goody, goody! It's our turn now, to go to the South Sea Island—to make a safari—to be exotic, far-off![21]

As Tom well knows, these myths compel Americans to adhere to as efficient an operation of economic machinery as possible; the machinery of war is simply an extension of already-extant systems of capitalism in which one

can "function as long as one is not a 'crank' or a 'cripple,' as long as [one] . . .
avoids the sin of inefficiency."[22]

While Babcock is right that Laura has a distinct "inability to standardize
herself," it is important to understand how the play looks not only to the
system which sees her as extraneous, but particularly embodies her
experience as a disabled woman in a society obsessed with compulsory able-
bodiedness (a critical concept articulated by Robert McRuer signifying the
presumption that everyone is non-disabled, or at least all things being equal,
would prefer to be).[23] (It is an experience that is inextricably intertwined
with the compulsory heteronormativity that seems to more obviously
oppress her in the shape of her mother's constant matrimonial "plans and
provisions" for her.) While as a "memory play" the work is not meant to be
strictly realistic, there are certainly resonant elements of Laura's experience
as a disabled woman to which attention must be paid. Disability studies
critic Deborah Kent argues as much:

> Regrettably, I cannot argue that Williams' portrayal of Laura is wholly
> unrealistic. A distressing number of women with disabilities (as well
> as men and women who are not disabled), convinced that they can
> never compete, do abandon the struggle. *The Glass Menagerie* is a
> heartbreakingly vivid story of a woman's wasted life—a story that
> deserves to be told. Williams, however, implies that Laura's tragedy is
> inevitable. He fails to convey that, born into a different family,
> encouraged to feel more positive about herself, she might have found
> love and happiness in spite of the brace on her leg. For most spectators,
> the play evokes no sense of outrage against the forces that have kept
> Laura from living fully. It is the image of the poor crippled girl—
> forever a child playing with her glass animals—that lingers on.[24]

As Kent suggests, Laura may be withdrawn and shy, but I do not agree that
Williams suggests Laura's "tragedy is inevitable." I contend that the play
clearly shows Laura's shyness is not simply an innate quality; rather, it is tied
directly to how she has been made conscious of her physical and emotional
difference. Indeed, Eric Levy argues that Laura's self-consciousness becomes
not just representative of an abandoned struggle, but a way of shaping
identity to which she eagerly clings: "Sensitivity to shame allows Laura to
identify with her worthiness, not of ridicule, but of delicate care and
compassion . . . lack of confidence is Laura's secret wish, for it protects from
confronting anything more threatening in her life than her own familiar

anxiety."[25] And so, late in the play, her mother bursts out with a frustrated cry: "Why can't you and your brother be *normal* people? Fantastic whims and behavior!"[26] But to counter Amanda, we see that a consciousness that she is distinctly *not* normal has been long ingrained in Laura. When Laura resists her mother's attempts to set her on the course for matrimony by protesting, "But, Mother— . . . I'm-crippled!" her mother reacts sharply:

> Nonsense! Laura, I've told you never, never to use that word. Why, you're not crippled, you just have a little defect—hardly noticeable, even! When people have some slight disadvantage like that, they cultivate other things to make up for it—develop charm—and vivacity—and—*charm!* That's all you have to do![27]

Amanda's protestations ("never . . . use that word") reinforce a sense of stigma, and Tom is hardly any better when he says about Laura, "We don't even notice she's crippled any more."[28] As Kent points out, there is a powerful directive against acknowledging disability identity performed in these exchanges:

> Amanda insists that the word "crippled" must never be spoken, refusing to let Laura stereotype herself as handicapped. But her extreme reaction whenever the word is uttered indicates a more insidious attitude. For Amanda there is something unspeakable about Laura's condition, something that must be denied and hidden away. To be "crippled" is somehow shameful, a disgrace. Laura has never been allowed to acknowledge her lameness as part of herself.[29]

Laura's options in dealing with her family's reactions to her disability, it would seem, are either to embrace overcoming and put the non-disabled person at their ease by "developing charm," or to try to completely ignore the fact of her disability as too terrible to be discussed. It is therefore hardly a surprise when she later describes to Jim how she perceived her own disability in high school, coming late into a choir class:

Laura Yes, it was so hard for me, getting upstairs. I had that brace on my
        leg—it clumped so loud!
Jim I never heard any clumping.
Laura (*wincing at the recollection*) To me it sounded like—thunder!
Jim Well, well, well, I never even noticed.

Laura   And everybody was seated before I came in. I had to walk in
front of all those people. My seat was in the back row. I had to go
clumping all the way up the aisle with everyone watching!

Jim   You shouldn't have been self-conscious.

Laura   I know, but I was. It was always a relief when the singing started.[30]

Laura has been schooled to read her disability as intrusive and dissonant, a
distinct contrast with the virtuosity, harmony, and sameness of the bodies
literally united in chorus.

The tyranny of patronizing attitudes is likewise held up for scrutiny. Such
condescension takes multiple forms, from do-gooderism to outright
paternalism. Laura is saddled with a mother, for example, whose
overprotectiveness emerges at least in part from a sense of desperation over
the limited choices that await a woman unable to mold herself to either
marriage or merchandising. Yet even Laura can see that Amanda immerses
herself into the role of selfless caregiver with just a bit too much relish:
"Mother, when you're disappointed, you get that awful suffering look on
your face, like the picture of Jesus' mother in the museum!"[31] Disabled
existence is also circumscribed by the medical model, and the play
mocks medical paternalism through Jim's diagnostic pretensions, prompt as
he is to tell Laura what he believes her psychological "problem" to be.
His bombast becomes satirical in itself, echoing rubrics of self-help familiar
to audiences then and now (and modeling an early version of what
would become a repetitive trope in television and film: the non-disabled
person who knows better than the disabled person what they should make
of their disability):

Now I've never made a regular study of it, but I have a friend who says
I can analyze people better than doctors that make a profession of it. I
don't claim that to be necessarily true, but I can sure guess a person's
psychology, Laura! . . . Yep—that's what I judge to be your principal
trouble. A lack of confidence in yourself as a person. You don't have the
proper amount of faith in yourself. I'm basing that fact on a number of
your remarks and also on certain observations I've made. For instance
that clumping you thought was so awful in high school. You say that
you even dreaded to walk into class. You see what you did? You
dropped out of school, you gave up an education because of a clump,
which as far as I know was practically non-existent! A little physical
defect is what you have. Hardly noticeable even! Magnified thousands

of times by imagination! You know what my strong advice to you is? Think of yourself as *superior* in some way![32]

We see echoed here Amanda's language in describing Laura's disability as a "little defect," Tom's determination not to even see Laura as disabled, the language of overcoming, and the insistence on faulting the disabled person, rather than the attitudes and conditions around them, for their "predicament." Linton emphasizes the cumulative effect of these things as a key element to Laura's character:

> Laura's behavior and view of the world is intensely real and accurate based on the way social norms and expectations—largely conveyed through Amanda—have relentlessly affected her. Her cognitive situation is not the result of any deficit, but instead of the psychological strain that has resulted from constant assault from dissonant and conflicting pressures on her: to overcome, to hide herself, to conform, to risk her heart's dignity even with an awareness of the possibility of rejection, and to simultaneously acknowledge and deny her condition.[33]

All these external pressures put on Laura as a disabled woman, layered with the language of diagnosis, shape an overweening sense of what ableist attitudes she has internalized over the years.

There is more to be located in this play that is relevant to disability than the testimony provided by a fictionalized experience, however, important as it is that that experience be made visible. Much has been made of when Jim, an inept diagnostician, mishears Laura telling him she had "pleurosis," instead thinking she has said "blue roses," which then becomes his nickname for her. As many critics (and Jim himself) assert, the appellation suggests Laura as rare, or at the very least, different; the slippage likewise references the mutability of language as well as the constructed nature of illness. Jim, and those critics, want to believe in the myth of Laura's exceptionalism. But I want to suggest another possibility: Williams also uses disability as manifestation of variation and indeterminacy, and in so doing actually moves us away from the easy binarism that, simply inverted, would now make Laura's "blue roses" a mark of superiority:

Jim The different people are not like other people, but being different is nothing to be ashamed of. Because other people are not such wonderful people. They're one hundred times one thousand. You're one times one! They walk all over the earth. You just stay here. They're common as—weeds, but—you—well, you're *Blue Roses!*[34]

We can of course mistrust Jim's speech as a variation on the rhetorics that assure disabled people that they are "special." Not only does this reveal the slipperiness of that rhetoric (how can one be exceptional and have to be referred to euphemistically at the same time?), to insist on Laura's specialness is to reify implicitly the hierarchies that the play is ostensibly attacking. The opposite of hypernormalcy is not hypervisibility, or a hierarchy in which Laura's blue roses supposedly outshine the weeds of common folk (which they never do), but rather an acceptance of a fuller range of human difference and variation. Siebers points out that disability in art "enlarges our vision of human variation and difference," and it is something like this that I believe happens here.[35] This ordinary in the seeming extraordinary is a significant aspect of *The Glass Menagerie*'s engagement with disability. It is not so much that Laura's disability makes her more special; it is that the world's masking of her variation reflects a larger tendency for it to willfully forget its own varied self.

It is understandable that disability studies scholars more recently wishing to reclaim Laura would want to revise the way she has been understood. Sarah Hosey's essay on teaching *The Glass Menagerie* from a disability studies perspective, for example, argues that students should be invited to regard "Laura's position at the end of the play ... as choice and accomplishment":

Laura may be emotionally and physically ill-suited for successful participation in what Williams portrays as brutal and dehumanizing labor and marriage markets; looked at in this way, Laura's limp and her preoccupations become not only markers of individuality, but potentially radical rejections of a capitalist-patriarchy.[36]

Does Laura need to be idealized for us to claim her as radical, however? I think, ironically, to see what makes Laura special, potentially even radical as a disabled character, we have to see how common she is; and by "common," I do not mean "conformist." There is something decidedly *ordinary* about Laura. In her wistful recollection of a teenaged crush, Laura echoes her mother's own girlish reverie; the "specialness" of her yearnings rather more reveal the spectacle of our wonder at a disabled woman *having* desire. Laura's visits to Forest Park, the penguins at the zoo, the Jewel Box, and the St. Louis Art Museum suggest less about a special poetic insight on Laura's part (thus feeding the myth of the disabled person as seer or having a Tiresias-like rarified insight), and instead show her inserting herself into a wider range of embodiment and identity. Neither tropical flowers nor penguins are rare taken out of their own context; all the bodies, paintings, animals, and flowers in the park, however, hold in common a lack of utility in *this* context, where they are simply preserved and displayed as "Other." Yet what they reference is that which lies beyond the "hive-like conglomeration" of St. Louis sameness: a rich, diverse planet, where multiplicity is more the way of the world. When she wanders the park, escaping the routinized strictures of Rubicam's Business College, Laura wends her way, on the move in *her* way, through as wide a range of experiences and embodiments as it is in her power to encounter. Though they are all circumscribed, literally and figuratively (each institution is a "container" of sorts within the rectangle of Forest Park, itself boxed in by the city of St. Louis), there is a kind of movement-as-engagement Laura performs here that sharply contrasts with her own brother's escapism and individualism (about which I will say more in a moment). He seeks illusion in the stasis of a movie seat; she moves through the real. As Linton observes: "she wants to know and see more, and is capable of it, as demonstrated when she ventures out alone."[37] Williams manages to show that movement alone is not in itself inherently better than stasis; note how Laura's explorations contrast with Tom's eventual movement, premised as it is on individualism rather than engagement with others, as he drifts aimlessly from city to city, disconnected and alone.

We also get a particular clue about why it matters to keep from mythologizing Laura as exceptional, either from a romanticized or a disability studies perspective, in Jim's *other* nickname for Laura; at least twice, he refers to her as "Shakespeare's sister" (Tom, as a poet, has been nicknamed "Shakespeare" by his co-workers at the shoe factory). This reference echoes that section of Virginia Woolf's famous feminist manifesto *A Room of One's Own* entitled "Shakespeare's Sister." In that portion, Woolf ponders the paradox of women who are celebrated in literature, yet non-existent in history: "Imaginatively she is of the highest importance; practically she is completely insignificant."[38] "What one must do," Woolf continues,

> to bring her to life was *to think poetically and prosaically at one and the same moment*, thus keeping in touch with fact—that she is Mrs. Martin, aged thirty-six, dressed in blue, wearing a black hat and brown

shoes; but not losing sight of fiction either—that she is a vessel in which all sorts of spirits and forces are coursing and flashing perpetually.[39]

Woolf imagines the fate of "Shakespeare's sister," the imaginary, equally gifted writer who, finding no place for her talents in a man's world, kills herself out of desperation. Certainly, Woolf further acknowledges, "it needs little skill in psychology to be sure that a highly gifted girl who had tried to use her gift for poetry would have been so thwarted and hindered by other people, so tortured and pulled asunder by her own contrary instincts, that she must have lost her health and sanity to a certainty."[40] Yet Woolf pulls us back from the myth of the romantic, tragic individual, a myth that would allow us simply to sentimentalize this tragic figure without actually striving to make her real, and pushes us instead to consider what it might take to *really* render Shakespeare's sister visible and functioning in the world. The potential for that visibility, Woolf points out, courses through all women (and, I would add, the disabled):

> She lives in you and in me, and in many other women who are not here tonight, for they are washing up the dishes and putting the children to bed. But she lives; for great poets do not die; they are continuing presences; they need only the opportunity to walk among us in the flesh ... For my belief is that if we live another century or so—I am talking of the common life which is the real life and not of the little separate lives which we live as individuals—and have five hundred a year each of us and rooms of our own; if we have the habit of freedom and the courage to write exactly what we think; if we escape a little from the common sitting room and see human beings not always in their relation to each other but in relation to reality; and the sky, too, and the trees or whatever it may be in themselves; ... if we face the fact, for it is a fact, that there is no arm to cling to, but that we go alone and our relation is to the world of reality and not only to the world of men and women, then the opportunity will come and the dead poet who was Shakespeare's sister will put on the body which she has so often laid down.[41]

Who is not here, Woolf asks? What would be needful for them to be here? What have we defined those absent figures in relation to, instead of esteeming them for themselves? Attitudes, as this simple reference to "Shakespeare's sister" reminds us, shape the material effect on what bodies are made visible and participatory in history.

Williams also reminds us, through Laura as well as the open-endedness of the play's treatment of her fate, not only of the body's variation, but of its contingency and impermanence. In this respect, there's an essential humanness in Laura's "march toward invisibility" that is something to be embraced, rather than feared or dismissed.[42] Disability is our shared experience and eventual fate; it is what not only underscores variation, but acknowledges the impermanence we flee. Certainly intimations of decay exist throughout the play; Mr. Wingfield was once a man invested in the latest technology of his time (the telephone) who fled his obligations; Jim seems well on his way to becoming yet another man who peaks early but settles into a life of mediocrity. Amanda's Scarlett O'Hara-like costume for the dinner party is yellowed and faded, and she is reduced to helping sell foundation garments at Famous-Barr department store to other aging belles. Technology, like femininity, is a kind of drag performance in that it becomes a satire of itself when outmoded. Williams' play encourages us to see contingency and indeterminacy as critical, and reflecting the human experience; it is an uncertainty embraced and valorized by being purposefully built into the conclusion of the play.

This seems a contradictory idea, since what happens next appears straightforwardly sad and set: Jim dances with Laura, Jim accidentally breaks the horn off of Laura's glass unicorn (a symbol for Laura's uniqueness), Jim kisses Laura, and Jim ultimately reveals he has a fiancée, and therefore cannot promise to see Laura again. And it is here that several critics have cemented their darkest views of the implications of Laura's disability in a fairly consistent reading of the play's end. In it, disability is a self-fulfilling prophecy victimizing her: she will not be able to be partnered with Jim, and so will retreat back into anonymity: "Laura cannot conform to the values of either business or marriage, so she renounces the real world in favor of the couch, where she plays with her glass figures and listens to records."[43] Louis K. Greiff's view of that end is even darker than Babcock's: '[by] the close of *The Glass Menagerie*, Laura has been torn from her fantasy world to become a figure without imaginative protection ... When she blows out her candles, to end the play, the glow of her own imagination is extinguished, and the resulting darkness seems utterly permanent."[44] For John Lahr, the close of the play is one in which Laura becomes part of a "dumb show" through which Tom (and, by extension, Tennessee Williams) is able to erase family memories in actuality in order to cope with loss and grief.[45] These several readings seem to differ only in the degree of pathos they ascribe to Laura, and they frequently lapse into ableist metaphors to describe her state. For example, when Jim breaks the glass unicorn's horn off, Gilbert Debusscher asserts that it "symbolizes a kind of emotional defloration, the girl's irreversible loss of childlike innocence, the *unavoidable mutilation* that Williams sees as necessarily accompanying the process of growing up."[46] Laura, as a result, "does not reproach Jim with clumsiness but, instead, indirectly expresses her gratitude for ending the *era of the lonely freak*."[47]

Perhaps most chillingly, Robert J. Cardullo shows us what happens when the paradox of exceptionality, i.e. romanticizing Laura as at once special and as a victim of her specialness, is taken to its logical extreme. Like Babcock, he identifies Laura as existing outside the slipstream of an industrialized age; hers, according to Cardullo, is a "fragile, almost unearthly ego brutalized by life in an industrialized, depersonalized Western metropolis filled with the likes of Gentleman Jim O'Connor."[48] Yet even Jim, for a moment, can see past his utilitarianism and recognize the rarified when he "beatifies Laura by emphasizing what is special, even divine about her and downplaying her physical disability."[49] We have already seen how such a selective reading of disability (i.e. it must be either ignored or the thing that makes one transcendent) is suspect. Indeed, for Cardullo, it reinforces the notion that Laura is a figure who, paradoxically, is rarified beyond her disability, yet too rarified because of this disability to exist in the world:

> She is too good for this world, the Romantics might say, and for this reason she could be said to be sadly beautiful or bluely roseate, like the soft-violet color of her kimono … in Scene 2—the first scene where the screen-image of blue roses appears.
>
> Indeed, Laura's physical as well as emotional frailty betokens an early demise, if not a death-wish on her part—a death that would bestow upon her the ultimate union with Nature so prized by Romantics and so elusive or unattainable in life.[50]

Such an interpretation of Laura's fate after Jim's rejection is chilling; it imagines her, Thomas Chatterton-like, embracing a beautiful death, hastened to it by her physical unsuitability for mortal existence:

> Yet it is the Gentleman Caller's departure rather than his arrival that provides a *final solution* to Laura's problems, for in intensifying her desperation and isolation, Jim's permanent disappearance after Scene

7—in combination with the subsequent permanent disappearance of Tom—could be said to hasten her physical and mental deterioration to the point of death ... It is there [in heaven] that Laura may finally know fully Mr. James Delaney O'Connor, a man who on earth remained for the most part a figment of her imagination. It is on earth, as well, that Laura's soul may have had the fortitude to endure the accent of Jim's coming foot, his opening of her apartment door, because that accent and that opening would mean not only momentary escape from the prisonhouse of her imagination along with her shyness, but also ultimate, perpetual release from the *cellblock of her physically crippled body, the wasteland of her emotionally crippled mind*, and the enslavement of urbanized subsistence.[51]

Laura's death, critically posited as "final solution" to the "cellblock" and "wasteland" of her emotional and physical disabilities, contains eerie echoes of another "final solution" being carried out at the time of the play's premiere—one whose methods were first practiced on disabled people in Germany's T-4 killing centers. Better, certain, logical, and more poetic, implies Cardullo's argument, that one will become dead because of being disabled. Laura will only ever be able to "know" Jim in the biblical sense in the afterlife; for most certainly, disabled people are disqualified from sexuality on earth.

Babcock makes culture the problem rather than the disabled person, recognizing that Williams is showing the commonality between bodies like his sister Rose's, Laura's, and those who deviate from a standardized norm, and what literally happens to them because of such fear of deviation:

Williams's sister Rose, of course, did not blow out her candles; she was the victim of a technological experiment, as were the citizens of Guernica. For Williams, both events were symptomatic of a historical crisis in which technology was increasingly being used to subdue or destroy human beings who did not conform to the dominant types, whether those types were American or Nazi. Both systems demanded that subjects conform to the whole, and resistance and difference were viewed with suspicion.[52]

Suspicion, of course, led to the policing of the disabled body. Indeed, Lahr argues that Williams believed his mother advocated for a lobotomy for his sister because of the shocking things, sometimes of a sexual nature, she would say. The lobotomy was "a result of Edwina's sexual hysteria, an enforcement of radical innocence through the surgical removal of the part of the brain that remembers."[53] Laura references, even satirizes, medical (and eugenicist) interventions such as the one Rose Williams suffered when she tells Jim she will pretend her broken unicorn "had an operation. The horn was removed to make him feel less—freakish!"[54] But even Babcock believes Laura capitulates in her own fashion, with her "renunciation of her difference ... made complete with the breaking of the horn."[55]

As part of their exchange over the broken unicorn, however, Laura also tells Jim, "I don't have favorites much. It's no tragedy, Freckles. Glass breaks so easily. No matter how careful you are. The traffic jars the shelves and things fall off them."[56] This would seem to be just another moment of the disabled person putting a non-disabled one at his ease. But Laura's affectionate nickname for Jim, "Freckles," is also a diminutive one that marks his face as imperfect, a gentle reminder to Jim that he is her equal: he, too, lives in a contingent body, one that is at once different (marked as it is) and ordinary (what could be more prosaic than freckles?). Laura gives Jim the horse—which is now, in fact, not normal at all, but disabled—as a souvenir. What is commemorated is not so much lost love as that moment of brief connection, and of a momentary move away from the rhetorics of hierarchy and exceptionalism toward a humbler, more real recognition of a fuller range of human embodiment; glass—like all bodies—breaks so easily. Laura does retreat at the play's end, and she is saddened, but one need not view that moment solely as a quick slide toward capitulation. Life is difficult, messy, and complex, but to re-romanticize Laura's embodiment of that merely as a tragic denouement offers only the opportunity to re-inscribe hierarchies of the kind that have already excluded Laura and those like her: because we fear her (and our) fate, we must see her example as special—and especially to be avoided.

It is, after all, worth remembering that the play's ending is rather more open-ended than the meanings critics have imposed on it would suggest. Laura does not speak after Jim reveals he is engaged, having been rendered speechless by the shock of the news. Yet her lack of speech also means we have a lack of closure on *really*, definitively knowing what has happened to her. Instead, as Tom steps forward to narrate his remembrance of Laura, Williams's stage directions are as follows:

> *We see, as through soundproof glass, that Amanda appears to be making a comforting speech to Laura, who is huddled upon the sofa. Now that*

we cannot hear the mother's speech, her silliness is gone and she has dignity and tragic beauty. Laura's hair hides her face until, at the end of the speech, she lifts her head to smile at the mother. Amanda's gestures are slow and graceful, almost dancelike, as she comforts her daughter.[57]

For the first time, we are not subject to Amanda's rhetoric. We have seen what about that rhetoric enforced normalcy and imposed self-loathing on Laura; but now there is a moment of communion and mutuality between them. But we are left to wonder as audience members what Amanda has said in place of her normal speeches; what would it take for Laura to connect with Amanda, and to be comforted? This hardly seems a death-wish, let alone a definitive defeat. Rather, it becomes a call to us to imagine what Amanda might be saying, to ourselves re-write a script of support and connection in the face of all the storytelling and mythologizing that has come before this point.[58]

In fact, the only character of whose defeat we can be sure is the one who has individuated his own ending. Tom's decision to put his own dreams ahead of his family's and follow ambition, to follow in his father's footsteps outside the apartment door, means he has merely traded the "celotex interior" of the shoe factory for a half-lit existence of memory and loneliness, as Bigsby suggests: "Fired from his job in the shoe warehouse, he wanders from city to city, looking for the companionship he had failed to offer his sister."[59] Tom's aimless meanderings seem created in pursuit of a dream of success and fortune as illusory as the memory of his sister, while his sister's more authentically lived life contains nuance, even if that nuance remains unappreciated, unvalued, and even punished by a standardized, and standardizing, world.

It is worth pointing out that my argument for differently envisioning *The Glass Menagerie* in turn suggests exciting opportunities for casting and directing. For example, rather than asking to what degree a non-disabled actor might imitate Laura's limp, casting a disabled actor in the role shifts things entirely, and in ways we might not entirely expect. As Bruno points out, "Laura, like most disabled characters, has traditionally been viewed through a non-disabled lens. By non-disabled people for sure, but I would argue, by most disabled people as well."[60] Linton underscores the importance of therefore casting a disabled actor as Laura:

Typically in *Menagerie*, Laura's disability is subtle, and "put-on" by the normatively able actresses who play her. Therefore, a question exists as to the extent of the disability, and the extent to which she is both physically and cognitively impaired. In order to achieve Laura's "disability" identity, I think many actresses often feel the need to effect an altered physical and cognitive state that get at the IDEA of disability. Which, in itself, is a construct ... Laura is therefore constructed based on a PERCEPTION of what it is to be disabled—which is often flawed from the outset—as opposed to a realistic experience. In my mind, it sets up the entire play for failure.[61]

Bruno played Laura in 2001 at The Fulton Opera House in Lancaster, Pennsylvania; Linton played Laura at the University of California, San Diego in 2012; Denver professional theatre company Phamaly staged the play with a cast entirely made up of disabled actors (as it stages all its productions) in 2014. The act of inclusive casting is a nod toward authenticity that disrupts the stage as a place where disability can only be simulated but never actually present, but it is important to emphasize that other opportunities for meaning-making also arise.

For example, that Linton, a wheelchair user, did not have a disability that aligned with Laura's as written is significant. An article at the time noted the way in which her presence changed how particular lines had resonance: "It's impossible to hear the line 'Glass breaks so easily' here and not think, in that moment, of a broken spine."[62] Beyond such literalism, however, Linton's presence retorted against the notion that Laura's limp might only be read as a metaphor for her supposed psychological disability—instead, it shows how the play can draw a line under the contingency of all bodies. Intriguingly, reviewer John Moore notes, "Linton would have pushed the envelope even further—she auditioned for the role of Amanda. Imagine: The woman most afraid that her daughter was damaged and unlovable—played from a wheelchair."[63] The envelope might have been pushed for Linton as an actor, but as Moore's comment begins to suggest, a disabled actor playing an ostensibly non-disabled role, one with Amanda's horror of "crippledom," could have also powerfully shown the insidious strength of internalized ableism. Phamaly took full advantage of the disability experience of its actors to more richly inform the play in such a way; in his notes, director Bryce Alexander observes:

The Glass Menagerie is not the story of any hero or villain, but of individuals who must walk their own paths—right or wrong—not by choice but by necessity, by circumstance, and even by the impenetrable influences within us all. The characters in the play must walk their own paths, but when coupled with Phamaly's performers—who navigate the path of disability every day—the play takes on an even greater and pervasive significance.[64]

The range of human embodiment represented by the Phamaly actors also echoes the argument I have made here about Williams' play valorizing such variability through Laura.

Both Bruno and Linton emphasize how they came to see Laura in ways that were radically different than how they had first perceived the character. Both actors speak of moving past that "non-disabled lens" through which they, like many audience members before them, had regarded her: "[The] more I prepared," noted Bruno, "the more I realized that all these years, I had been complicit in perpetuating every stereotype ever written about Laura." But now, "[her] vulnerability, dreams, invisibility, generosity, isolation, beauty, imagination were mine. My joy, longing, physicality, empathy, pain, wisdom, fear, desire were hers."[65] Linton, too, emphasizes Laura's importance as a disabled character, and explains why it therefore matters even more that a disabled actor play her:

I think the play is a beautiful illustration of how the construct of disability—and other forms of otherness—are forced upon individuals with real, heartbreaking consequences; individuals who under more supportive circumstances would live full, unsheltered lives ... When Laura's disability is real and embodied, her inner struggle becomes more tangible: how to honestly acknowledge that she is "different" but then tease out the extent to which she accepts or refuses the proscribed realities of how her differences rule her life. In my opinion, the only way to truly do justice to this play, and find the beauty of Laura, her strength, her imagination, her heart, and the nuances of her situation, is to have a non-normative body playing the role.[66]

As the experiences of these actors remind us, lived disability experience can importantly intersect through casting and direction to underscore how *The Glass Menagerie* is an exemplum of what modern drama can do for a richer, more nuanced understanding of disability. As Linton simply, yet powerfully affirms: "It has become, for me, one of the few plays that aptly represents the complicated story of disability."[67]

Disability haunts the corners of this play; as Cardullo points out, Laura's physical frailty manifests itself multiply: "not only ... the childhood illness that left her crippled, with one leg held in a brace, but also ... her frequent faintness, nausea, and colds, together with her bout of pleurosis as a teenager."[68] It is striking, however, that the play opens not with any of these images of Laura's disability, but with America-as-disabled, as when Tom introduces his reverie by saying:

> To begin with, I turn back time. I reverse it to that quaint period, the thirties, when the huge middle class of America was matriculating in a school for the blind. Their eyes had failed them, or they had failed their eyes, and so they were having their fingers pressed forcibly down on the fiery Braille alphabet of a dissolving economy.[69]

This is no simple ableist metaphor. Tom's reversal of the metaphor ("they had failed their eyes") purposefully uncouples the metaphor from physical ability, making the ability to see irrelevant to having real insight. Braille in this image becomes punishing, but also prophetic and truthful, a reconnection to reality accomplished through alternative means of reading. If we, similarly, can find these alternative means of reading cultural texts, perhaps we can likewise reclaim insights that do suggest a burgeoning disability presence in art, and do not deserve to be relegated to invisibility within the context of disability history.[70]

CHAPTER 7

ACCESS AESTHETICS AND MODERN DRAMA: AN INTERVIEW WITH JENNY SEALEY ON GRAEAE THEATRE COMPANY'S *THE THREEPENNY OPERA* AND *BLOOD WEDDING*

Kirsty Johnston

Graeae Theatre Company, founded in 1980, is one of the world's leading disabled-led theatre companies, recognized for its envelope-pressing artistry, inclusive and accessible practices, and strong reception by audiences and critics. Graeae has produced its own devised work and commissioned scripts, but has also offered challenging, risk-taking, and powerful productions of modern plays. To gain a sense of how Graeae moves from modern drama texts to accessible performance, I asked Jenny Sealey, Graeae's Artistic Director since 1997, to respond to a range of questions about her art and practice and that of Graeae Theatre Company.

Sealey's work is well known and lauded. In 2009, she was awarded an MBE (Member of the Most Excellent Order of the British Empire) in the Queen's Honours and became an Artistic Advisor for the Unlimited 2012 Festival, part of London's Cultural Olympiad. She also co-directed the London 2012 Paralympic Opening Ceremony with Bradley Hemmings. Sealey is the recipient of honorary doctorates from the Royal Conservatoire of Scotland and Middlesex University and an Honorary Fellow of the Central School of Speech and Drama and Rose Bruford College. In 2012 she won the Liberty Human Rights Arts Award. As Artistic Director of Graeae, Sealey has directed and produced a diverse range of performances which have toured nationally and internationally.

In the interview, she refers to several productions, the details about which are available in the company's online production archive. Further information about other Graeae workshops and programs can also be found on the company's website: www.graeae.org. In the interview, I have added endnotes to provide readers additional context or links to programs or work that may not be generally known.

Kirsty Johnston (KJ): What are your artistic goals as the Artistic Director of Graeae Theatre Company?

Jenny Sealey (JS): Well, everything that Graeae does is absolutely fueled by accessibility, and that's functional, practical, and artistic accessibility. Further, our mission is to create high-quality theatre and to profile the excellence of Deaf and disabled artists. We absolutely know that we have a right to be on a real diversity of platforms, whether it's a small black box, or large mainstage, or an outdoor theatre arena, or, as with the Paralympics, a stadium. So, our goals are to be as ambitious as any mainstream theatre company, but always to work with a strong cohort of Deaf and disabled artists.

KJ: How do you understand the concepts of theatre accessibility and inclusion?

JS: Accessibility and inclusion are absolutely permeated within Graeae's DNA. So, it's not a question of understanding it, it's a question of feeling it and knowing that it's your right and responsibility to create accessible theatre. As a Deaf person, I want to go to see more theatre, and I can't because there is such a lack of signed performances or captioned performances. So, for me, making the work that I do at Graeae, it has to be accessible for me, for my Deaf actors on stage; it also has to be accessible for a Deaf audience. But at the same time, it has to be accessible to blind and visually impaired people, and the set and everything has to be accessible for any wheelchair users or people with mobility issues in the play. We only perform in theatres where the backstage is accessible, and the auditorium has access for more than one wheelchair user, which sometimes is the case with some old theatres. Inclusion is, well, it's everything we do. Some of the mainstream theatres now are including at least one disabled person. I'm waiting for the day when they might include more than one. And I'm waiting for the day when they might include real accessibility in terms of sign language, captioning, and audio-description into their main productions.

KJ: What modernist drama and theatre have you and Graeae Theatre Company produced?

JS: I've had the most extraordinary time creating productions of plays like *Blasted* by Sarah Kane, Brecht's *Threepenny Opera*, which was adapted by Robert David MacDonald with lyrics by Jeremy Sams and recently, we've just done Lorca's *Blood Wedding*. It has been said that my approach to theatre is very Brechtian, but I'm not an academic and I'm not a Brechtian expert by any stretch of the imagination. All I know is that the work that I do is informed by the script which will always determine how the artistic access will work. And if that in a sense becomes Brechtian, then so be it. Obviously, *Threepenny Opera* was Brechtian because that was Brecht!

With *Blasted*, the most curious thing was that I didn't understand what Sarah Kane meant when she said in her opening notes, everything in round brackets functions as a line. I thought, wow, Sarah Kane is way ahead of her game. She is writing audio-description, because most of the things in the round brackets were saying what people were doing: Ian gulps down a gin. Cate takes off her dress. Cate looks around the room. Ian gets his gun.[1] And I thought, well, that's audio-description, that is wonderful. So, that's exactly what I did in my naïveté. I had the actors voicing those very lines. With the stage directions, we made some decisions around who was a protagonist in each scene. In the first act, Ian is very much the protagonist. So we had the character of Ian lead on some of those stage directions and the character Cate leading on others so she could make a comment on how she feels about him being in the hotel room with her, her observations about his health and how she feels about him carrying a gun.

To ensure access for Deaf people, we filmed Deaf actors signing on a big screen behind the actors on the stage. For Act One, the main protagonist is Ian, so we had Neil Fox dressed the same as Ian, and he had the same mannerisms as Ian, but signed everything that Ian said, literally translating the action, for example gulping gin or smoking. Cate is the protagonist in Act Two. Adele Ward signed for Cate. And in Act Three, the soldier is the main protagonist. Daryl Jackson signed the soldier's lines, dressed in combats. And when the stage soldier, played by David Toole, spoke the stage directions "takes a sausage sandwich and devours it," we had a close-up of Daryl eating a sandwich with the grease and sauce running down his chin.

We were able to play with all the visceral elements, but they were on film, while spoken by the actor on stage. What this pairing and its effect did for me was exactly what I thought Kane wanted. She did not want anyone to escape. Every single word she had to say was about our apathy and our lack of engagement with Bosnia and also our own wars at home. Our production of *Blasted* forced everyone to hear or see every single word. It became so claustrophobic, you couldn't switch off. And at the end of the first show, a young woman in the toilets was heard to be saying, "I am traumatized by that. I am traumatized. I did not want the soldier to be talking about what he was doing. Bad enough having to see it." We didn't show a rape but we did have David revealing his stump to give the impression that this was how he was going to rape Ian. This physical positioning was in and around the character of Ian, played by Gerard McDermott, but it was a still picture. The emotion and violence of the act came through by voicing Kane's stage directions. This was pushed further by the BSL translation on screen. So I think we really messed with people's minds and made them really understand what it was Sarah Kane was saying.

For *Threepenny Opera*, having the most glorious, diverse Deaf and disabled cast and having our narrator John Kelly who is a wheelchair user saying very publicly, "Up there are the words in case we forget what we're saying and over there we'll be tapping a laptop making sure the words come up so we'll remember. And we will also be muttering into a microphone, telling the blind lot what's happening." We were very upfront about what our means of access were. And because it's Brecht, you can be that upfront. We also had some glorious in-jokes with some of the disabled performers, being very, very self-deprecating about their physicality. Max Runham, who played Filch, has a prosthetic arm, which he would sometimes take off; it would get lost in and around the set. He would find it, or somebody would trip over it, or he'd take it off to scratch his back. By having such a gloriously motley crew, we were able to be so irreverent, naughty, in your face. And Brechtian, I think! The other thing that I think Brecht would have loved was how the songs were signed. Jude Mahon won Best Supporting Actress for her role as a sign language interpreter/whore at Nottingham playhouse.[2] And just having two people, one person singing, one person signing, you get a different, three-dimensional sense of those songs. In some of the songs we also had a running photo track. Not all Deaf people find sign language easy; not all Deaf people read; and having visuals also serves people who may have English as a second language. The visual stimulus put the songs into context, so we were able to have some quite horrid images of very, very topical issues and people, of Jimmy Savile, the Pope, David Cameron, and so placing the events of the play absolutely in 2014. This allowed us to really, really push issues around austerity and the treatment of disabled people and poverty, explaining the landscape of inequality, really spelling it out to an audience.

We recently produced Lorca's *Blood Wedding*. David Ireland's adaptation brought it right up to 2015. Our adaptation was very much about the inner city, not the hot landscape of Spain, but inner city—Glasgow, for example—it is about what goes on behind closed doors. The heat of it is the proximity of all the families and people. One review which I liked said we didn't have any elephants in the room as issues around disability, deafness, and race all came to the fore. What was interesting about this particular production is that we set up who everybody was right at the beginning. And all the audio-description was live, so sighted and hearing people heard it and some of it was signed for Deaf people. All of the text was captioned. It was a really diverse, radical way of doing *Blood Wedding*. What we discovered in rehearsal as we were practicing audio-description was that every single person in the cast was constantly viewing the scene that they were not in; therefore, by audio-describing the text or operating the PowerPoint for these scenes everyone was complicit in the action; and by breaking down the fourth wall it served to make the audience complicit in what happens at the end, the death of two young men.

The other thing was that we had a Deaf Mother with a profoundly Deaf voice on stage. She spoke and signed with her son in a typical family way of signing but when she was meeting the Bride's family she signed in fluent BSL and switched her voice off and expected her son to voice over for her. This gave us some wonderful comic moments (and Ireland's text was extremely funny, which is not what one expects from Lorca) where the Mother is signing to her son (in front of everyone), asking if his bride is a whore. The power of EJ Raymond's Deaf voice gave the grief of having lost her son and husband and then later her other son a guttural and raw dimension; not having a "normal voice" was crucial to this. In her final speech, she signed and spoke in BSL syntax (which has a different grammatical order from English). The Bride and the Wife echoed the same words, creating a choral finale of grief.

KJ: What drew you to these works and what were your artistic goals for each production?

JS: I am a fan of Sarah Kane and I've always wanted to do *The Threepenny Opera* and *Blood Wedding*. Actually I really want to do *The House of Bernarda Alba*, but it was thought that that wouldn't sell as well as *Blood Wedding*. As an Artistic Director, I love doing extant plays because when you put a Deaf or disabled person into the fabric of the narrative, that's not normally allowed for us, there is an embarrassment of riches, because we can add so many layers of meaning, of content. When we did *Bent* by Martin Sherman, about what happened to gay men during the Holocaust, I had every character played by two people. Each character had one hearing actor and one actor who was a Deaf BSL user. I also played around with diverse ethnicity. We had a black cellist, two black actors as Max, an Irish performer for Horst and two white actors as Rudy. The multiple diversity of casting really, really hit home that disabled people were also the first to go during the Holocaust, along with gay men, Jews, and anybody of a different ethnicity. This added an emotional texture and understanding of that period of time and the impact was profound.

And the same is really true of all the other plays we do. After productions of *Blood Wedding*, we asked audiences in Dundee, Derby, and in Bangladesh, what does love mean? And who has a right to love? It's a perceived myth that disabled people are just different, they're "Other"—we don't love or have lives.

KJ: What casting, rehearsal and production procedures best served your goals for inclusive production?

JS: When I'm casting, I cast the best person for the job. It's very rare that I cast to type. When I did *A Lovely Sunday for Creve Coeur* by Tennessee Williams, I cast Deaf actor Caroline Parker to play the Deaf character in the script. But in *Blood Wedding* I cast EJ Raymond because she was brilliant and happened to be Deaf. And suddenly it made absolute sense that the character of the Mother was Deaf as it made her relationship with her son become even more profound because not only is she losing him but she is also losing him as a form of communication with the outside world.

With all of our plays, it is about getting the right person to do the job and then we have very intense conversations around what are the best means for them to access the play and access rehearsals. And all of that becomes permeated within everything. What I love about Graeae is that we do access as a team and it is everyone's responsibility. When we have Deaf actors, we have to have the script translated into BSL. So the hearing actors work with Deaf actors and sign language interpreters to translate. When you translate it to BSL you have to really know the meaning of every single line, which you should do as an actor anyway. But translating into BSL really forces that point. And so that becomes really useful for Deaf and hearing actors. You get the right translation and the hearing actors really get to know what it is they are saying. The same is also true when we are trying to audio-describe the set, or to audio-describe what it is we are doing. The actors get a different sense of ownership over the play that they are in, the costumes they are wearing, the set design that they inhabit. All of this goes into creating a preamble on a CD which we give to blind audiences so that they get a sense of who the key actors are, their physicalities, their ethnicity, and some things about them, their little foibles, their idiosyncrasies of who they are as people. And then they go on to talk about their characters and how their characters dress and move and what is the deep inner secret of their character. As a result, for a blind audience, when they hear those actors on stage, they've already heard the voices. So it helps them to have a richer engagement and experience.

KJ: Is there anything you would do differently in subsequent productions?

JS: I tend not to dwell on what I didn't get right or what wasn't explored. A director is only as good as their last production. I think there are some things you wish for, like you would want to have more time, more R and D to start with, but when you are up against time pressures, I think you get more done. The Royal Shakespeare Company has eleven weeks of rehearsal. I don't think I could cope with eleven weeks! On second thought, I think if I were devising, then I would like to have a bit longer. I did a show called *Belonging* with Brazilian and UK circus performers, all disabled and all still relatively new to the genre. My UK cast had been part of the Paralympics Opening Ceremony, as my professional cast, and this had been their first venture into the arts! Some were former Royal Marines, Army or graphic designers, or stay-at-home mums, and their journey to the arts was still new. With *Belonging*, I should have given them more time because we were also working in English, Portuguese, British Sign Language, and Libras (Brazilian sign language), which added to the complexity of the process.

KJ: Do you plan to produce more modernist drama? Which plays and why?

JS: Amit Sharma, who is my Associate Director, is directing at present, a new play by Jack Thorne, a very up-and-coming and prolific disabled writer. It's called *The Solid Life of Sugar Water* and is about two people trying to have sex for the first time after having a stillbirth. It's a beautifully, beautifully written piece, very painful, very raw, very open, and very sexually provocative.

Plays I have swimming around in my head are *La Cage Aux Folles* and of course *Bernarda* and I will be doing *The Hunchback of Notre Dame* for Manchester Royal Exchange adapted by Canadian writer Alex Bulmer, who is blind and really wants to push the notion of audio-description within the adaptation. She and Jack adapted it for radio some years ago but radio is so wasted on me so I am excited about this becoming a stage show. Graeae is doing a lot of new writing, and we have a new project called "Write to Play."[3] We've just finished our first year with National Theatre Studio, Soho Theatre, and the Royal Court, and we've been working with five disabled writers, who as I talk now, are all working towards a second draft of a full length play. And Year Two writers are at the moment writing their miniatures, which are monologues and duologues. Our partners for this are the Royal Exchange Theatre, Manchester, the Octagon Theatre, Bolton and the Everyman Theatre, Liverpool. Year Three of the program will take place in the North East. We're just about to start working on that. So some of those plays will absolutely fit into a more modernist drama. I'm not absolutely sure what is meant by modernist drama. I think my line is always: "I just do plays, if you know what I mean!"

KJ: How do you respond to any particular praise or criticism which you receive in reviews?

JS: When we have been absolutely slated by the press, I remember feeling quite joyous, because that meant that they were criticizing Graeae in the same way that they would a mainstream theatre. Our problem with some of the criticisms we have received has been with how they talk about impairment, so we have written some responses correcting terminology.

KJ: Does Graeae have explicit accessibility policies and procedures? If yes, how are these policies and procedures communicated within and without the institution?

JS: As I have said, everything that Graeae does is in and around accessibility, profiling the excellence and skills of Deaf and disabled people. We are partners mainly as access consultants on *Ramps on the Moon*, which is a collaboration with seven regional reps with a grant from Arts Council England to produce one big show a year, of which the first is *The Government Inspector*.[4] The aim of this is to promote real cultural shifts with all the reps in terms of access and employment of disabled actors, writers, producers, designers, etc. and really pushing working with the broad diversity of Deaf, blind, visually impaired, physically disabled, learning disabled people, and people who are users/survivors of the mental health system and others who have hidden disabilities.

Over the last eighteen months Graeae has gone back to its political roots with a capital P! The biggest issue facing us here in the UK at the moment is that we have had a very good scheme, called Access to Work and the Independent Living Fund.[5] The Independent Living Fund means people can live independently. That is now being closed so people who need personal care may well end up going back to live in residential homes. Changes to Access to Work may mean that I'm going to have to re-figure how I do my job. If I'm not allowed to bank my hours, and if I have to save them just for rehearsals, it means I can no longer be an ambassador for the company, representing the company at Arts Council England, the British Council, in and around academia and other public events. So, there's a lot of change happening. But we have to keep fighting to make sure that we can still stay true to our belief and our passion that great art, great theatre really does have the ability to challenge and to change perception, and take people on a whole other journey of what is possible.

CHAPTER 8
SHATTERING THE GLASS MENAGERIE
*Terry Galloway, M. Shane Grant, Ben Gunter,
and Carrie Sandahl*

Characters

Carrie Sandahl, *herself*
Terry Galloway, *herself*
Tom, **Amanda**, **Laura**, **Jim**, **Eager Audience Member**, *Ben Gunter and M. Shane Grant*

Shattering the Glass Menagerie is a multi-media performance art piece. It was first presented by the authors at the Association for Theatre in Higher Education (ATHE) conference entitled "Tomorrow's Stages: Blueprints for Transforming Theatre" held in New York in August 2003. It was subsequently performed by the authors in March 2011 as part of the "At the Hip: Conjoining Queerness and Disability" conference held at the State University of New York (SUNY), Buffalo.

*(**Slide #1 Legend: Shattering the Glass Menagerie**)*

Scene: Two chairs DC and a small table in between them with two coffee cups sitting on it.

*(**Slide #2 Legend: The Glass Menagerie**)*

A few beats . . .

*(**Slide #3 Legend: The Accent of a Coming Foot**)*

Carrie and Terry enter simultaneously (from UR and UL, respectively), limping like crazy, waving to each other, thumping our canes like mad, falling all over the place, Terry cupping her hand over her ear. When they get to their chairs, the dialogue begins.

Terry   God. I'm so embarrassed.

Carrie   Don't be. It was hardly noticeable. A slight defect.

Terry   I still feel so embarrassed.

Carrie   Your problem is you lack confidence. You know what my strong advice to you is? You've got to think of yourself as superior in some way!

Terry   Carrie, thanks for saying that. I'll let those nuggets of advice you just quoted from Tennessee Williams's play *Glass Menagerie* inspire me to adopt a more aloof, superior—critical attitude. So. From a disability perspective, *The Glass Menagerie* is a cringingly embarrassing play.

Carrie   OK, Terry. If we have criticism, we need evidence. And with this play, it is not hard to find. Time and again scenes like this play themselves out:

The Glass Menagerie Clip #1

Tom   One little warning. He doesn't know about Laura . . .

Amanda   . . . He'll know about Laura when he gets here. When he sees how lovely and sweet and pretty she is, he'll thank his lucky stars he was asked to dinner.

Tom   Mother, you mustn't expect too much of Laura.

Amanda   What do you mean?

Tom   Laura seems all those things to you and me because she's ours and we love her. We don't even notice she's crippled any more.

Amanda   Don't say crippled! You know that I never allow that word to be used!

Tom   But face facts, Mother. She is and—that's not all.

Amanda   What do you mean "not all"?

Tom   Laura is very different from other girls.

Amanda   I think the difference is all to her advantage.

Tom   Not quite all—in the eyes of others—strangers—she's terribly shy and lives in a world of her own and those things make her seem a little peculiar to people outside the house.

Amanda   Don't say peculiar.

Tom Face the facts. She is—she lives in a world of her own—a world of little glass ornaments, Mother. She plays old phonograph records and—and that's about all.

As we watch the scenes we become more and more cringingly embarrassed and end up holding our heads and our crotches in agonized shame.

Terry I'm holding my crotch because I'm feeling the loss of the horn, the fragile horn that represents the power of imagination and desire. A power that has been shattered by everything we now know of the real, lived experience of disability.

Carrie And I'm holding my crotch because I'm so pissed off I can hardly restrain my ire.

Terry Do tell.

Carrie This play pisses me off because I've always longed to play the part of Laura. After all, she was the only crippled girl who limped her way into the dramatic canon. I never got to play the pretty girl. Even in my late teens and early twenties, I was cast as the old lady, the crazy inmate, the wacky servant, or as a man. As if my disability cancelled out my femininity. But Laura would give me the chance to play a pretty girl, crippled and all. I always believed that part belonged to me. She was the girl that I loved to hate. I hated her so much that I didn't trust anyone else to play her.

Terry One of my most memorable childhood roles was Wilbur in *Wilbur's Close Shave*, which if I remember correctly had something to do with Wilbur mistaking the word "coughing" for the word "coffin." Which given my deafness might have been a bit of typecasting. No matter. I liked playing the boy. As the boy I could indulge my exterior cripple—the inky, dirty, breakneck, loud, constant messy misadventure that mimicked Helen Keller pre-Anne Sullivan—that savage and biting (literally), often uncomprehending presence that indulged in its own freedom from meaning. But my interior cripple was another story.

(Slide #4 Legend: Blue Roses)

Carrie By your "interior cripple" do you mean your queer identity?

Terry No. My queer identity was perfectly happy being breakneck, physical, and totally freely irresponsible. My interior cripple was busy trying to figure out how to survive the critical eye that even then, young as I was, I knew was going to be turned upon me the minute my role as boygirl hoyden ceased to charm. When my body could no longer be strapped down enough to contain its fleshy uncouthness; when I would start to metamorphose from child at play to adult. That's when I'd be exposed under the unforgiving light of the world's stage in all my quintessentially female, quintessentially disabled, quintessentially queer and useless imperfection.

Carrie How does the role of Laura fit in?

Terry I coveted the role of Laura for much the same reasons as did my friend Bobby with whom I traded sneakers (he liked my light blue low-tops; I preferred his black high-tops). He was a burly, freckled, burr-cut redhead with a gang of older brothers who were constantly bullying him to act like a man, get tough, quit whining and most of all take off those fucking baby blue low-tops. We both felt at odds with the perception that was layered upon us by our appearances. We both imagined that we had an inner sensitivity, a nobility that was being unfairly overlooked, a grace, a gentleness, an imaginative sweetness of spirit that ought to be honored, cherished even—a fragility that should have given us—like Laura—reason enough for being.

Laura I went in the art museum and the bird-houses at the Zoo. I visited the penguins every day! Sometimes I did without lunch and went to the movies. Lately I've been spending most of my afternoons in the Jewel-box, that big glass house where they raise the tropical flowers.

Terry Toss in going to the movies, that's my perfect day! If only we could play the role of Laura, be convincing in that role, people would see us in another light, a more forgiving one—see that we weren't as tough as we were pretending; that, rough beasts though we seemed, we needed all the kindness, all the consideration, all the love we could get so we'd be relieved—like Williams relieved Laura—of the burden of having to justify ourselves, our existence. The burden of having to take action, to grow up, get out, get married, get a job, get capitalistic, get responsible, and work our busy butts off the rest of our existence. When all we really wanted to do—like Laura—like Tennessee Williams—was play, fantasize.

(Slide #5 Legend: Do you think I'm in love with Continental Shoemakers?)

Carrie   What are you suggesting? That by buying into the role of Laura, you and I were not only buying into Williams's supposed portrayal of what it means to be crippled, but we were also buying into Williams's supposed portrayal of what it means to be queer?

Laura   Most of them are little animals made out of glass, the tiniest little animals in the world. Mother calls them the glass menagerie. Here's an example of one, if you'd like to see it! This one is the oldest, it's nearly thirteen. Oh, be careful—if you breathe, it breaks!

Terry   And sexual and uselessly imaginative.

Carrie   I agree that Williams's plays are studded (so to speak) with homosexual coda. That has been a given for a long while now.

Terry   I've always suspected that, but I'm not an academic—I'm free to form my impressions from out of the air—and never feel compelled to cite sources. But, Carrie, you're welcome to if you know any.

Carrie   Off the top of my head?

Terry   That's where a true academic would be carrying them.

(Slide #6 Legend: Ha!)

Carrie   Well, obviously, there's Clum's *Acting Gay*. And there's Bronski's *Culture Clash*, Beaver's "Homosexual Signs," Sinfield's *Out on Stage*, Shackelford's "The Ghost of a Man," Phillips' "Blanche's Phantom Husband," Savran's "By Coming Suddenly into a Room that I Thought was Empty" . . .

(Terry interrupts at any point here.)

Terry   Impressive. But I would have simply pointed my sex decoder ring at these particular passages from *Glass Menagerie* replete with queer clues to, uh, crack it (so to speak).

Amanda   I took that horrible novel back to the library—that hideous book by that insane MR. LAWRENCE. I cannot control the output of a DISEASED MIND or people who cater to them, but I won't allow such filth in my house. No nonnonononono, I think you've been DOING

THINGS YOU'RE ASHAMED OF. That's why you act like this. I don't believe that you go EVERY NIGHT TO THE MOVIES. Nobody goes to the movies night after night. Nobody in their right mind goes to the movies as often as you pretend to. People don't go to the MOVIES AT NEARLY MIDNIGHT, and MOVIES DON'T LET OUT AT 2 AM. Come in stumbling, muttering to yourself like a maniac.

OH I can see the handwriting on the wall as plain as I see the nose in front of my face! It's terrifying! More and more you remind me of your father! He was OUT ALL HOURS WITHOUT EXPLANATION then left! Good-bye! And me with the bag to hold. I saw that letter you got from **the** MERCHANT MARINE I know what YOU'RE DREAMING OF. I'm not standing here blindfolded! Yes well, then, Then do it! But not till there's somebody to take your place.

(Carrie and Terry applaud)

Terry   Once upon a time this passage could simply have been read without the subtext we know Williams either consciously or unconsciously attached to it. Again, it's all speculative conjecture to me. But since I'm a homosexual you can trust me to more authentically interpret the lingo.

Carrie   Puh-lease! If you're arguing that Williams protected his homosexual subtext by hiding it within the actions of a heterosexual female character, then I, as a disabled heterosexual woman (like Laura), should represent queerness in the extreme. And that gives me as much a right to decode queerness in the text as you do.

Terry   As I was saying . . . Once upon a time, a straight audience not in any way "in the know" would have thought Tom spends his spare time in bars drinking and dreaming of abandoning his nagging mother and crippled sister to sail off to adventures of his own.

Carrie   But Tom is suspect. I get it. You know, though, in retrospect alcohol just doesn't seem a shameful enough excuse for being out at all hours. That it takes the suggestion of the male homoeroticism of D.H. Lawrence to merit the exaggeration of "diseased minds." That in order to merit Amanda's hysteria "the movies" has to be interpreted as porn.

Terry   That the letter from **the** Merchant Marine has to be read in the singular rather than the plural, as He rather than It.

(Slide #7 Legend: Love!)

Carrie That leaving duty to concentrate on self, abandoning one's family and dreaming things you're ashamed of doing has got to be somehow sexually reconstituted in order to be something Tom should be ashamed of.

Terry Otherwise, the contemporary mind finds itself impatient with the text—its sources of agony and shame seem unauthentic, dated, more than a little ridiculous.

Carrie OK. But that's Tom's queerness. What about Laura's queerness? Is Williams saying that being queer is being a kind of a wimp who ought to be pitied? What good does pity do for Laura? For us? Do you really think being pitied relieves you of the burden of having to make your own way in the world?

Amanda What is there left for us now but dependency all our lives? I tell you, Laura, I know so well what happens to unmarried women who aren't prepared to occupy a position in life. I've seen such pitiful cases in the South—barely tolerated spinsters living on some brother's wife or a sister's husband—tucked away in some mouse-trap of a room—encouraged by one in-law to go on and visit the next in-law—little bird-like women—without any nest—eating the crust of humility all their lives!

Terry I don't care what relieves me of that burden as long as something does. What I'm arguing is that what will relieve Laura of that burden isn't marriage but imagination. That pity is a form of imagining. In some ways the disabled could embrace Laura's fate or at least re-articulate it—what's wrong with being peculiar? With being different? With being imaginative? With turning your back on capitalistic expectation? With wanting to be pitied—wanting empathetic, imaginative understanding of your differences?

Carrie Come on, Terry, history shows us that the non-disabled relieve themselves of the burden of disability by trying to eliminate the disabled themselves. Pity is one step away from contempt, which is one step away from hate, which is one step away from eugenics, which is one step away from euthanasia, which is one step away from . . . you see where I'm going with this?

In poll after poll, people say they'd rather be dead than disabled. Consider the fact that Williams based the character of Laura on his schizophrenic sister, Rose, who was institutionalized most of her life and later lobotomized. Some good pity did her in real life. Also, consider the fact that after Tom leaves, we have no idea of what happens to Laura. In the play's time period, people with disabilities were institutionalized in record numbers, suffered involuntary sterilizations, and most were banned from public schools. Clouding this reality with the haze of Laura's fantasy life is reprehensible. Her fantasy life serves the play dramaturgically as a kind of self-negation; her "peculiar behavior" a convenient justification for her loneliness.

Terry   And in my book that alone makes her unremarkable in any way. Who doesn't use fantasy for self-negation? Who doesn't use peculiar behavior to justify loneliness? And that's what I find to be so radical about her. Her absolute determination not to Be. I love it.

Carrie   I hate it. (*Slide #8 Legend: Terror!*) Laura embodied my worst fears as a disabled girl: that no man would ever love me … that I would never be able to make my way in the world … that I wouldn't have any friends … that I was an embarrassment to my family, that people just patronized me when they told me that my disability was what made me "special."

Laura   I never did have much luck at making friends.

Jim   Well, I don't see why you wouldn't.

Laura   Well, I started out badly.

Jim   You mean being ———?

Laura   Well, yes, it—sort of—stood between me …

Terry   So I'll say again, cripples are always called upon to be remarkable to justify ourselves. It is not enough for someone who is disabled or queer and disabled or simply disabled, queer, and uninvested in mores of this world to simply be.

Carrie   I always thought if I could play Laura I could rescue her, play her with a vengeance!

(Slide #9 Legend: The Opening of a Door)

I believed that only I could understand the depth of Laura's suffering. I would bring an authenticity to the role, relieving audiences of the torture of watching yet another able-bodied beauty fake a limp and wallow in Laura's wimpiness. I would, à la Artaud, "signal through the flames" with my brilliant acting.[1]

Amanda   I don't understand you at all, honey. Every time I try to do anything for you that's the least bit different you just seem to set yourself against it. Now take a look at yourself. No, wait! Wait just a minute—I forgot something.

Laura   What is it?

Amanda   A couple of improvements. When I was a girl we had round little lacy things like that and we called them "Gay Deceivers."

Laura   I won't wear them!

Amanda   Of course you'll wear them.

Laura   Why should I?

Amanda   Well, to tell you the truth, honey, you're just a little bit flat-chested.

Laura   You make it seem like we were setting a trap.

Amanda   We are. All pretty girls are a trap and men expect them to be traps.

Carrie   Ha! Gay Deceivers, you can say that again.

Terry   Again, we have to constantly justify our being. By being brilliant. But really it would be enough if we would simply stay special.

Carrie   When you are disabled, people are always telling you how special you are then rejecting you because you're just too fucking special. *(Slide #10 Legend: It's a pretty trap)* It's a mixed message we always hear.

Terry   So to speak.

Carrie   And it's the mixed message that makes me both love and hate Laura. Love her because we want that spotlight, we want to be told that we're special, we want to be that ethereal and fragile and pretty. But—

Terry   But—

Carrie   Laura is told constantly that her disability isn't noticeable, that it's only a slight defect, that she's got wonderful qualities that she just needs to have confidence in.

Amanda   Girls that aren't cut out for business careers usually wind up married to some nice man. Sister, that's what you'll do.

Laura   But, Mother—

Amanda   Yes?

Laura   I'm—crippled!

Amanda   NONSENSE, Laura, I've told you never, never to use that word. Why you're not crippled, you just have a little defect—hardly noticeable, even. When people have some slight disadvantage like that, they cultivate other things to make up for it—develop charm—and vivacity—and *charm*! That's all you have to do. [. . .]

Carrie   Jim tells her the same thing.

Jim   (*to Laura*) [. . .] Yep—that's what I judge to be your principal trouble. A lack of confidence in yourself as a person. Now I'm basing that fact on a number of your remarks and on certain observations I've made. For instance, that clumping you thought was so awful in high school. You say that you dreaded to go upstairs? You see what you did? You dropped out of school, you gave up an education all because of a little clump, which as far as I can see is practically non-existent! Oh, a little physical defect is all you have. It's hardly noticeable even! Magnified a thousand times by your imagination!

Carrie   You know what my strong advice to you is? You've got to think of yourself as superior in some way!

Terry   You said much of the same thing to me when we first started this conversation.

Carrie   Well in this context it makes me want to puke! Who does Jim think he is? Her doctor?

Terry You'd think so, given the way he diagnoses her problems throughout the entire scene.

Carrie And did you ever notice that Jim treats Laura just like Amanda does: he dismisses her as a disabled woman, tries to replace who she really is with some vague platitudes, then he gives her a pity kiss! And worst of all she falls for it! Then he dumps her. He even takes the broken glass! What are her special qualities? The ability to fondle glass animals? Big whoop.

Terry So the question you're asking is what use is she? And I'm saying that's the question always asked of anyone who is disabled. And of many of us who are homosexual. Of most of us who live primarily in our imaginations. How do we justify the money spent, the attention paid, the care given? How do we weigh in human regard if we are regarded as flawed, less than whole, unable or uninterested in actual or symbolic procreation—yet unwilling to stand aside, cease to demand. In short, the selfish embodiment of human imperfection.

Carrie Right, the imperative to be productive. I'll give you that. But what's wrong with expecting disabled people to be productive? I don't live in my imagination. I've got a faculty position, a husband, two kids, two cars, a great job in Chicago with tenure! [...]

Terry Well, isn't that SPECIAL? (*angry, accusatory*)

Carrie Touché.

(*Slide #11 Legend: The Crust of Humility*)

Terry You seem to be buying into that whole super gimp mentality. Your glass horn has been broken off and now you're like all the other horses. Is that what you think disability identity is all about—BECOMING JUST LIKE EVERYONE ELSE?

Jim We knocked the little glass horse over.

Laura Yes.

Jim Is he broken?

Laura Now he's just like all the other horses.

Jim You mean he lost his ...?

Laura He's lost his horn. It doesn't matter. Maybe it's a blessing in disguise. [. . .] I'll just imagine he had an operation. The horn was removed to make him feel less—freakish! Now he will feel more at home with the other horses, the ones who don't have horns.

Carrie Ugh. (*waves them away*) I guess I see your point. So, you are arguing that Williams is using Laura's disability as a metaphor for the ways in which queers were viewed as non-reproductive?

Terry Well, we've just seen that Williams, like Tom, is haunted by the memory of a Laura who cannot bring herself to "mean" in any conventional way. She can't earn a living.

Carrie She can't type,

Terry she can't eat,

Carrie she can't get her own dates,

Terry she can't get upset without fainting. She can't do this, that, or the other. Her life, whether she means it or not, is selfish. She exists for her own sake. And for her own pleasure—which again is imaginative.

Carrie So you're rehabilitating Laura, seeing her as somewhat aggressively passive?

(*Slide #12 Legend: Annunciation*)

Terry Why not? Gay men who read themselves into Williams have also presumably read themselves past its articulation of the social condemnation of homosexuality and freed themselves from male heterosexual duty as articulated by Amanda.

Amanda I mean that as soon as Laura has got somebody to take care of her, married, a home of her own, independent—why then you'll be free to go wherever you please, on land, on sea, whichever way the wind blows you! But until that time you've got to look out for your sister. I don't say me because I'm old and don't matter! I say for your sister because she's young and dependent. I put her in business college—a dismal failure! Frightened her so it made her sick at the stomach. . . .

Tom What can I do about it?

Amanda Overcome selfishness. Self, self, self is all that you ever think of! [...] Go to the movies, go! Don't think about us, a mother deserted, an unmarried sister who's crippled and has no job! Don't let anything interfere with your selfish pleasure! Just go, go, go—to the movies.

Carrie But Tom—gay or straight—does escape. It is an escape that Williams cannot imagine for a crippled girl. The women in Williams's landscapes brood, they have no recourse. They rely all too heavily on the kindness of strangers. They keep all too fresh and pretty for gentlemen callers who never come and when they do, they give you pity kisses or they're rapists like Stanley Kowalski.

Terry Yes, but nonetheless, I find it interesting that the sentiments of duty come out of the mouth of Amanda, a role so many of my drag queen friends say was written just for them.

(Slide #13 Legend: The Opening of a Door)

Carrie She's a man, duh! Wingfield!

Amanda [...] Honey, don't push your food with your fingers. If you have to push your food with something, the thing to use is a crust of bread. You must chew your food. Animals have secretions in their stomachs which enable them to digest their food without mastication, but human beings must chew their food before they swallow it down, and chew, chew—chew!

Terry (interrupting) Look, this is overkill. We've already established that strand of queer sensibility that's been imposed on the play. But I'm not interested in the drag queen shtick. I'm interested in the other queer sensibility being evoked in the play, in Laura's disability. Because in truth, Laura is as much Williams the queer as Amanda and Tom are.

Eager Audience Member Dr. Sandahl?

Carrie Yes.

Eager Audience Member Remember when you asked Terry about whether her "interior cripple" was her queer identity?

Carrie Why indeed I do.

Eager Audience Member   What strikes me as somewhat problematic is that, to some degree, your little "play about the play" points toward disability as external and visible, while sexuality is relegated to the internal.

Carrie   Is this about Judith Butler?

Eager Audience Member   Ya. Ok. People don't identify me (or other queers, for that matter) as queer from being able to see my hypothalamus or that pesky "gay gene." If we accept biological determinist arguments, then the root of queerness is invisible. Therefore, sexuality is communicated either through performative or verbal utterance. When this occurs, sexuality becomes signed and signified externally, the same way some disabilities do. Of course, there are "non-visual" disabilities (such as Terry's deafness). However, when she puts in her hearing aids her internal disability becomes externally visible ... much in the same way that sexuality becomes externally visible through performative or verbal utterance.

(*We think he's done and clap.*)

Also, I think you could go so far as to say, that the materiality of the non-visible disabled body and the queer body change once the queerness or disabledness has been uttered. I don't mean that my body actually physically changes, but others' perceptions of it do. What my body means, physically, to someone else changes when they know I'm gay (either to something gross or something yummy, depending on their sexuality ... hee hee). The material worth/value of my body also changes when my queerness is uttered for capitalistic reasons I'm sure you understand.

Terry   You postmodern scholars have created a monster.

Carrie   Thank you, random audience member, you're absolutely right. That would make an excellent dissertation topic. Too bad for you, I wrote an article on that very same topic: refer to my seminal (so to speak) article in *Gay and Lesbian Quarterly*.[2] (*holds up journal*) Terry, so, you were saying that the selfishness that informs the characters in the play is an aspect of queerness?

Terry   And disability and the imaginative and academic narcissism. So maybe I'm arguing that Laura's usefulness in this play is that she's performing not just another aspect of Williams's queerness, but queerness as a critique of dutiful assumptions? Laura allows him his free reign not just as a homosexual but as an ungendered soul—he uses her to contain and deflect criticism for longings, which expressed as himself, as a man, as a queer would engender contempt rather than pity, disgust rather than any attempt to comprehend, empathize.

Carrie   I see. So Williams is borrowing some of the pity automatically ascribed to gimps for queers in order to argue for the purely imaginative? Pity doesn't work! I dunno, Terry, I think in the light of the historical treatment of disabled people that what you're suggesting is a really shaky proposition.

Terry   Why? It's a proposition that allows me to love this play again. I know the play ought to stand on its own two feet, sans comment, criticism, apologia or autobiography, but in these terms I'm able to discover something to love in a play I loathe; I'm able to find something in his portrayal of crippled helpless Laura that I like, that I identify with. For the first time I can see the profundity of Williams's investment in Laura—her sweetness, her gentle fragility, her stubborn willfulness in pursuit of the unconventional, her abiding belief in the deeply symbolic world of her own imagining. Does it matter that I see her limp, her defect, as his signifier of both the vulnerability and the endurance of the purely imagined self?

Carrie   Why are you so invested in finding something to like about this play?

Terry   Because, as we keep bending and twisting this play, its language, its intentions, we keep discovering our own purposes. I know when I reread it now, I won't be able to rid myself of the presence of the troubled, sweet, gay man who sat at his typewriter and pecked it all out. And I like reading his play more when I'm imagining him longing to be Laura.

Carrie   Terry, I can hardly bear to sit here! Let me repeat: the play is not about Laura! It's not about anything we recognize to be true about disability. I mean listen to Williams's stage direction at the beginning of the play: '*The light upon Laura should be distinct from the others, having a peculiar pristine clarity such as light used in early religious portraits of female saints or madonnas.*' Gag me. No, gag him (*points to image of Tennessee Williams*). Laura's merely a symbol, a cipher for whatever the hell Williams was trying to say about queerness. I resent being used for someone else's purposes. I want to do this play again and do it differently— or just tear around and rip things up, smash the rest of the fucking glass animals.

Laura, shove that fucking unicorn horn up your ass and use it as a backbone!

Terry   Why not? Carrie, there is some amazing language in this play, reflecting the beauty of both Laura's and Williams's imaginative world. And I think any interpretation that completely disregards that beauty is juvenile—like thugs at our high school productions of the play who laughed their guts out when Laura fell down the stairwell.

Terry/Carrie   (*Both laugh maniacally*)

(*Slide #14 Legend: The Sky Falls!*)

Carrie   Maybe . . . It's funny how we keep going back to junior high and high school because that's when so much of what goes unspoken or repressed in this play is constantly in your face.

Tom   I had known Jim slightly in high school. In high school, Jim was a hero. He had a tremendous Irish good nature and vitality with the scrubbed and polished look of white chinaware. He seemed to move in a continual spotlight. He was a star in basketball, captain of the debating club, president of the senior class and the glee club, and he sang the male lead in the annual light opera.

Carrie   In high school, one of my best friends, Peter, and I developed a ritual to survive walking from his locker to the lunchroom. Peter was frequently a target for queer bashing in high school. He must've weighed 90 lbs, max, and had one of those new wave haircuts: you remember the 80s? The swooshing bangs in the front, slightly asymmetrical, cut short in the back. Well, that haircut, the trench coat he wore no matter what the weather, and his popularity with the drama geeks was enough to make him a target.

On his way to lunch every day, he had to make his way through a gauntlet lined by the "back hallers"—you know, those kids who wore rock concert T-shirts, black jeans, and lots of eyeliner. These kids pushed Peter, called him a fag, threatened to kill him.

We'd walk down the hall holding hands, pretending to be boyfriend and girlfriend. No one would bother us then. No one would dare threaten a crippled girl. Even the back hallers had ethics. Holding my hand, we performed straight couple together. The pity I engendered, in a way, protected Peter. In return, I got that coveted cultural capital of the high school girl set: a boyfriend. Peter was my date to homecoming; he gave me the male attention and affection I craved; and he always made me laugh. I'm starting to see what you mean, Terry. We can think about Williams forging a queer–cripple alliance, in a way, to make it down the hall.

Terry   Well, yes. But too bad, don't you think, that it's too late.

Carrie   What do you mean?

Terry   That it's too late, too old, too far beyond its own obvious conclusions. Carrie, you are a disability scholar and an activist. I'm an artist and an activist. Don't tell me there isn't even a part of your scholarly self that has questioned the purpose of this so-called play about a play we're performing right now instead of a talk featuring the up-and-coming work of actual queer disabled artists and scholars themselves.

Carrie   You're reversing yourself?

Terry   Yeah, yeah. That's our prerogative until we reach a point of thought where we feel we've gotten somewhere new, somewhere more contemplative and hence dynamic.

Carrie   For once, I totally agree. Even given the queered overlay, watching *The Glass Menagerie* is too much like watching the Jerry Lewis Telethon. He actually once told activists who disagreed with his portrayal of poster children, "You don't want to be pitied because you're in a wheelchair? Stay in your house!"

Terry   Part of the problem is that there is no real way to revisit the play.

Carrie   Point taken.

Terry   But the play can't, like *Taming of the Shrew*, for instance, be revisited in any fundamental way because fundamentally it is a deeply dated, deeply offensive piece of work—a monument to the fear and repression of the time in which it was written.

Carrie   And that fear and that repression is still playing itself out, despite the fact that so many disabled theatre artists are rising from the ranks to create really good work about their own experiences.

Terry   I think you're right. But the only way to rehabilitate the play may be to play up its repression—

Carrie   Remind people of where the ongoing attempt to repress has its roots—

Terry   Exaggerate the play's claustrophobia, use it as a tool to remind people that once

Carrie   and now again

Terry   there was a time when it was criminal for queer desire to be voiced,

Carrie   a time when it was impossible to imagine disabled yearning, to imagine a gay man or a crippled girl taking on life.

(Slide #15 Legend: The World is Waiting for the Sunrise!)

Terry   And that time is now.

Jim   Don't tighten up, relax. Loosen your backbone. Let yourself go.

Carrie   So maybe now's the time to look at Williams with a cool eye and put him aside—as a cautionary tale.

Terry   It's not as if his work was pure art, untainted by politics. His art could never be that pure because it already was so tainted by politics.

Carrie   We owe it to him

Terry   if we are indeed going to forge some queer–crip alliance inspired by his work

Carrie   to look at what he wrote and vow to help create playwrights that are never that coded,

Terry   never that afraid of their own voices

Carrie   or their own desire

(*Carrie and Terry pick up copies of the play and begin to read.*)

Carrie as Amanda   "Let those dishes go and come in front. Laura, come here and make a wish on the moon. A little silver slipper of a moon. Look over your left shoulder, Laura and make a wish!"

Terry as Laura   "Yes, Mother. What shall I wish for, Mother?"

Carrie as Amanda   "Happiness!"

Terry as Laura   "And just a little bit of good fortune."

Terry   The Opening of a Door!

Carrie   The Sky Falls!

Terry   The World is Waiting for the Sunrise!

(*Slide #16 Legend: Things have a way of turning out so badly*)

Carrie   Things Have a Way of Turning Out So Badly . . .

From the film   Laura, Laura. I tried to leave you behind me, but I am more faithful than I intended to be.

NOTES

Introduction

1. Tobin Siebers, *Disability Aesthetics*, Ann Arbor: University of Michigan Press, 2010, p. 4.

2. Readers interested in a contemporary disabled playwright's engagement with Buchner's pivotal work will be interested in *Private Battle*, a 1997 play by award-winning American playwright and actor Lynn Manning. Inspired by *Woyzeck*, the play is available in Lynn Manning's *Private Battle and Other Plays*, South Gate CA: No Passport Press, 2014, pp. 9–81. Also, as this book goes to press, Deaf West's *Spring Awakening* featuring Marlee Matlin, Camryn Mannheim, and a young cast of Deaf and hearing actors has just opened to overwhelmingly positive reviews on Broadway following its successful 2014 Los Angeles run.

3. While this book focuses on drama, readers should note that Petra Kuppers has helpfully surveyed critical readings of Antonin Artaud's theatre manifestos from a disability studies perspective. See the chapter entitled "Outsider Energies" in her book *Disability and Contemporary Performance: Bodies on Edge*, New York: Routledge, 2003, pp. 70–86.

4. Siebers, *Disability Aesthetics*, p. 20.

5. Carrie Sandahl, "The Tyranny of Neutral: Disability and Actor Training," in Carrie Sandahl and Philip Auslander (eds), *Bodies in Commotion: Disability and Performance*, Ann Arbor: University of Michigan Press, 2005, p. 255; Carrie Sandahl, "Ahhhh Freak Out! Metaphors of Disability and Female-ness in Performance," *Theatre Topics* Vol. 9, No. 1 (1999), p. 15; Victoria Ann Lewis, *Beyond Victims and Villains: Contemporary Plays by Disabled Playwrights*, New York: Theatre Communications Group, 2006, p. xxii.

6. Kanta Kochhar-Lindgren, "Disability" in Susan Crutchfield and Marcy Epstein (eds), *Keywords for American Cultural Studies*, New York: New York University Press, 2014, p. 83.

7. Ibid.

8. Janet Lyon, "Disability and Generative Form," *Journal of Modern Literature*, Vol. 38, No. 1 (2014), p. vi.

9. Peter Gay, *Modernism: The Lure of Heresy from Baudelaire to Beckett and Beyond*, New York: Norton, 2008, p. 3.

10. Ric Knowles, Joanne Tompkins, and W.B. Worthen (eds), *Modern Drama: Defining the Field*, Toronto: University of Toronto Press, 2003.

Notes

11. Ric Knowles, 'Introduction,' in ibid., p. vii.

12. Ibid.

13. Ibid., p. xiii.

14. Catherine Kudlick, "Disability History: Why We Need Another 'Other,'" *American Historical Review*, Vol. 108, No. 3 (2003), p. 764.

15. Marvin Carlson, *The Haunted Stage: The Theatre as Memory Machine*, Ann Arbor: University of Michigan Press, 2001, p. 1.

16. Ibid., p. 1.

17. Ibid., p. 7

18. Lewis, *Beyond Victims and Villains*, p. xiv.

19. Ibid., p. xxii.

20. Ibid.

21. See, for example, David Feeney, "Sighted Renderings of a Non-Visual Aesthetics: Exploring the Interface between Drama and Disability Theory," *Journal of Literary and Cultural Disability Studies*, Vol. 3, No. 1 (2009), pp. 85–99; Ann M. Fox, 'Battles on the Body: Disability, Interpreting Dramatic Literature, and the Case of Lynn Nottage's *Ruined*,' *Journal of Literary & Cultural Disability Studies*, Vol. 5, Issue 1 (2011), pp. 1–15; Ann M. Fox and Joan Lipkin, "Res(Crip)ting Feminist Theater Through Disability Theater Selections from The DisAbility Project," *Feminist Formations*, Vol. 14, No. 3 (2002), pp. 77–98.

22. Quoted in Mike Levin, "The Art of Disability: An Interview with Tobin Siebers," *Disability Studies Quarterly*, Vol. 30, No. 2 (2010), http://dsq-sds.org/article/view/1263/1272 (accessed 30 May 2015).

23. Ibid.

24. Tobin Siebers, *Disability Aesthetics*, pp. 10–11.

25. Fox, "Battles on the Body," p. 3.

26. Ibid., p. 2.

27. Fox cites Michael Davidson, *Concerto for the Left Hand: Disability and the Defamiliar Body*, Ann Arbor: University of Michigan Press, 2008; David T. Mitchell and Sharon L. Snyder, *Narrative Prosthesis: Disability and the Dependencies of Discourse*, Ann Arbor: University of Michigan Press, 2001; Ato Quayson, *Aesthetic Nervousness: Disability and the Crisis of Representation*, New York: Columbia University Press, 2007; Tobin Siebers, *Disability Theory*, Ann Arbor: University of Michigan Press, 2008; Siebers, *Disability Aesthetics*.

28. Davidson, *Concerto for the Left Hand*, p. 225.

29. Ibid., pp. 5–6.

30. Jenny Sealey interview, this book, p. 155.

31. Victor Shklovsky, "Art as Technique," in Lee T. Lemon and Marion J. Reis (eds.), *Russian Formalist Criticism: Four Essays*, Lincoln: University of Nebraska Press, 1965, p. 12, quoted in Michael Davidson, *Concerto for the Left Hand*, p. 5.

32. Simi Linton, "Disability and Conventions in Theatre," http://www.similinton.com/about_topics_2.htm (accessed 1 June 2015).

33. Michael Davidson, this book, p. 116.

34. Ibid.

35. Ann M. Fox, this book, p. 131.

36. Ibid., p. 133.

37. Ibid., p. 132.

38. Ibid.

39. Michael Davidson, *Concerto for the Left Hand. Disability and the Defamiliar Body*, Ann Arbor: University of Michigan Press, 2008, p. 1.

1 What is Disability Theatre?

1. Maya Sabatello, "A Short History of the International Disability Rights Movement," in Maya Sabatello and Marianne Schulze (eds.), *Human Rights and Disability Advocacy*, Philadelphia: University of Pennsylvania Press, 2014, p. 18.

2. Sharon L. Snyder and David T. Mitchell, *Cultural Locations of Disability*, Chicago: University of Chicago Press, 2006, p. 12.

3. Lennard Davis, "Constructing Normalcy," in Lennard Davis (ed.), *The Disability Studies Reader* (Third Edition), New York: Routledge, 2010, p. 3.

4. Snyder and Mitchell, *Cultural Locations*, p. 70.

5. Ibid., p. 71.

6. Davis, "Constructing Normalcy," p. 17.

7. Colin Barnes and Geof Mercer, *Disability*, Cambridge: Polity, 2003, pp. 124–5.

8. Doris Zames Fleischer and Frieda Zames, *The Disability Rights Movement: From Charity to Confrontation*, Philadelphia: Temple University Press, 2001, pp. 33–48.

9. Theresia Degener, "Disability Discrimination Law: A Global Comparative Approach," in Caroline Gooding and Anna Lawson (eds.), *Disability Rights in Europe: From Theory to Practice*, Oxford: Hart Publishing, 2006, pp. 87–106; Michael Prince, "Canadian Federalism and Disability Policy Making," *Canadian Journal of Political Science*, Vol. 34, No. 4 (2001), pp. 791–817; Richard Skotch, "American Disability Policy in the Twentieth Century," in Paul K. Longmore and Lauri Umansky (eds.), *The New Disability History*, New York: New York University Press, 2001, pp. 375–92.

10. Sabatello, "A Short History of the International Disability Rights Movement," pp. 12–24.

11. Recent cuts to the Access to Work program in the UK have prompted a number of disability activists to speak out. See, for example, Jenny Sealey's online conversation of 29 August 2014 with John Kelly on the Graeae website: https://www.youtube.com/watch?v=dxjVeJQySDQ (accessed 22 May 2015). Producer Jo

Notes

Verrent also places these cuts within the context of disability arts in the UK in her article "Disability and the arts: the best of times, the worst of times," *The Guardian*, 23 March 2015, http://www.theguardian.com/culture-professionals-network/2015/mar/23/disability-arts-best-worst-of-times (accessed 22 May 2015).

12. Victoria Ann Lewis, *Beyond Victims and Villains: Contemporary Plays by Disabled Playwrights*, New York: Theatre Communications Group, 2006, p. xix.

13. Ibid., p. xx.

14. Paul K. Longmore, *Why I Burned My Book and Other Essays on Disability*, Philadelphia: Temple University Press, 2003, p. 1.

15. Tom Shakespeare, "The Social Model of Disability," in Lennard Davis (ed.), *The Disability Studies Reader* (Third Edition), New York: Routledge, 2010, p. 268.

16. Mike Oliver, "The Social Model in Action: If I Had a Hammer," in Colin Barnes and Geof Mercer (eds.), *Implementing the Social Model of Disability Theory and Research*, Leeds: The Disability Press, 2004, p. 19.

17. Longmore, *Why I Burned My Book*, p. 2.

18. Tobin Siebers, *Disability Theory*, Ann Arbor: University of Michigan, 2008, p. 3.

19. Longmore, *Why I Burned My Book*, p. 2.

20. Tom Shakespeare and Nicholas Watson, "The Social Model of Disability: An Outdated Ideology? Exploring Theories and Expanding Methodologies," in *Research in Social Science and Disability 2*, Stamford, CT: JAI Press, 2001, pp. 9–28.

21. Snyder and Mitchell, *Cultural Locations of Disability*, p. 6.

22. Ibid.

23. Ibid., p. 10.

24. Ibid.

25. Colette Conroy, *Theatre and the Body*, New York: Palgrave Macmillan, 2010, pp. 55–6.

26. Kanta Kochhar-Lindgren, "Disability," in Bruce Burgett and Glen Hendler (eds.), *Keywords for American Cultural Studies*, New York: New York University Press, 2014, pp. 81–4.

27. See, for example, Barnes and Mercer, *Disability*; Ayesha Vernon and John Swain, "Theorizing divisions and hierarchies: Toward a commonality or diversity?" in Colin Barnes, Mike Oliver, and Len Barton (eds.), *Disability Studies Today*, Cambridge: Polity, pp. 77–97.

28. Ayesha Vernon, "The Dialectics of Multiple Identities and the Disabled People's Movement," *Disability and Society*, Vol. 14, No. 3 (1999), p. 394.

29. Simi Linton, *Claiming Disability: Knowledge and Identity*, New York: New York University Press, 1998, p. 4.

30. Kochhar-Lindgren, "Disability," p. 84.

31. Ibid.

32. Ibid., p. 83.

33. In Vancouver, under the leadership of filmmaker Bonnie Sherr Klein and disability scholar and activist Catherine Frazee, the Society for Disability Arts and Culture launched in 2001 an international festival series called "kickstART! A Celebration of Disability Arts and Culture" to press disability arts and culture forward in Canada.

34. For details concerning the dates, sites and programming of these and other disability arts festivals in the UK, please see the Chronology of Disability Arts prepared by Allan Sutherland, director of the Edward Lear Foundation. This resource is available at the Disability Arts Online website: http://www.disabilityartsonline.org.uk/Chronology_of_Disability_Arts (accessed 24 September 2015).

35. Drawing on her experience as General Manager of Arts in Action and Creative Producer of Australia's High Beam Festival, Jayne Leslie Boase has written about the challenges and opportunities of disability arts festivals. See her article, "Festivals: Agents of Change? Dynamics and Humanism within Disability and Arts Collaborations," *The International Journal of the Humanities*, Vol. 3, No. 10, 2006, pp. 133–6.

36. Paul Anthony Darke, "Now I Know Why Disability Arts is Drowning in the River Lethe (with thanks to Pierre Bourdieu)," in Sheila Riddell and Nick Watson (eds.), *Disability, Culture and Identity*, Harlow, England: Pearson Education, 2003, p. 132.

37. Bonnie Sherr Klein, quoted in *Arts Smarts: Inspiration and Ideas for Canadian Artists with Disabilities*, Vancouver: Society for Disability Arts and Culture, 2002, p. 41.

38. Carol Padden and Tom Humphries, "Deaf People: A Different Center," in Lennard Davis (ed.), *The Disability Studies Reader* (Third Edition), New York: Routledge, 2010, p. 396.

39. Ibid.

40. For a further overview of the politics surrounding Deaf culture in light of disability culture, please see Colin Barnes and Geof Mercer's book *Disability* (Cambridge: Polity Press, 2003), pp. 104–6.

41. Petra Kuppers, *Disability Culture and Community Performance: Find a Strange and Twisted Shape*, London: Palgrave, 2013, p. 23.

42. Ibid, p. 4.

43. Susan Crutchfield and Marcy Epstein, 'Introduction,' in Susan Crutchfield and Marcy Epstein (eds), *Points of Contact: Disability, Art, and Culture*, Ann Arbor: University of Michigan Press, 2000, p. 5.

44. Ibid.

45. "The Republic of Inclusion" was an event presented as part of the Progress International Festival of Performance and Ideas, held in Toronto, Canada from 4 to 15 February 2015. Curators Alex Bulmer and Sarah Garton Stanley explained the impulse and practical access details for the event as follows:

Notes

> [We] call for a rigorous and provocative discussion about the state of inclusion in our theatre community. A conversation for theatre makers, audiences, leaders, funders, all those in the performance world, and those who are being left out. Progress: it's about accessing the arts and about the arts being accessible. The Theatre Centre is fully accessible for wheelchair users. The event will also include ASL interpretation, Live Captioning, Audio Description, Tactile Map of the space and a supportive listener, and will be live-streamed via SpiderWebShow.ca in partnership with HowlRound: A commons by and for people who make performance.
> http://thisisprogress.ca/2014/11/dramatic-action-the-republic-of-inclusion/
> (accessed 22 May 2015)

46. Snyder and Mitchell, *Cultural Locations of Disability*, p. 10.

47. Ann M. Fox and Joan Lipkin, "Res(Crip)ting Feminist Theater Through Disability Theater: Selections from the DisAbility Project," *NWSA Journal*, Vol. 14, No. 3 (2002), p. 81.

48. Jason Bogaard Dorwart, "Phamaly and the DisAbility Project: Models of Theater by Disabled Actors," MA thesis, Department of Theatre and Dance, University of Colorado, 2012, p. 13.

49. http://www.phamaly.org (accessed 31 May 2015).

50. The following four founding artists remain active in the company: Kevin Ahl, Kathleen Traylor, Gregg Vigil, and Teri Westerman.

51. John Sefel, "Finding Phamaly," *Stage Directions* (2012), http://www.stage-directions.com/4600-finding-phamaly.html (accessed 24 September 2015).

52. Quoted in ibid.

53. Sefel, "Finding Phamaly," Matthew Swartz and Ali Zimmerman, "Distinguishing Sounds," *Theatre Design & Technology* (2005), pp. 14–20; Dorwart, "Phamaly and the DisAbility Project," p. 31.

54. Ibid.

55. Peter Eckersall and Helena Grehan (eds.), *"We're People who do Shows": Back to Back Theatre: Performance, Politics, Visibility*, Aberystwyth: Performance Research Books, 2013.

56. Ibid., p. 15.

57. Ibid., p. 31.

58. Bryoni Trezise and Caroline Wake, "Disabling Spectacle: Curiosity, contempt and collapse in performance theatre," in Peter Eckersall and Helena Grehan (eds.), *"We're People who do Shows": Back to Back Theatre: Performance, Politics, Visibility*, Aberystwyth: Performance Research Books, 2013, p. 119.

59. Fiona Gruber, "Performance more than a question of ability," *The Australian*, Vol. 19, 2008, p. 10.

60. Trezise and Wake, "Disabling Spectacle," pp. 122–3.

61. Ibid., p. 123.

62. Fox and Lipkin, "Res(Crip)ting Feminist Theater," p. 82.

63. The company website notes that Joan Lipkin and Fran Cohen began the DisAbility Project in 1995. Also on the site are details concerning the company's awards. http://www.uppityco.com/dp.html?pnl=1_3 (accessed 22 May 2015).

64. Fox and Lipkin, "Res(Crip)ting Feminist Theater," p. 82.

65. Details concerning this company are derived from their website: http://extant. org.uk/about_us (accessed 24 September 2015).

66. Oshodi clarifies her rationale and primary impulses for producing the piece:

    The play is a tragic farce, where an old couple of 94 and 95 have lived for years in isolation in their home surrounded by miles of water. Repetitious enactments of aspects of their past are interrupted by the need now to welcome an ever-growing crowd of invisible visitors. The old man and old woman accumulate many chairs for the invisible guests who wait for the arrival of an orator to deliver the old man's world changing speech, but to what effect ...? ... Having cast blind actors in the two main roles, Extant has shifted focus on the interpretation of this classic text, describing a unique relationship between unseeing actors interacting with what is visible and what is not. If the audience understands that the old man and woman are blind, are they to believe that the old man and woman really relate to these characters as unseen? Or is it the audience themselves who are in fact somehow lacking an ability—to see these other people?
       This quote and further material about the production may be found at http:// extant.org.uk/chairs/background (accessed 12 June 2015).

67. Rose Jacobson and Geoff McMurchy, "Focus on Disability and Deaf Arts in Canada: A Report from the Field by Rose Jacobson and Geoff McMurchy," Canada Council for the Arts, December 2010, p. 17.

68. Please see note 40.

69. A primary way they have done this is through their establishment of the Madness and Arts World Festival held first at Toronto's Harbourfront Arts Centre in 2003. The company has been involved in further iterations of the festival in Münster, Germany and Haarlem, near Amsterdam. Another company that participated in more than one of these festivals was Germany's Theater Sycorax which, interestingly given the focus on modern drama and disability theatre in this volume, brought their production of Buchner's *Woyzeck* to Toronto, staging it with clinicians in white coats and a set with doors reminiscent of Russian avant-garde theatre artist Meyerhold's famous production of *The Government Inspector*.

70. Barnes and Mercer, *Disability*, p. 102.

71. Carrie Sandahl and Philip Auslander, "Introduction: Disability Studies in Commotion with Performance Studies," in Carrie Sandahl and Philip Auslander (eds.), *Bodies in Commotion: Disability and Performance*, Ann Arbor: University of Michigan Press, 2005, p. 6.

Notes

72. Ibid., p. 5.

73. Richard Tomlinson, *Disability, Theatre and Education*, London: Souvenir Press, 1982, pp. 11–13.

74. Kochhar-Lindgren, 'Disability'.

75. Kuppers, *Disability Culture and Community Performance*, pp. 23–4.

76. Tomlinson, *Disability, Theatre and Education*, p. 21; Nabil Shaban, "Early History of Graeae" (2006), http://www.oocities.org/jinghiz53/The_Beginning_of_ Graeae.htm (accessed 22 May 2015).

77. David Mitchell and Sharon Snyder, *Vital Signs: Crip Culture Talks Back*, documentary, Fanlight Productions, 1995.

78. Kuppers, *Disability Culture and Community Performance*, p. 23.

79. Carrie Sandahl, "Queering the Crip or Cripping the Queer?: Intersections of Queer and Crip Identities in Solo Autobiographical Performance," *GLQ: A Journal of Lesbian and Gay Studies*, Vol. 9, Nos. 1-2 (2003), p. 36.

80. Eli Clare, *Exile and Pride: Disability, Queerness, and Liberation*, Cambridge, MA: South End, 1999, p. 70.

81. Sandahl, 'Queering the Crip or Cripping the Queer?,' pp. 52–3, fn. 1.

82. Rosemarie Garland-Thomson, *Extraordinary Bodies: Figuring Physical Disability in American Culture and Literature*, New York: Columbia University Press, 1997, p. 8.

83. Quoted in Garland-Thomson, *Extraordinary Bodies*, p. 8. Original source is Erving Goffman, *Stigma: Notes on the Management of Spoiled Identity*. Englewood Cliffs, NJ: Prentice-Hall, 1963, p. 128.

84. Michael Davidson, *Concerto for the Left Hand: Disability and the Defamiliar Body*, Ann Arbor: University of Michigan Press, 2008, p. 226.

85. Charles Mee, *the (re)making project*, http://www.charlesmee.org/casting.shtml (accessed 22 May 2015).

86. Rosemarie Garland-Thomson, "Introduction: From Wonder to Error—A Genealogy of Freak Discourse in Modernity," in Rosemarie Garland Thomson (ed.), *Freakery: Cultural Spectacles of the Extraordinary Body*, New York: New York University Press, 1996, pp. 1–22.

87. Ibid., p. 1.

88. Bree Hadley, *Disability, Public Space, Performance and Spectatorship: Unconscious Performers*, London: Palgrave, 2014, pp. 4–5.

2 Critical Embodiment and Casting

1. Bertolt Brecht, *The Messingkauf Dialogues*. Translated by John Willett, London: Methuen, 1965, p. 87. In a footnote on the same page, the Willett translation

links Amtsdiener Mitteldorf to "*Biberpelz und Roter Hahn*, an adaptation from Hauptmann."

2. Quoted in Daniel Banks, "The Welcome Table: Casting for an Integrated Society," *Theatre Topics*, Vol. 23, No. 1 (2013), p. 2. That imbalances persist has been made evident by more recent research, reported by Banks (p. 2) from the Asian American Performers Action Coalition (AAPAC) revealing that 80 percent of the New York area's shows from the 2006–7 to 2010–11 seasons were cast with European heritage actors.

3. Quoted in ibid., p. 3.

4. Quoted in ibid., p. 4.

5. Angela Pao, *No Safe Spaces: Re-Casting Race, Ethnicity, and Nationality in American Theatre*, Ann Arbor: University of Michigan Press, 2010, p. 178.

6. Banks, "The Welcome Table," p. 4.

7. Alliance for Inclusion in the Arts, website, 2015, http://inclusioninthearts.org (accessed 28 April 2015).

8. Ibid.

9. Betsy Goolian, "Alliance Takes a Much-Deserved Bow. Alumna Sharon Jensen Wins Tony Honor for Excellence in Theater," *Michigan Muse*, Vol. 6, No. 1 (2011). http://www.music.umich.edu/muse/2011/fall/Alliance-Takes-A-Bow.html (accessed 29 April 2015).

10. Ibid.

11. Alliance for Inclusion in the Arts, website.

12. Ibid.

13. Ibid.

14. Ibid.

15. Ibid.

16. Ibid.

17. Carrie Sandahl, "Why Disability Identity Matters: From Dramaturgy to Casting in John Belluso's *Pyretown*," *Text and Performance Quarterly*, Vol. 28, Nos. 1–2 (2008), p. 226.

18. Ibid., p. 225.

19. Ibid., p. 226.

20. Alliance for Inclusion in the Arts, "Written on the Body: A Conversation about Disability," http://inclusioninthearts.org/projects/written-on-the-body-a-conversation-about-disability (accessed 1 June 2015).

21. Quoted in ibid.

22. Sandahl, 'Why Disability Identity Matters,' p. 225.

23. Ibid., p. 240, fn. 5. In this footnote, Sandahl explains, "I became aware of the term 'cripping up' from the disability arts community describing non-disabled

actors playing disabled roles. I believe that this term was coined by Kaite O'Reilly, a disabled U.K. playwright." Sandahl then refers readers to the work of Jozefina Komporály: "'Cripping Up is the Twenty-first Century's Answer to Blacking Up': Conversation with Kaite O'Reilly on Theatre, Feminism, and Disability – 6 June 2005, British Library, London," *Gender Forum: Illuminating Gender*, Vol. 12 (2005), http://www.genderforum.org/issues/illuminating-gender-i/cripping-up-is-the-twenty-first-centurys-answer-to-blacking-up (accessed 25 September 2015).

24. Sandahl, "Why Disability Identity Matters," p. 236.

25. Frances Ryan, "We wouldn't accept actors blacking up, so why accept 'cripping up'?" *The Guardian*, 13 January 2015, http://www.theguardian.com/commentisfree/2015/jan/13/eddie-redmayne-golden-globe-stephen-hawking-disabled-actors-characters (accessed 13 May 2015).

26. Quoted in Kathleen Tolan, "We are not a Metaphor: A Conversation About Representation," *American Theatre* (2001), p. 21.

27. Quoted in ibid.

28. Christopher Shinn, "Disability Is Not Just a Metaphor," *The Atlantic*, 23 July 2014, http://www.theatlantic.com/entertainment/archive/2014/07/why-disabled-characters-are-never-played-by-disabled-actors/374822/ (accessed 1 June 2015).

29. Quoted in Tolan, 'We Are Not a Metaphor,' p. 21.

30. Quoted in Ibid.

31. Banks, "The Welcome Table," p. 12.

32. Kwame Kwei-Armah, Keynote Address, Theatre Communications Group Fall Forum on Governance, 2012, www.tcg.org/events/fallforum/2012/recordings.cfm (accessed 1 June 2015).

33. Ibid.

34. Quoted in Tolan, 'We Are Not a Metaphor,' p. 18.

35. Quoted in ibid., p. 19.

36. Quoted in ibid., pp. 18–19.

37. Sandahl, "Why Disability Identity Matters," p. 236.

38. Carrie Sandahl, "The Tyranny of Neutral: Disability and Actor Training," in Carrie Sandahl and Philip Auslander (eds), *Bodies in Commotion: Disability and Performance*, Ann Arbor: University of Michigan Press, 2005, pp. 255–67.

39. Ibid., p. 255.

40. Ibid.

41. Ibid., p. 260.

42. Ibid., p. 261.

43. Ibid., p. 262.

44. Quoted in ibid., p. 262.

45. Ibid., pp. 264–5.

46. Victoria Ann Lewis, "Disability and Access: A Manifesto for Actor Training," in Ellen Margolis and Lissa Tyler Renaud (eds.), *The Politics of American Actor Training*, New York: Routledge, 2010, pp. 187–8.

47. Kathy Dacre and Alex Bulmer, "*Into the Scene* and its Impact on Inclusive Performance Training," *Research in Drama Education: The Journal of Applied Theatre and Performance*, Vol. 14, No. 1 (2009), p. 134.

48. Lewis, "Disability and Access," p. 190.

49. Ibid., p. 192.

50. Ibid.

51. "Realwheels Mission and History," Realwheels website, http://realwheels.ca/house-lights-on-realwheels/our-mission-and-history/ (accessed 9 June 2015).

52. "Wheel Voices," Realwheels website, http://realwheels.ca/wheel-voices/ (accessed 9 June 2015).

53. Dacre and Bulmer, "*Into the Scene*," p. 135.

54. Ibid., p. 136.

55. Ibid., p. 138.

56. Ibid., p. 137.

57. Ibid., pp. 138–9.

58. Roberta Barker and Kim Solga, "Introduction: Reclaiming Canadian Realisms, Part Two," in Roberta Barker and Kim Solga (eds.), *New Canadian Realisms*, Toronto: Playwrights Canada Press, p. 3.

59. Quoted in Patrick Healy, "Advocacy Group Opposes 'Miracle Worker' Casting Choice," *New York Times* ArtsBeat blog, 29 October 2009, artsbeat.blogs.nytimes.com/2009/10/29/advocacy-group-opposes-miracle-worker-casting-choice (accessed 2 June 2015)

60. Ibid.

61. Quoted in Barker and Solga, "Introduction: Reclaiming Canadian Realisms," pp. 3–4.

62. Ibid., p. 3.

63. Natalie Alvarez, "Realisms of Redress: Alameda Theatre and the Formation of a Latina/o-Canadian Theatre and Politics," in Roberta Barker and Kim Solga (eds.), *New Canadian Realisms*, Toronto: Playwrights Canada Press, p. 155.

64. Ibid., p.156.

65. Alvarez follows this word with an explanatory footnote: "I place 'race' in quotation marks here in order to acknowledge the ways in which this category has been complicated by historians and scholars of race theory and dismantled by biologists and geneticists." Ibid., p. 161.

66. Ibid., p. 161

67. Ibid., p. 162.

68. Sandahl, "Why Disability Identity Matters," p. 236.

Notes

69. Ann M. Fox, 'Reclaiming the Ordinary Extraordinary Body: Or, The Importance of *The Glass Menagerie* for Literary Disability Studies', This book, p. 148.

70. Nabil Shaban, "The performer and disability" textbox under the entry "Disability" by Linda Moss and Sharon Jensen in Colin Chambers (ed.), *The Continuum Companion to Twentieth Century Theatre*, London: Continuum, 2006, pp. 212–13.

3 Staging Inclusion

1. Tanya Titchkosky, *The Question of Access: Disability, Space, Meaning*, Toronto: University of Toronto Press, 2011.

2. James Fagan Tait (playwright and director) *The Idiot*. Frederic Wood Theatre, University of British Columbia, co-produced by Neworld Theatre and Vancouver Moving Theatre and presented by the PuSh International Performing Arts Festival and Theatre at UBC, 20–29 January 2012.

3. Sarah G. Stanley and Michael Rubenfeld, *The Book of Judith*, co-produced by The Theatre Centre, Absit Omen, and Die In Debt Theatre on the Centre for Addiction and Mental Health Queen Street site lawn, Toronto, Ontario, 19–31 May 2009.

4. Carrie Sandahl, "Considering Disability: Disability Phenomenology's Role in Revolutionizing Theatrical Space," *Journal of Dramatic Theory and Criticism*, Vol. 16, No. 2 (2002), p. 30.

5. Ibid.

6. Ibid., p. 23.

7. Victoria Ann Lewis, "The Theatrical Landscape of Disability," *Disability Studies Quarterly* Vol. 24, No. 3 (2004), http://dsq-sds.org/article/view/511/688 (accessed 30 May, 2015).

8. Ibid.

9. Ibid.

10. Janet Lyon, *Manifestoes: Provocations of the Modern*, Ithaca: Cornell University Press, 1999, p. 2.

11. Ibid., 3.

12. Titchkosky, *The Question of Access*, p. 16.

13. Ibid.

14. Ibid pp. 15-16.

15. President Barack Obama, cited on the White House government webpage: https://www.whitehouse.gov/blog/2015/07/21/president-obama-celebrates-25-years-ada (accessed 30 July 2015).

16. Robert L. Burgdorf Jr., "Why I wrote the Americans with Disabilities Act," *Washington Post*, 24 July 2015, https://www.washingtonpost.com/

posteverything/wp/2015/07/24/why-the-americans-with-disabilities-act-mattered/ (accessed 30 July 2015).

17. Robert L. Burgdorf Jr., "A Dozen Things to Know About the ADA on Its Twenty-Fifth Anniversary," University of the District of Columbia, David A. Clarke School of Law website, http://www.law.udc.edu/?ADAAnniversary (accessed 30 July 2015).

18. Ibid.

19. Ibid.

20. Lewis, "The Theatrical Landscapes of Disability."

21. Ibid.

22. Ibid.

23. Ibid.

24. See the campaign website at http://stopchanges2atw.com/about/ (accessed 30 July 2015).

25. Bulmer quoted in Diane Flacks, "Life is a Five-Star Performance," *Toronto Star*, 26 May 2009, http://www.thestar.com/life/2009/05/26/life_is_a_fivestar_performance.html (accessed 30 July 2015).

26. Lyn Gardner, "Disability arts left hanging by a thread," *The Guardian*, 29 July 2014, http://www.theguardian.com/stage/theatreblog/2014/jul/29/disability-arts-cuts-access-to-work-theatre (accessed 30 July 2015).

27. "Accessing the Arts Symposium" presented by Selfconscious Theatre and Abilities Centre with generous support from the Equity Office of the Canada Council for the Arts. 13 June 2014 conference at the Abilities Centre in Whitby, Ontario, Canada.

28. Abilities Centre website, http://www.abilitiescentre.org (accessed 30 July 2015).

29. Judith Snow in "Keynote Conversation between Alex Bulmer & Judith Snow" at the "Accessing the Arts Symposium" presented by Selfconscious Theatre and Abilities Centre with generous support from the Equity Office of the Canada Council for the Arts. 13 June 2014 conference at the Abilities Centre in Whitby, Ontario, Canada.

30. Canada Council for the Arts, *Expanding the Arts: Deaf and Disability Arts Access Equality*, 2012, pp. 21–5, http://canadacouncil.ca/council/research/find-research/2012/expanding-the-arts-deaf-and-disability-arts (accessed 30 July 2015).

31. Ibid., p. 14. The document cites the work of Heather Hollins in its use of the term "tiers": Heather Hollins, "Reciprocity, Accountability, Empowerment: Emancipatory Principles and Practices in the Museum," in Richard Sandell, Jocelyn Dodd, and Rosemarie Garland-Thomson (eds.), *Re-presenting Disability: Activism and Agency in the Museum*, London: Routledge, 2012. On page 235, Hollins, in turn, cites Janice Majewski and Lonnie Bunch's article concerning tiers of access: "The Expanding Definition of Diversity: Accessibility and

Disability Culture Issues in Museum Exhibitions," *Curator: The Museum Journal*, Vol. 41, Issue 3 (1998), pp. 153–61.

32. Canada Council for the Arts, *Expanding the Arts*.

33. Ibid.

34. Please see the conference website which provides descriptions of each of the sessions: http://www.bookofjudith.com/symposium/session-details (accessed 30 July 2015).

35. The two-day program took place from 4 to 5 March 2011 at the Club Row Gallery, Rochelle School, London.

36. Mary Paterson, "Reflections on *Access All Areas*," in Lois Keidan and C.J. Mitch (eds.), *Access All Areas: Live Art and Disability*, London: Live Art Development Agency, 2012, p. 55.

37. Lyn Gardner, "Putting Disability Centre Stage," in Keidan and Mitch (eds.), *Access All Areas*, p. 60.

38. Mat Fraser quoted in Lois Keidan, "'It doesn't stop here': An Introduction to *Access All Areas*," in Keidan and Mitch (eds.), *Access All Areas*, p. 7.

39. Aaron Williamson and Sinead O'Donnell, "In Alien Couch Territory," in Keidan and Mitch (eds.), *Access All Areas*, pp. 20–22.

40. Brian Lobel, "Confrontation and Celebration," in Keidan and Mitch (eds.), *Access All Areas*, p. 71.

41. The Disabled Avant-Garde [Katherine Araniello and Aaron Williamson], "Sicknotes" in Keidan and Mitch (eds.), *Access All Areas*, pp. 129–35.

42. Titchkosky, *The Question of Access*, pp. 28–9.

43. Edward Steinfeld and Jordana Maisel, *Universal Design: Creating Inclusive Environments*, Hoboken, NJ: John Wiley & Sons, p. 15.

44. Ibid., p. 23.

45. Ibid., p. 24.

46. Tobin Siebers quoted in Jos Boys, *Doing Disability Differently: An Alternative Handbook on Architecture, Dis/ability and Designing for Everyday Life*, London: Routledge, 2014, p. 190.

47. Boys, *Doing Disability Differently*, p. 1.

48. Ibid.

49. See artist blog at http://www.araniello-art.com/Biog-Statement (accessed 30 July 2015).

50. Boys, *Doing Disability Differently*, p. 1.

51. Lyon, *Manifestoes*, p. 3.

52. Petra Kuppers, "Landscapings: Spacings," *Women & Performance: A Journal of Feminist Theory*, Vol. 13, No. 2, p. 42.

53. Ibid., pp. 42–4.

54. Ibid., p. 44.

55. Ibid., pp. 44–46.

56. James Sanders quoted in Peter Birnie, "'What happens if an avatar takes you over?' Play explores disability issues, including those of people addicted to technology as an escape,' *Vancouver Sun*, 4 March 2010: D9.

57. The Earl of Snowdon, GCVO, "Foreword," in C. Wycliffe Noble and Geoffrey Lord, *Access for Disabled People to Arts Premises: The Journey Sequence*, Amsterdam: Architectural Press, Elsevier, 2004, p. xi.

58. Noble and Lord, *Access for Disabled People to Arts Premises*, pp. 2–3.

59. Ibid., pp. 3–5.

60. Ibid., p. xiii.

61. Erik Piepenburg, "Parents and Kids Say They Appreciated Autism-Friendly 'Lion King' Matinee," *New York Times*, ArtsBeat, 3 October 2011, http://artsbeat.blogs.nytimes.com/2011/10/03/parents-and-kids-say-they-appreciated-autism-friendly-lion-king-matinee (accessed 30 July 2015).

62. Theatre Development Fund, "Autism Theatre Initiative: Making Theatre Accessible to Autistic Children and Adults," https://www.tdf.org/nyc/40/Autism-Theatre-Initiative (accessed 30 July 2015).

63. Lewis, "The Theatrical Landscapes of Disability."

64. Bree Hadley, "Participation, politics and provocations: People with disabilities as non-conciliatory audiences," *Participations: Journal of Audience & Reception Studies*, Vol. 12, No. 1 (2015), p. 155.

65. Ibid., p. 168.

66. Titchkosky, *The Question of Access*, p. 149.

67. Ric Knowles, *How Theatre Means*, London: Palgrave, 2014, p. 2.

68. Ric Knowles, *Reading the Material Theatre*, Cambridge: Cambridge University Press, 2004, p. 63.

4 Inherited Plays and New Approaches

1. Lyn Gardner, "My disability helped me understand Blanche DuBois, says Streetcar actor," http://www.theguardian.com/stage/2014/jun/02/disabled-actor-plays-blanche-dubois-streetcar-named-desire (accessed 8 June 2015).

2. Ibid.

3. Bertolt Brecht, "The Literarization of the Theatre," in John Willett (ed.), *Brecht on Theatre: The Development of an Aesthetic*, New York: Hill and Wang, 1986, p. 44.

4. Michael Davidson, *Concerto for the Left Hand: Disability and the Defamiliar Body*, Ann Arbor: University of Michigan Press, 2008, p. 226.

Notes

5. Readers interested in Graeae's development of new drama should refer to Jenny Sealey (ed.), *Graeae Plays 1: New Plays Redefining Disability*, London: Aurora Metro Publications Ltd., 2002.

6. Richard Tomlinson, *Disability, Theatre and Education*, London: Souvenir Press, 1982, p. 9.

7. Nabil Shaban, "Early History of Graeae," 2006, http://www.oocities.org/ jinghiz53/The_Beginning_of_Graeae.htm (accessed 22 May 2015).

8. Tomlinson, *Disability, Theatre and Education*, p. 19.

9. Ibid., pp. 41–3.

10. Shaban, "Early History of Graeae."

11. Tomlinson, *Disability, Theatre and Education*, pp. 44–5.

12. Ibid., p. 40.

13. Ibid., p. 43. Please note that Tomlinson does not give the actors' names.

14. Ibid., p. 44.

15. Ibid., p. 45.

16. Jenny Sealey, "Introduction," in Jenny Sealey (ed.), *Graeae Plays: New Plays Redefining Disability*, London: Aurora Metro Press, 2002, p. 10.

17. Ibid., p. 11.

18. Ibid.

19. Ibid., p. 12.

20. Maeve Walsh, "Theatre: On the Fringe," *The Independent*, 24 March 1999.

21. Ibid.

22. Graeae Theatre Company, *A Guide to Inclusive Teaching Practice in Theatre: For Teachers, Directors, Practitioners and* Staff, London, 2009, p. 20. Available as a download at www.graeae.org (accessed 22 May 2015).

23. www.graeae.org/get-involved/training-courses/missing-piece (accessed 29 September 2014). The website entry concludes by noting that "the 49 actors all went on to work in theatre, radio, TV, film and performance art." For a firsthand account of an actor's journey to Missing Piece 5, please see Penny Pepper, "Missing Piece Marvellous," an article in which the author "talks to some of the actors who have come through Graeae Theatre Company's performance training for aspiring actors with sensory and physical disabilities as she experiences Missing Pieces for herself." http://www.disabilityartsonline.org.uk/missing-pieces (accessed 8 June 2015).

24. Dennis A. Klein, *Blood Wedding, Yerma, and The House of Bernarda Alba: García Lorca's Tragic Trilogy*, Boston: Twayne Publishers, 1991, p. 27.

25. Paul F. Cockburn, "Graeae Theatre tackle a new adaptation of 'Blood Wedding,'" *Disability Arts Online,* 16 February 2015, www.disabilityartsonline.org.uk/ jenny-sealey-graeae-theatre-interview (accessed 8 June 2015). In this interview with Cockburn, Sealey explains that she had first been invited by Levick to "do

some workshops in and around the aesthetics of access, the way Graeae likes to work." This led to the idea of a co-production. Derby Theatre then became interested and the three co-produced *Blood Wedding* in 2015. The production toured to Dundee Rep Theatre (4–14 March), Derby Theatre (17–28 March), Beacon Arts Centre, Greenock (1–3 April), Traverse Theatre, Edinburgh (8–11 April), New Wolsey Theatre, Ipswich (14–16 April) and Liverpool Everyman (21–25 April).

26. "Graeae Theatre Take Lorca's 'Blood Wedding' on tour to Dundee, Derby, Greenock, Edinburgh, Ipswich and Liverpool", *Disablity Arts Online*, www.disabilityartsonline.org.uk/Events?item=7069 (accessed 8 June 2015).

27. Cockburn, "Graeae Theatre tackle a new adaptation."

28. Alex Chisholm, "*Blood Wedding* at Everyman Theatre," *Exeunt Magazine*, April 2015, http://exeuntmagazine.com/reviews/blood-wedding/ (accessed 3 June 2015).

29. Andrew Haydon, "*Blood Wedding* – Everyman, Liverpool," *Postcards from the Gods* blog, 23 April 2015, http://postcardsgods.blogspot.co.uk/2015/04/blood-wedding-everyman-liverpool.html (accessed 3 June 2015).

30. Mark Fisher, "Blood Wedding Review—Lorca's Tragedy Turned into a Soap Opera," *The Guardian*, 10 March 2015, www.theguardian.com/stage/2015/mar/10/blood-wedding-review-lorca (accessed 8 June 2015).

31. As quoted in Alfred Hickling, "Graeae's The Threepenny Opera: 'it dissipates the fear of disability,'" *The Guardian*, 25 February 2014, www.theguardian.com/stage/2014/feb/25/jenny-sealey-disabled-actors-graeae-threepenny-opera (accessed 7 June 2015). Hickling explains that the company's past collaborations included the Ian Dury musical *Reasons to be Cheerful* and Richard Cameron's *Flower Girls*.

32. Hickling, "Graeae's The Threepenny Opera," notes that Sams' translation was an update of the one produced by the Donmar Warehouse in 1994.

33. For a rich account of the historical context informing this collaborative work and the questions of authorship and interpretation associated with text and music, see Stephen McNeff, "The Threepenny Opera," in Peter Thomson and Glendyr Sacks (eds.), *The Cambridge Companion to Brecht*, Cambridge: Cambridge University Press, 2006, pp. 78–89.

34. Bertolt Brecht, "The Literarization of the Theatre," p. 46.

35. Bertolt Brecht, *The Threepenny Opera*, translated by Ralph Manheim and John Willett in John Willett and Ralph Manheim (eds.), *Collected plays [of] Bertolt Brecht*, Vol. 2, Part 2, London: Methuen, 1970–2003. London: Methuen Drama, p. 8.

36. Ibid. p. 78.

37. Brecht quoted in Kim H. Kowalke, "Accounting for success: misunderstanding *Die Dreigroschenoper*," *The Opera Quarterly*, Vol. 6, No. 3 (1989), p. 29.

38. Brecht, "The Literarization of the Theatre," pp. 43–4.

39. Matt Trueman, "Threepenny Opera Review: 'All the More Furious from Disabled Actors,'" *Guardian*, 18 March 2014, www.theguardian.com/stage/2014/mar/18/threepenny-opera-nottingham-playhouse-graeae-review (accessed 1 June 2015).

40. Hickling, "Graeae's The Threepenny Opera."

41. Jenny Sealey and Carissa Hope Lynch, "Graeae: an aesthetic of access: (de) cluttering the clutter," in Susan Broadhurst and Josephine Machon (eds.), *Identity, Performance and Technology: Practices of Empowerment, Embodiment and Technicity*, London, Palgrave Macmillan, 2012, p. 73.

42. Ibid., p. 62.

43. Mat Fraser, "Mat Fraser on The Threepenny Opera," *Graeae's Blog*, 7 March 2014, https://graeaetheatrecompany.wordpress.com/2014/03/07/mat-fraser-on-the-threepenny-opera/ (accessed 7 June 2015).

44. Quoted in Roz Laws, "Themes of Class Struggle and Corruption Make Opera So Relevant Today," *Birmingham Post*, 27 March 2014, www.birminghampost.co.uk/whats-on/arts-culture-news/threepenny-opera-plays-birmingham-rep-6874862 (accessed 3 June 2015).

45. Peter Kirwan, "The Threepenny Opera at Nottingham Playhouse," *Exeunt Magazine*, February-March 2014, http://exeuntmagazine.com/reviews/the-threepenny-opera/ (accessed 2 June 2015).

46. Ibid.

47. Liz Porter, "Graeae Theatre present The Threepenny Opera," *Disability Arts Online*, 18 March 2014, www.disabilityartsonline.org.uk/graeae-the-threepenny-opera-review (accessed 1 June 2015).

48. Ibid.

49. Ibid.

50. Ibid.

51. Ibid.

52. Ibid.

53. Ibid.

54. Hickling, "Graeae's The Threepenny Opera."

55. Kirwan, "The Threepenny Opera at Nottingham Playhouse."

56. Colin Hambrook, "Graeae Theatre Stage a New Production of The Threepenny Opera," *Disability Arts Online*, 19 February, 2014, www.disabilityartsonline.org.uk/graeae-the-threepenny-opera (accessed 1 June 2015).

57. Mounted with additional support from the Scottish Executive as part of The Year of The Disabled, that production played "to full houses in Glasgow's Tramway, Aberdeen and Edinburgh's Festival Theatre," www.theatre-workshop.com/events/2004/june/thrp_opera.html (accessed 7 June 2015).

58. Neil Cooper, "Brecht and to the point. The Threepenny Opera is low-life, an in-your-face howl from the left. Will Theatre Workshop's production be shabby enough to shock?" *The Herald* [Scotland], 15 June 2004, www.heraldscotland. com/sport/spl/aberdeen/brecht-and-to-the-point-the-threepenny-opera-is-low-life-an-in-your-face-howl-from-the-left-will-theatre-workshop-s-production-be-shabby-enough-to-shock-1.83079 (accessed 8 June 2015).

59. Carol Poore, *Disability in Twentieth-Century German Culture*, Ann Arbor: University of Michigan Press, 2009, p. 16. See also pp. 27–28.

60. Tobin Siebers, *Disability Aesthetics*, Ann Arbor: University of Michigan Press, 2010, p. 10.

61. National Library of Scotland, Theatre Workshop Edinburgh Accession Inventory (Acc.13521) [2014], www.nls.uk/catalogues/online/cnmi/inventories/acc13521. pdf (accessed 31 May, 2015).

62. Robert Rae website, www.robertrae.co.uk (accessed 29 September 2015).

63. Theatre Workshop Scotland, "History," www.theatre-workshop.com/aboutus/history/ (accessed 31 May 2015).

64. Ibid.

65. Critics' Awards for Theatre in Scotland (CATS), "2004–05 Shortlists," www.criticsawards.theatrescotland.com/Shortlists%20by%20year/04-05.html (accessed 31 May 2015).

66. "Disability Arts Festival Begins," *BBC News*, 8 August 2007, news.bbc.co.uk/2/hi/uk_news/scotland/edinburgh_and_east/6937245.stm (accessed 31 May 2015).

67. At the time of writing, the TWS's future remains uncertain; Rae concluded his term as artistic director in 2014.

68. Michael Davidson, "'Every Man His Specialty': Beckett, Disability, and Dependence," *Journal of Philosophy: A Cross Disciplinary Inquiry*, Vol. 6, No. 13 (2010), p. 2.

69. Ibid.

70. Ato Quayson, *Aesthetic Nervousness: Disability and the Crisis of Representation*, New York: Columbia University Press, 2007, p. 56.

71. Davidson, "'Every Man His Specialty,'" p. 7.

72. Quayson, *Aesthetic Nervousness*, p. 78.

73. Ibid., p. 54.

74. Ibid., p. 67.

75. Quoted in Jonathan Kalb, *Beckett in Performance*, Cambridge: Cambridge University Press, 1989, p. 79.

76. Mark Brown, "Endgame: Another Side of Beckett," *The Telegraph*, 28 November 2007, www.telegraph.co.uk/culture/theatre/3669567/Endgame-Another-side-of Beckett.html (accessed 10 July 2013).

77. Ibid.

Notes

78. Samuel Beckett, *Endgame*, New York: Grove Press, 1958, p. 1.

79. Ibid.

80. Joyce McMillan, "Endgame," *The Scotsman*, 6 November 2007. Available at http://joycemcmillan.wordpress.com/2007/11/06/endgame/ (accessed 10 July 2013).

81. Mark Fisher, "Endgame," *Northings Blog*, 13 February 2008, http://northings.com/2008/02/05/endgame/ (accessed 8 June 2015).

82. Brown, "Endgame: Another Side of Beckett."

83. Steve Cramer, 'Endgame,' *The List,* 15 November 2007, www.list.co.uk/article/5642-endgame/ (accessed 10 July 2013).

84. McMillan, "Endgame"; Sita Ramamurthy and Robert Rae, "Theatre Workshop Artistic Evaluation Endgame," Scottish Arts Council, 12 November 2007. Since I first accessed this report online in 2013, the Scottish Arts Council website has changed so that it now directs visitors to Creative Scotland (http://www.creativescotland.com). The formerly available PDFs of the artistic reports are no longer accessible online but Creative Scotland can provide copies. The first section of the document contains Sita Ramamurthy's assessment of the production. The third and final part of the document includes Rae's response.

85. Rae's response is appended to Ramamurthy's evaluation.

86. Siebers, *Disability Aesthetics*, p. 4.

5 "Every Man his Specialty"

1. Lennard Davis, *Bending Over Backwards: Disability, Dismodernism and Other Difficult Positions*, New York: New York University Press, 2002, p. 18.

2. Ibid., p. 30.

3. Eva Feder Kittay, *Love's Labor: Essays on Women, Equality, and Dependency*, New York: Routledge, 1999, p. xi.

4. Not all persons with a disability are dependent or share an equal relationship to caregiving. A person in a wheelchair is only dependent when she encounters a building without ramps or elevators; a deaf person is not dependent when signing ASL among deaf family members but becomes so when encountering a classroom without a sign-language interpreter or captioner. Disability rights advocates have been critical of seeing themselves as dependent, based on their long and troubled history with the medical and rehabilitation model. Yet the absence of any discourse about dependency has reinforced a "supercrip" mentality that disregards the various forms dependence takes within disability.

5. Alasdair MacIntyre, *Dependent Rational Animals: Why Human Beings Need the Virtues*, Chicago: Open Court, 1999, p. 8.

6. Quoted in Martha C. Nussbaum, *Frontiers of Justice: Disability, Nationality, Species Membership*, Cambridge, MA: Harvard University Press, 2006, p. 27.

7. Ibid., p. 70.

8. From a disability standpoint, we could see the grimmer application of this model in global development where resources are distributed based on the productivity of able-bodied persons or when healthcare is restricted to clinics that only preach abstinence but do not mention abortion.

9. The phrase "phantom public" was used by Walter Lippmann in 1925 to describe (and decry) the large number of citizens who choose not to participate in political life. The phrase has been appropriated by Bruce Robbins to describe the various debates within the Left about the loss of the public intellectual or the decline of participatory democracy. Robbins' anthology, *The Phantom Public Sphere*, attempts to define those "counter publics" left out of much public sphere discourse, from Lippmann to Habermas. Not surprisingly, the book does not mention persons with disabilities. Robbins, Bruce (ed.), *The Phantom Public Sphere*, Minneapolis: University of Minnesota Press, 1993.

10. Nussbaum, *Frontiers of Justice*, p. 104.

11. Ato Quayson, *Aesthetic Nervousness: Disability and the Crisis of Representation*, New York: Columbia University Press, 2007, p. 56.

12. Ibid., p. 54.

13. Ibid., p. 76.

14. Ibid., p. 79.

15. On "compulsory able-bodiedness," see the Introduction to Robert McRuer's *Crip Theory*. Robert McRuer, *Crip Theory: Cultural Signs of Queerness and Disability*, New York: New York University Press, 2006, pp. 1–32.

16. According to many Beckett scholars, this parable does not appear in this exact form anywhere in Augustine, although it seems to resemble a remark from his letters. Beckett quotes it in a statement to Harold Hobson in 1956: "I take no sides. I am interested in the shape of ideas even if I do not believe them. There is a wonderful sentence in Augustine . . . 'Do not despair; one of the thieves was saved. Do not presume: one of the thieves was damned.' That sentence has a wonderful shape. It is the shape that matters." Quoted in Michael Worton, "*Waiting for Godot* and *Endgame*: Theatre as Text," in John Pilling (ed.), *The Cambridge Companion to Beckett*, Cambridge: Cambridge University Press, 2005, p. 75.

17. Samuel Beckett, *Waiting for Godot*, New York: Grove Press, 1982, p. 44.

18. Ibid., p. 49.

19. As Nussbaum and Kittay point out, dependency is often gendered. Those who deliver care or who are presumed to be responsible for dependent children and the aged and infirm are invariably women who are either not compensated, because they are part of the family structure, or poorly compensated, because they are components of the caregiving industry.

20. Samuel Beckett, *Molloy. Three Novels of Samuel Beckett: Molloy, Malone Dies, The Unnamable*, New York: Grove Press, 1958, p. 25.

Notes

21. *Malone Dies. Three Novels of Samuel Beckett*, p. 218.

22. All of the plays discussed here are now available on a DVD set, *Beckett on Film*, produced in 2005 by Blue Angel Films for Radio Telefis Eireann and Channel 4. *Rough for Theatre I* appears in Samuel Beckett, *The Collected Shorter Plays of Samuel Beckett*, New York: Grove Press, 1984, pp. 65–73.

23. Ibid., p. 68.

24. Ibid., p. 67.

25. Ibid., p. 69.

26. Ibid., p. 70.

27. Ibid., p. 71.

28. In this sense, the prosthetic body differs from Yoshiki Tajiri's use of the phrase to describe "the body that harbours the inorganic other within it." Tajiri is interested in those aspects of Beckett's characters in which parts of the body are felt to be alien or whose body and organs are experienced as a 'broken machine'. Dependency theory, at least in my understanding of it, treats the other's body as a prosthesis for one's own. Yoshiki Tajiri, *Samuel Beckett and the Prosthetic Body: The Organs and Senses in Modernism*, Houndsmills: Palgrave Macmillan, 2007, p. 5.

29. *Rough for Theatre*, p. 71.

30. Samuel Beckett, *Happy Days*, New York: Grove Press, 1961, p. 28.

31. Ibid., p. 40.

32. Ibid., p. 10.

33. Steven Connor, *Samuel Beckett: Repetition, Theory and Text*, London: Basil Blackwell, 1988, pp. 184–4.

34. *Happy Days*, p. 56.

35. Ibid., p. 58.

36. Ibid., p. 20.

37. Ibid., p. 62.

38. *Malone Dies*, p. 195.

39. Ibid., p. 199.

40. *Happy Days*, p. 46.

41. Nels Pearson, "'Outside of here it's death': Co-dependency and the Ghosts of Decolonization in Beckett's *Endgame*," *ELH* Vol. 68, No. 1 (2001), pp. 215–16.

42. Albert Memmi, *Dependence*, Boston: Beacon Press, 1984.

43. Samuel Beckett, *Endgame*, New York: Grove Press, 1958, p. 58.

44. Ibid., p. 76.

45. Ibid., p. 36.

46. Stanley Cavell, "Ending the Waiting Game: A Reading of Beckett's *Endgame*," in Harold Bloom (ed.), *Samuel Beckett's Endgame*, New York: Chelsea House Publishers, 1988, p. 61.

47. *Endgame*, p. 10.

48. Memmi, *Dependence*, p. 24.

49. *Endgame*, pp. 32–3.

50. Ibid., p. 33.

51. Theodor Adorno, "Trying to Understand *Endgame*," in Harold Bloom (ed.), *Samuel Beckett's Endgame*, New York: Chelsea House Publishers, 1988, p. 27.

52. *Endgame*, p. 29.

53. Ibid., p. 44.

54. Lukács sees Beckett's *Molloy* as the "*ne plus ultra*" of modernism's treatment of social neurosis by reducing man to an animal state: "In Beckett's novel we have the same vision twice over. He presents us with an image of the utmost human degradation—an idiot's vegetative existence. Then, as help is imminent from a mysterious unspecified source, the rescuer himself sinks into idiocy." By focusing entirely on subjective states, Beckett, in Lukács' mind, lacks historical perspective by which value can be ascertained. However, by regarding Beckett's work through theories of dependence and care, rather than existential interiority, we may understand the deeply social nature of his work. Georg Lukács, *Realism in our Time*, New York: Harper, 1964, p. 31.

55. Kittay, *Love's Labor*, p. xii.

56. *Endgame*, p. 81.

57. Adorno, "'Trying to Understand *Endgame*," p. 13.

58. Ibid., p. 32.

59. Quoted in Nussbaum, *Frontiers of Justice*, p. 59.

60. William Blake, "The Human Abstract," in W.H. Stevenson (ed.), *Songs of Innocence and Experience. The Poems of William Blake*, London: Longman, 1971, p. 216.

61. MacIntyre, *Dependent Rational Animals*, p. 5.

6 Reclaiming the Ordinary Extraordinary Body

1. I first heard Garland-Thomson use the phrase "disability gain" in her keynote address at the conference "Avoidance and the Academy: The International Conference on Disability, Culture, and Education," Centre for Culture and Disability Studies, Liverpool Hope University, Liverpool, United Kingdom, 12 September 2013. In it, she expanded upon the concept of Deaf Gain, one itself discussed at greater length by H. Dirksen Bauman and Joseph J. Murray in their introduction to their co-edited *Deaf Gain: Raising the Stakes for Human Diversity*, Minneapolis: University of Minnesota Press, 2014.

2. Christine Bruno, "Disability in American Theater: Where is the Tipping Point?" *HowlRound*, 7 April 2014, http://howlround.com/disability-in-american-theater-where-is-the-tipping-point (accessed 26 May 2015).

Notes

3. The problem with non-disabled actors playing disabled roles, and the importance of casting disabled actors instead, has been discussed by disability studies critics from Paul K. Longmore, "Screening Stereotypes: Images of Disabled People in Television and Motion Pictures," in *Why I Burned My Book and Other Essays on Disability*, Philadelphia: Temple University Press, 2003, pp. 131–46 to Carrie Sandahl (see, for example, her book with Phillip Auslander (eds.), *Bodies in Commotion: Disability and Performance,* Ann Arbor: University of Michigan Press, 2005), or Kathleen Tolan, "We Are Not a Metaphor: A Conversation About Representation," *American Theatre* (2001), pp. 17–21, 57–9, and explored in films including *Code of the Freaks*, Carrie Sandahl, Aly Patsavas, Susan Nussbaum, and Salome Chasnoff (dirs.), Personal Hermitage Productions, 2011 and *Cinemability*, Jenni Gold (dir), Gold Pictures, 2013. It is finally garnering some attention in the popular press, including an essay in *The Atlantic* by playwright Christopher Shinn, "Disability Is Not Just a Metaphor," *The Atlantic,* 23 July 2014, www.theatlantic.com/entertainment/archive/2014/07/why-disabled-characters-are-never-played-by-disabled-actors/374822/ (accessed 22 May 2015), as well as the slew of articles that followed Eddie Redmayne's 2015 Best Actor Oscar Award for playing Stephen Hawking in *The Theory of Everything*. Yet the presumption that a non-disabled actor can not only assume, but masterfully execute, an authentic representation of disability remains fairly persistent. For example, in two talkbacks for Broadway shows I attended in 2011 (*Time Stands Still* and *The Whipping Man*), both of which featured actors playing disabled characters, the first question to the actors was about the challenges of playing a disability. In each case, the fact of disability simulation was of more immediate interest than the meaning of either representation.

4. Victoria Ann Lewis, *Beyond Victims and Villains: Contemporary Plays by Disabled Playwrights*, New York: Theatre Communications Group, 2005.

5. See my essay " 'But, Mother—I'm—crippled!' Tennessee Williams, Queering Disability, and Dis/Membered Bodies in Performance," in Bonnie G. Smith and Beth Hutchison (eds.), *Gendering Disability*, New Brunswick, NJ: Rutgers University Press, 2004, pp. 233–50.

6. Doris Baizley and Victoria Ann Lewis, "P.H.*reaks: The Hidden History of People with Disabilities," in Victoria Ann Lewis (ed.), *Beyond Victims and Villains: Contemporary Plays by Disabled Playwrights*, New York: Theatre Communications Group, 2005, pp. 303–32.

7. Michael Davidson, *Concerto for the Left Hand: Disability and the Defamiliar Body*, Ann Arbor: University of Michigan Press, 2008, p. 1.

8. Christine Bruno, message to the author, "Re: *Glass Menagerie*," 26 May 2015 and 28 May 2015, and Regan Linton, message to the author, "Re: Menagerie," 21 May 2015. Linton and Bruno both recounted funny stories around the presumption that disabled women could only play Laura: Linton noted that "*The Glass Menagerie* often comes to people's minds as the ONE play that could accommodate a girl with a disability. (So much that one of my disabled actor friends has joked about an idea for a play where a disabled actress is stuck in an

alternative world, doomed to a perpetual and ceaseless playing of Laura.)"
Bruno also recalled that "another agent in the firm that represented me, said to
my agent (while I was in the room), 'What's she going to do . . . play Laura for
her whole career?'" It's not a little ironic, then, that Bruno was only able to
secure an audition for the production of *The Glass Menagerie* in which she
eventually starred by circumventing a casting director who assumed that the
production director would not want to consider a disabled actor for the role of
Laura, and (illegally) refused her an audition. Such lack of access to disabled
roles is, according to Bruno, far more the norm for disabled actors.

9. Deborah Kent, "In Search of a Heroine: Images of Women with Disabilities in
Fiction and Drama," in Michelle Fine and Adrienne Asch (eds.), *Women with
Disabilities: Essays in Psychology, Culture, and Politics*, Philadelphia: Temple
University Press, 1988, p. 96.

10. John Lahr, *Tennessee Williams: Mad Pilgrimage of the Flesh*, New York: W.W.
Norton & Company, 2014, p. 60.

11. For a more extensive discussion of how drama studies and disability studies can
invigorate one another, see my essay, "Fabulous Invalids Together: Why
Disability in Mainstream Theater Matters," in David Bolt and Clare Penketh
(eds.), *Disability, Avoidance and the Academy: Challenging Resistance*, London:
Routledge, 2015, pp. 122–32.

12. Jill Dolan, "Feminist Performance Criticism and the Popular: Reviewing Wendy
Wasserstein," *Theatre Journal*, Vol. 60, No. 3 (2008), p. 435.

13. Ibid., p. 435.

14. Davidson, *Concerto for the Left Hand*, p. 2.

15. Tobin Siebers, *Disability Aesthetics*, Ann Arbor: University of Michigan Press,
2010, p. 20.

16. Lahr, *Tennessee Williams*, pp. 35 and 59.

17. C.W.E. Bigsby, "Entering *The Glass Menagerie*," in Matthew Roudané (ed.), *The
Cambridge Companion to Tennessee Williams*, New York and Cambridge:
Cambridge University Press, 1997, p. 35.

18. Fox, " 'But, Mother—I'm—crippled!'"

19. Granger Babcock, "*The Glass Menagerie* and the Transformation of the Subject,"
Journal of Dramatic Theory and Criticism, Vol. 14, No. 1 (1999), p. 18.

20. Ibid., p. 21.

21. Tennessee Williams, *The Glass Menagerie*, New York: New Directions, 1999,
p. 61.

22. Babcock, "*The Glass Menagerie* and the Transformation of the Subject," p. 24.

23. Quoted in ibid., p. 25; see Robert McRuer, "Compulsory Able-Bodiedness and
Queer/Disabled Existence,"' in Lennard J. Davis (ed.), *The Disability Studies
Reader*, Fourth edition, New York: Routledge, 2013, pp. 369–78.

24. Kent, "In Search of a Heroine," p. 98.

Notes

25. Eric Levy, "'Through Soundproof Glass': The Prison of Self-Consciousness in *The Glass Menagerie*," *Modern Drama*, Vol. 36, No. 4 (1993), p. 531.

26. Williams, *The Glass Menagerie*, p. 57, emphasis added.

27. Ibid., pp. 17–18.

28. Ibid., p. 47.

29. Kent, "In Search of a Heroine," p. 97.

30. Williams, *The Glass Menagerie*, p. 75.

31. Ibid., p. 15.

32. Ibid., p. 81.

33. Linton, "Re: Menagerie."

34. Williams, *The Glass Menagerie*, p. 87.

35. Siebers, *Disability Aesthetics*, p. 3.

36. Sarah Hosey, "Resisting the S(crip)t: Disability Studies Perspectives in the Undergraduate Classroom," *Teaching American Literature: A Journal of Theory and Practice*, Vol. 6, No. 1 (2013), pp. 26 and 30.

37. Linton, "Re: Menagerie."

38. Virginia Woolf, "Shakespeare's Sister," from *A Room of One's Own* in Sandra Gilbert and Susan Gubar (eds.), *The Norton Anthology of Literature by Women: The Traditions in English*, Vol. 2, Third edition., New York: W.W. Norton and Co., 2007, p. 239.

39. Ibid., emphasis added.

40. Ibid., p. 242.

41. Ibid., p. 243.

42. I am indebted to my colleague, C. Shaw Smith, who mentioned this phrase to me as one his brother, Graham Smith, an actor, uses to describe our journey toward death.

43. Babcock, "*The Glass Menagerie* and the Transformation of the Subject," p. 28.

44. Louis K. Greiff, "Fathers, Daughters, and Spiritual Sisters: Marsha Norman's *'night Mother* and Tennessee Williams's *The Glass Menagerie*," *Text and Performance Quarterly*, Vol. 9, No. 3 (1989), p. 226.

45. Lahr, *Tennessee Williams*, p. 60.

46. Gilbert Debusscher, "Tennessee Williams's Unicorn Broken Again," in Harold Bloom (ed.), *Tennessee Williams's The Glass Menagerie*, New York: Chelsea House Publishers, 1988, p. 54; emphasis added.

47. Ibid., emphasis added.

48. Robert J. Cardullo, "*Liebestod*, Romanticism, and Poetry in *The Glass Menagerie*," *ANQ: A Quarterly Journal of Short Articles, Notes and Reviews*, Vol. 23, No. 2 (2010), p. 76.

49. Ibid., p. 77.

50. Ibid., p. 78.

51. Ibid., p. 81; emphasis added.

52. Babcock, "*The Glass Menagerie* and the Transformation of the Subject," p. 32.

53. Lahr, *Tennessee Williams*, p. 58.

54. Williams, *The Glass Menagerie*, p. 86.

55. Babcock, "*The Glass Menagerie* and the Transformation of the Subject," p. 28.

56. Williams, *The Glass Menagerie*, p. 86.

57. Ibid., p. 96.

58. Linton, "Re: Menagerie." Linton notes that in the production in which she starred at the University of California, San Diego in 2012, this final moment was staged as one in which Laura rejects comfort if it only means a perpetuation of that paternalism to which she has been so painfully subject: "at the conclusion of our play, Amanda moved to comfort Laura, who then forcefully rejected her mother's smothering 'comfort,' choosing to face the rejection, hurt, and sadness head-on." She will no longer, in the words of Linton, be a "bystanding pawn tormented by others' neuroses that kidnap her disability as their battlefield."

59. Bigsby, "Entering *The Glass Menagerie*," p. 38.

60. Bruno, "Re: *Glass Menagerie.*"

61. Linton, "Re: Menagerie."

62. John Moore, "PHAMALy Actor Regan Linton Works Her Magic in San Diego," *The Denver Post* 3 February 2012, www.denverpost.com/ci_19880409 (accessed 22 December 2014).

63. Ibid.

64. Bryce Alexander, "Director's Notes—*The Glass Menagerie*," Lone Tree Arts Center, http://lonetreeartscenter.org/ckeditor/userfiles/images/1392744251_GlassDirectorsNotes.pdf (accessed 22 December 2014).

65. Bruno, "Re: *Glass Menagerie.*"

66. Linton, "Re: Menagerie."

67. Ibid.

68. Cardullo, "*Liebestod*, Romanticism, and Poetry," p. 78.

69. Williams, *The Glass Menagerie*, p. 5.

70. For generously sharing their thoughtful observations about playing Laura Wingfield, I would like to thank Christine Bruno and Regan Linton.

7 Access Aesthetics and Modern Drama

1. The stage directions to which Sealey refers read as follows in the opening notes of *Blasted*: "Words in square brackets [ ] are not spoken, but have been included

in the text to clarify meaning. Stage directions in brackets () function as lines."
Sarah Kane, *Blasted*, in *Sarah Kane: Complete Plays*, introduced by David Greig,
London: Methuen Drama, 2001, p. 2.

2. The Backstage Pass Award for Best Supporting Actress in 2013–14 was juried by
the Nottingham Playhouse backstage pass members. *The Threepenny Opera*
received several other awards, including best direction and best ensemble:
www.nottinghamplayhouse.co.uk/news/backstage-pass-members-pick-the-
winners/ (accessed 27 May 2015).

3. "Training Course: Write to Play," www.graeae.org/get-involved/training-courses/
write-to-play/ (accessed 27 May 2015).

4. The *Ramps on the Moon* project is described by Arts Council England as follows:
"Led by New Wolsey Theatre, Ipswich, 'Ramps on the Moon' will bring together
a collaborative network of seven National portfolio organisation theatres
including New Wolsey Theatre, Ipswich and strategic partner Graeae Theatre
Company—Birmingham Repertory Theatre, Theatre Royal Stratford East,
Nottingham Playhouse, West Yorkshire Playhouse, Liverpool Everyman and
Playhouse and Sheffield Theatres. The network, which spans the country,
includes theatres that are committed to offering opportunities to disabled people
by putting disabled artists and audiences at the centre of their programmes, to
help the mainstreaming of disability arts and culture." www.artscouncil.org.uk/
news/arts-council-news/new-strategic-touring-funding-recipients-announced/
(accessed 27 May 2015).

5. Access to Work and Independent Living Fund policies are outlined by the UK
government at the following websites: www.gov.uk/access-to-work/overview
and www.gov.uk/government/organisations/independent-living-fund/about.
Jenny Sealey's criticisms of the cuts to the Access to Work program may be
viewed on YouTube in two videos: www.youtube.com/watch?v=gk0i6vd305o
and www.youtube.com/watch?v=CUvsO8wGzpM. Sealey also published an
op-ed about the cuts on the *Guardian* Theatre Blog on 13 April 2015: "Deaf
and disabled artists: we will not let government cuts make us invisible,"
www.theguardian.com/stage/theatreblog/2015/apr/13/deaf-and-disabled-
artists-we-will-not-let-government-cuts-make-us-invisible (all websites
accessed 27 May 2015).

8 Shattering The Glass Menagerie

1. Please see Antonin Artaud, *The Theatre and its Double*, New York: Grove Press,
1958, p. 13.

2. Please see Carrie Sandahl, "Queering the Crip or Cripping the Queer?
Intersections of Queer and Crip Identities in Solo Autobiographical
Performance," *GLQ: A Journal of Lesbian and Gay Studies*, Vol. 9, Nos. 1–2
(2003), pp. 25–56.

BIBLIOGRAPHY

Abilities Centre, www.abilitiescentre.org (accessed 30 July 2015).

"Accessing the Arts Symposium," presented by Selfconscious Theatre and Abilities Centre with generous support from the Equity Office of the Canada Council for the Arts, 13 June 2014, Abilities Centre, Whitby, Ontario, Canada.

Accessing the Arts, "The Book of Judith Symposium," www.bookofjudith.com/symposium/session-details/ (accessed 30 July 2015).

Adorno, Theodor, "Trying to Understand *Endgame*," in Harold Bloom (ed.), *Samuel Beckett's Endgame*. New York: Chelsea House Publishers, 1988, pp. 9–40.

Alexander, Bryce, "Director's Notes—*The Glass Menagerie*," Lone Tree Arts Center. http://lonetreeartscenter.org/ckeditor/userfiles/images/1392744251_GlassDirectorsNotes.pdf (accessed 22 December 2014).

Alliance for Inclusion in the Arts, website, 2015. http://inclusioninthearts.org/ (accessed 28 April 2015).

Alliance for Inclusion in the Arts, "Written on the Body: A Conversation about Disability," 2006. http://inclusioninthearts.org/projects/written-on-the-body-a-conversation-about-disability (accessed 1 June 2015).

Alvarez, Natalie, "Realisms of Redress: Alameda Theatre and the Formation of a Latina/o-Canadian Theatre and Politics," in Roberta Barker and Kim Solga (eds.), *New Canadian Realisms*. Toronto: Playwrights Canada Press, 2012, pp. 144–62.

Araniello, Katherine, Artist Blog, www.araniello-art.com/Biog-Statement (accessed 30 July 2015).

Araniello, Katherine and Aaron Williamson, "Sicknotes: The Disabled Avant-Garde," in Lois Keidan and C.J. Mitch (eds.), *Access All Areas: Live Art and Disability*. London: Live Art Development Agency, 2012, pp. 129–35.

Artaud, Antonin, *The Theatre and its Double*. New York: Grove Press, 1958.

Arts Council England, "New Strategic touring funding recipients announced: including a pioneering disability and diversity partnership," www.artscouncil.org.uk/news/arts-council-news/new-strategic-touring-funding-recipients-announced/ (accessed 27 May 2015).

Arts Smarts: Inspiration and Ideas for Canadian Artists with Disabilities. Vancouver: Society for Disability Arts and Culture, 2002.

Babcock, Granger, "*The Glass Menagerie* and the Transformation of the Subject," *Journal of Dramatic Theory and Criticism*, Vol. 14, No. 1 (1999), pp. 17–36.

Baizley, Doris and Victoria Ann Lewis, "P.H.*reaks: The Hidden History of People with Disabilities," in Victoria Ann Lewis (ed.), *Beyond Victims and Villains: Contemporary Plays by Disabled Playwrights*. New York: Theatre Communications Group, 2005, pp. 303–32.

Bibliography

Banks, Daniel, "The Welcome Table: Casting for an Integrated Society," *Theatre Topics*, Vol. 23, No. 1 (2013), pp. 1–18.

Barker, Roberta and Kim Solga, "Introduction: Reclaiming Canadian Realisms, Part Two," in Roberta Barker and Kim Solga (eds.), *New Canadian Realisms*. Toronto: Playwrights Canada Press, 2012, pp. 1–15.

Barnes, Colin and Geof Mercer, *Disability*. Cambridge: Polity, 2003.

Bauman, H. Dirksen and Joseph J. Murray, "Introduction," in H. Dirksen Bauman and Joseph J. Murray (eds.), *Deaf Gain: Raising the Stakes for Human Diversity*. Minneapolis: University of Minnesota Press, 2014, pp. xv–xlii.

BBC News, "Disability Arts Festival Begins," 8 August 2007, news.bbc.co.uk/2/hi/uk_news/scotland/edinburgh_and_east/6937245.stm (accessed 31 May 2015).

Beckett, Samuel, *The Collected Shorter Plays of Samuel Beckett*. New York: Grove Press, 1984.

Beckett, Samuel, *Endgame*. New York: Grove Press, 1958.

Beckett, Samuel, *Happy Days*. New York: Grove Press, 1961.

Beckett, Samuel, *Molloy*, in *Three Novels of Samuel Beckett: Molloy, Malone Dies, The Unnamable*. New York: Grove Press, 1958.

Beckett, Samuel, *Waiting for Godot*. New York: Grove Press, 1982.

Bigsby, C.W.E., "Entering *The Glass Menagerie*," in Matthew Roudané (ed.), *The Cambridge Companion to Tennessee Williams*. New York and Cambridge: Cambridge University Press, 1997, pp. 29–44.

Birnie, Peter, "'What happens if an avatar takes you over?' Play explores disability issues, including those of people addicted to technology as an escape," *Vancouver Sun*, 4 March 2010.

Blake, William, "The Human Abstract," in W.H. Stevenson (ed.), *Songs of Innocence and Experience: The Poems of William Blake*. London: Longman, 1971, p. 216.

Blue Angel Films for Radio Telefis Eireann and Channel 4, *Beckett on Film*, 2005.

Boase, Jayne Leslie, "Festivals: Agents of Change? Dynamics and Humanism within Disability and Arts Collaborations," *The International Journal of the Humanities* Vol. 3, No. 10, 2006, pp. 133–6.

Boys, Jos, *Doing Disability Differently: An Alternative Handbook on Architecture, Dis/ability and Designing for Everyday Life*. London: Routledge, 2014.

Brayton, Jenna, "President Obama Celebrates 25 Years of the ADA," The White House webpage, www.whitehouse.gov/blog/2015/07/21/president-obama-celebrates-25-years-ada (accessed 30 July 2015).

Brecht, Bertolt, "The Literarization of the Theatre," in John Willett (ed.), *Brecht on Theatre: The Development of an Aesthetic*. New York: Hill and Wang, 1986, pp. 43–6.

Brecht, Bertolt, *The Messingkauf Dialogues*, translated by John Willett. London: Methuen, 1965.

Brecht, Bertolt, *The Threepenny Opera*, translated by Ralph Manheim and John Willett in John Willett and Ralph Manheim (eds.), *Collected Plays [of] Bertolt Brecht*, Vol. 2, Part 2. London: Methuen, 1979.

Brown, Mark, "Endgame: Another Side of Beckett," *The Telegraph*, 28 November 2007, www.telegraph.co.uk/culture/theatre/3669567/Endgame-Another-side-of-Beckett.html (accessed 10 July 2013).

Bruno, Christine, "Disability in American Theater: Where is the Tipping Point?" *HowlRound*, 7 April 2014, http://howlround.com/disability-in-american-theater-where-is-the-tipping-point (accessed 26 May 2015).

Bulmer, Alex and Sarah Garton Stanley, 'HowlRound: A commons by and for people who make performance,'" http://thisisprogress.ca/2014/11/dramatic-action-the-republic-of-inclusion (accessed 22 May 2015).

Burgdorf Jr., Robert L, "Why I wrote the Americans with Disabilities Act," *Washington Post*, 24 July 2015, www.washingtonpost.com/posteverything/wp/2015/07/24/why-the-americans-with-disabilities-act-mattered/ (accessed 30 July 2015).

Burgdorf Jr., Robert L, "A Dozen Things to Know About the ADA on Its Twenty-Fifth Anniversary," University of the District of Columbia, David A. Clarke School of Law website, www.law.udc.edu/?ADAAnniversary (accessed 30 July 2015).

Canada Council for the Arts, *Expanding the Arts: Deaf and Disability Arts Access Equality,* 2012, pp. 21–5, http://canadacouncil.ca/council/research/find-research/2012/expanding-the-arts-deaf-and-disability-arts (accessed 30 July 2015).

Cardullo, Robert J., "*Liebestod*, Romanticism, and Poetry in *The Glass Menagerie*," *ANQ: A Quarterly Journal of Short Articles, Notes and Reviews*, Vol. 23, No. 2 (2010), pp. 76–85.

Carlson, Marvin, *The Haunted Stage: The Theatre as Memory Machine*. Ann Arbor: University of Michigan Press, 2001.

Cavell, Stanley, "Ending the Waiting Game: A Reading of Beckett's *Endgame*," in Harold Bloom (ed.), *Samuel Beckett's Endgame*. New York: Chelsea House Publishers, 1988, pp. 59–77.

Chisholm, Alex, "*Blood Wedding* at Everyman Theatre," *Exeunt Magazine*, April 2015, http://exeuntmagazine.com/reviews/blood-wedding/ (accessed 3 June 2015).

Clare, Eli, *Exile and Pride: Disability, Queerness, and Liberation*. Cambridge, MA: South End, 1999.

Cockburn, Paul F., "Graeae Theatre tackle a new adaptation of 'Blood Wedding,'" *Disability Arts Online,* 16 February 2015, www.disabilityartsonline.org.uk/jenny-sealey-graeae-theatre-interview (accessed 8 June 2015).

Connor, Steven, *Samuel Beckett: Repetition, Theory and Text*. London: Basil Blackwell, 1988.

Conroy, Colette, *Theatre and the Body*. New York: Palgrave Macmillan, 2010.

Cooper, Neil, "Brecht and to the point. The Threepenny Opera is low-life, an in-your-face howl from the left. Will Theatre Workshop's production be shabby enough to shock?" *The Herald* [Scotland], 15 June 2004, www.heraldscotland.com/sport/spl/aberdeen/brecht-and-to-the-point-the-threepenny-opera-is-low-life-an-in-your-face-howl-from-the-left-will-theatre-workshop-s-production-be-shabby-enough-to-shock-1.83079 (accessed 8 June 2015).

Cramer, Steve, "Endgame," *The List*, 15 November 2007, www.list.co.uk/article/5642-endgame/ (accessed 10 July 2013).

Bibliography

Critics' Awards for Theatre in Scotland (CATS), "2004–05 Shortlists," www.criticsawards.theatrescotland.com/Shortlists%20by%20year/04-05.html (accessed 31 May 2015).

Crutchfield, Susan and Marcy Epstein (eds.), *Points of Contact: Disability, Art, and Culture*. Ann Arbor: University of Michigan Press, 2000.

Dacre, Kathy and Alex Bulmer, "*Into the Scene* and its Impact on Inclusive Performance Training," *Research in Drama Education: The Journal of Applied Theatre and Performance*, Vol. 14, No. 1 (2009), pp. 133–9.

Darke, Paul Anthony, "Now I Know Why Disability Arts is Drowning in the River Lethe (with thanks to Pierre Bourdieu)," in Sheila Riddell and Nick Watson (eds.), *Disability, Culture and Identity*. Harlow, England: Pearson Education, 2003, pp. 131–42.

Davidson, Michael, *Concerto for the Left Hand: Disability and the Defamiliar Body*. Ann Arbor: University of Michigan Press, 2008.

Davidson, Michael, "'Every Man His Specialty': Beckett, Disability, and Dependence," *Journal of Literary and Cultural Disability Studies*, Vol. 1, No. 2 (2007), pp. 55–68.

Davis, Lennard, *Bending Over Backwards: Disability, Dismodernism and Other Difficult Positions*. New York: New York University Press, 2002.

Davis, Lennard, "Constructing Normalcy," in Lennard Davis (ed.), *The Disability Studies Reader* (Third Edition). New York: Routledge, 2010, pp. 3–19.

Debusscher, Gilbert, "Tennessee Williams's Unicorn Broken Again," in Harold Bloom (ed.), *Tennessee Williams's The Glass Menagerie*. New York: Chelsea House Publishers, 1988, pp. 47–57.

Degener, Theresia, "Disability Discrimination Law: A Global Comparative Approach," in Caroline Gooding and Anna Lawson (eds.), *Disability Rights in Europe: From Theory to Practice*. Oxford: Hart Publishing, 2006, pp. 87–106.

Disability Arts Online, "Graeae Theatre Take Lorca's 'Blood Wedding' on tour to Dundee, Derby, Greenock, Edinburgh, Ipswich and Liverpool," *Disability Arts Online*, www.disabilityartsonline.org.uk/Events?item=7069 (accessed 8 June 2015).

Dolan, Jill, "Feminist Performance Criticism and the Popular: Reviewing Wendy Wasserstein," *Theatre Journal*, Vol. 60, No. 3 (2008), pp. 433–57.

Dorwart, Jason Bogaard, "Phamaly and the DisAbility Project: Models of Theater by Disabled Actors," MA thesis, Department of Theatre and Dance, University of Colorado, 2012.

Eckersall, Peter and Helena Grehan (eds.), *"We're People who do Shows": Back to Back Theatre: Performance, Politics, Visibility*. Aberystwyth: Performance Research Books, 2013.

Extant Theatre website. http://extant.org.uk/about_us (accessed 12 June 2015).

Feeney, David, "Sighted Renderings of a Non-Visual Aesthetics: Exploring the Interface between Drama and Disability Theory," *Journal of Literary and Cultural Disability Studies*, Vol. 3, No. 1 (2009), pp. 85–99.

Fisher, Mark, "Blood Wedding Review—Lorca's Tragedy Turned into a Soap Opera," *The Guardian*, 10 March 2015, www.theguardian.com/stage/2015/mar/10/blood-wedding-review-lorca (accessed 8 June 2015).

Fisher, Mark, "Endgame," *Northings Blog*, 13 February 2008, http://northings. com/2008/02/05/endgame/ (accessed 8 June 2015).

Flacks, Diane, "Life is a Five-Star Performance," *Toronto Star*, 26 May 2009, www. thestar.com/life/2009/05/26/life_is_a_fivestar_performance.html (accessed 30 July 2015).

Fleischer, Doris Zames and Frieda Zames, *The Disability Rights Movement: From Charity to Confrontation*. Philadelphia: Temple University Press, 2001.

Fox, Ann M., "Battles on the Body: Disability, Interpreting Dramatic Literature, and the Case of Lynn Nottage's *Ruined*," *Journal of Literary & Cultural Disability Studies*, Vol. 5, Issue 1 (2011), pp. 1–15.

Fox, Ann M., "'But, Mother—I'm—crippled!' Tennessee Williams, Queering Disability, and Dis/Membered Bodies in Performance," in Bonnie G. Smith and Beth Hutchison (eds.), *Gendering Disability*. New Brunswick, NJ: Rutgers University Press, 2004, pp. 233–50.

Fox, Ann M., "Fabulous Invalids Together: Why Disability in Mainstream Theater Matters," in David Bolt and Clare Penketh (eds.), *Disability, Avoidance and the Academy: Challenging Resistance*. London: Routledge, 2015, pp. 122–32.

Fox, Ann M. and Joan Lipkin, "Res(Crip)ting Feminist Theater Through Disability Theater: Selections from the DisAbility Project," *NWSA Journal*, Vol. 14, No. 3 (2002), pp. 77–98.

Fraser, Mat, "Mat Fraser on The Threepenny Opera," *Graeae's Blog*, 7 March 2014, https://graeaetheatrecompany.wordpress.com/2014/03/07/mat-fraser-on-the-threepenny-opera/ (accessed 7 June 2015).

Gardner, Lyn, "Disability arts left hanging by a thread," *The Guardian*, 29 July 2014. http://www.theguardian.com/stage/theatreblog/2014/jul/29/disability-arts-cuts-access-to-work-theatre (accessed 30 July 2015).

Gardner, Lyn, "My disability helped me understand Blanche DuBois, says Streetcar actor," *The Guardian*, 2 June 2014. www.theguardian.com/stage/2014/jun/02/disabled-actor-plays-blanche-dubois-streetcar-named-desire (accessed 8 June 2015).

Gardner, Lyn, "Putting Disability Centre Stage," in Lois Keidan and C.J. Mitch (eds.), *Access All Areas: Live Art and Disability*. London: Live Art Development Agency, 2012, pp. 60–62.

Garland-Thomson, Rosemarie, "Avoidance and the Academy: The International Conference on Disability, Culture, and Education," Centre for Culture and Disability Studies, Liverpool Hope University, Liverpool, United Kingdom, 12 September 2013.

Garland-Thomson, Rosemarie, *Extraordinary Bodies: Figuring Physical Disability in American Culture and Literature*. New York: Columbia University Press, 1997.

Garland-Thomson, Rosemarie, "Introduction: From Wonder to Error—A Genealogy of Freak Discourse in Modernity," in Rosemarie Garland Thomson (ed.), *Freakery: Cultural Spectacles of the Extraordinary Body*. New York: New York University Press, 1996, pp. 1–22.

Gay, Peter, *Modernism: The Lure of Heresy from Baudelaire to Beckett and Beyond*. New York: Norton, 2008.

Bibliography

Goffman, Erving, *Stigma: Notes on the Management of Spoiled Identity*. Englewood Cliffs, NJ: Prentice-Hall, 1963.

Gold, Jenni (dir.), *Cinemability*, Gold Pictures, 2013.

Goolian, Betsy, "Alliance Takes a Much-Deserved Bow. Alumna Sharon Jensen Wins Tony Honor for Excellence in Theater," *Michigan Muse*, Vol. 6, No. 1 (2011), www.music.umich.edu/muse/2011/fall/Alliance-Takes-A-Bow.html (accessed 29 April 2015)

Graeae Theatre Company, *A Guide to Inclusive Teaching Practice in Theatre: For Teachers, Directors, Practitioners and Staff*, London, 2009, www.graeae.org/wp-content/uploads/2011/01/AGuideto2.pdf (accessed 22 May 2015).

Graeae Theatre Company, "Training Course: Missing Piece," www.graeae.org/get-involved/training-courses/missing-piece (accessed 29 September 2015).

Graeae Theatre Company, "Training Course: Write to Play," www.graeae.org/get-involved/training-courses/write-to-play/ (accessed 27 May 2015).

Greiff, Louis K., 'Fathers, Daughters, and Spiritual Sisters: Marsha Norman's *'night Mother* and Tennessee Williams's *The Glass Menagerie*," *Text and Performance Quarterly*, Vol. 9, No. 3 (1989), pp. 224–8.

Gruber, Fiona, "Performance more than a question of ability," *The Australian*, Vol. 19 (2008), p. 10.

Hadley, Bree, *Disability, Public Space, Performance and Spectatorship: Unconscious Performers*. London: Palgrave, 2014.

Hadley, Bree, "Participation, politics and provocations: People with disabilities as non-conciliatory audiences," *Participations: Journal of Audience & Reception Studies*, Vol. 12, No. 1 (2015), pp. 154–74.

Hambrook, Colin, "Graeae Theatre Stage a New Production of The Threepenny Opera," *Disability Arts Online*, 19 February 2014, www.disabilityartsonline.org.uk/graeae-the-threepenny-opera (accessed 1 June 2015).

Haydon, Andrew, "*Blood Wedding* – Everyman, Liverpool," *Postcards from the Gods* blog, 23 April 15, http://postcardsgods.blogspot.co.uk/2015/04/blood-wedding-everyman-liverpool.html (accessed 3 June 2015).

Healy, Patrick, "Advocacy Group Opposes 'Miracle Worker' Casting Choice," *New York Times* ArtsBeat blog, 29 October 2009, artsbeat.blogs.nytimes.com/2009/10/29/advocacy-group-opposes-miracle-worker-casting-choice (accessed 2 June 2015).

Hickling, Alfred, "Graeae's The Threepenny Opera: 'it dissipates the fear of disability,'" *The Guardian*, 25 February 2014, www.theguardian.com/stage/2014/feb/25/jenny-sealey-disabled-actors-graeae-threepenny-opera (accessed 7 June 2015).

Hollins, Heather, "Reciprocity, Accountability, Empowerment: Emancipatory Principles and Practices in the Museum," in Richard Sandell, Jocelyn Dodd, and Rosemarie Garland-Thomson (eds.), *Re-presenting Disability: Activism and Agency in the Museum*. London: Routledge, 2012, pp. 228–43.

Hosey, Sarah, "Resisting the S(crip)t: Disability Studies Perspectives in the Undergraduate Classroom," *Teaching American Literature: A Journal of Theory and Practice*, Vol. 6, No. 1 (2013), pp. 23–44.

Jacobson, Rose and Geoff McMurchy, "Focus on Disability and Deaf Arts in Canada: A Report from the Field by Rose Jacobson and Geoff McMurchy," Canada Council for the Arts, December 2010.

Kalb, Jonathan, *Beckett in Performance*. Cambridge: Cambridge University Press, 1989.

Kane, Sarah, *Blasted*, in *Sarah Kane: Complete Plays*, introduced by David Greig. London: Methuen Drama, 2001, pp. 1–61.

Keidan, Lois, "'It doesn't stop here': An Introduction to *Access All Areas*," in Lois Keidan and C.J. Mitch (eds.), *Access All Areas: Live Art and Disability*. London: Live Art Development Agency, 2012, pp. 6–13.

Kent, Deborah, "In Search of a Heroine: Images of Women with Disabilities in Fiction and Drama," in Michelle Fine and Adrienne Asch (eds.), *Women with Disabilities: Essays in Psychology, Culture, and Politics*. Philadelphia: Temple University Press, 1988, pp. 90–110.

Kirwan, Peter, "The Threepenny Opera at Nottingham Playhouse," *Exeunt Magazine*, February–March 2014, http://exeuntmagazine.com/reviews/the-threepenny-opera/ (accessed 2 June 2015).

Kittay, Eva Feder, *Love's Labor: Essays on Women, Equality, and Dependency*. New York: Routledge, 1999.

Klein, Dennis A., *Blood Wedding, Yerma, and The House of Bernarda Alba: García Lorca's Tragic Trilogy*, Boston: Twayne Publishers, 1991.

Knowles, Ric, *How Theatre Means*. London: Palgrave, 2014.

Knowles, Ric, *Reading the Material Theatre*. Cambridge: Cambridge University Press, 2004.

Knowles, Ric, Joanne Tompkins and W.B. Worthen (eds.), *Modern Drama: Defining the Field*. Toronto: University of Toronto Press, 2003.

Kochhar-Lindgren, Kanta, "Disability," in Bruce Burgett and Glen Hendler (eds.), *Keywords for American Cultural Studies*. New York: New York University Press, 2014, pp. 81–4.

Komporály, Jozefina, "'Cripping Up is the Twenty-first Century's Answer to Blacking Up': Conversation with Kaite O'Reilly on Theatre, Feminism, and Disability – 6 June 2005, British Library, London," *Gender Forum: Illuminating Gender*, Vol. 12 (2005), 29 August 2007, www.genderforum.org/issues/illuminating-gender-i/cripping-up-is-the-twenty-first-centurys-answer-to-blacking-up/ (accessed 25 September 2015).

Kowalke, Kim H., "Accounting for success: misunderstanding *Die Dreigroschenoper*," *The Opera Quarterly*, Vol. 6, No. 3 (1989), pp. 18–38.

Kudlick, Catherine, "Disability History: Why We Need Another 'Other,'" *American Historical Review*, Vol. 108, No. 3 (2003), pp. 763–93.

Kuppers, Petra, *Disability and Contemporary Performance: Bodies on Edge*. New York: Routledge, 2003.

Kuppers, Petra, *Disability Culture and Community Performance: Find a Strange and Twisted Shape*, London: Palgrave, 2013.

Kuppers, Petra, "Landscapings: Spacings," *Women & Performance: A Journal of Feminist Theory*, Vol. 13, No. 2 (2003), pp. 41–56.

Bibliography

Kwei-Armah, Kwame, Keynote Address, Theatre Communications Group Fall Forum on Governance, 2012, www.tcg.org/events/fallforum/2012/recordings. cfm (accessed 1 June 2015).

Lahr, John, *Tennessee Williams: Mad Pilgrimage of the Flesh*. New York: W.W. Norton & Company, 2014.

Laws, Roz, "Themes of Class Struggle and Corruption Make Opera So Relevant Today," *Birmingham Post*, 27 March 2014, www.birminghampost.co.uk/whats-on/arts-culture-news/threepenny-opera-plays-birmingham-rep-6874862 (accessed 3 June 2015).

Levin, Mike, "The Art of Disability: An Interview with Tobin Siebers," *Disability Studies Quarterly* Vol. 30, No. 2 (2010), http://dsq-sds.org/article/view/1263/1272 (accessed 30 May 2015).

Levy, Eric, "'Through Soundproof Glass': The Prison of Self-Consciousness in *The Glass Menagerie*," *Modern Drama*, Vol. 36, No. 4 (1993), pp. 529–37.

Lewis, Victoria Ann, "The Theatrical Landscape of Disability," *Disability Studies Quarterly*, Vol. 24, No. 3 (2004), http://dsq-sds.org/article/view/511/688 (accessed 30 May 2015).

Lewis, Victoria Ann, *Beyond Victims and Villains: Contemporary Plays by Disabled Playwrights*. New York: Theatre Communications Group, 2005.

Lewis, Victoria Ann, "Disability and Access: A Manifesto for Actor Training," in Ellen Margolis and Lissa Tyler Renaud (eds.), *The Politics of American Actor Training*. New York: Routledge, 2010, pp. 177–97.

Linton, Simi, *Claiming Disability: Knowledge and Identity*. New York: New York University Press, 1998.

Linton, Simi, "Disability and Conventions in Theatre," www.similinton.com/about_topics_2.htm (accessed 1 June 2015).

Lipkin, Joan and Ann M. Fox, "Res(Crip)ting Feminist Theater Through Disability Theater Selections from The DisAbility Project," *Feminist Formations*, Vol. 14, No. 3 (2002), pp. 77–98.

Lobel, Brian, "Confrontation and Celebration," in Lois Keidan and C.J. Mitch (eds.), *Access All Areas: Live Art and Disability.* London: Live Art Development Agency, 2012, pp. 63–71.

Longmore, Paul K., *Why I Burned My Book and Other Essays on Disability*. Philadelphia: Temple University Press, 2003.

Lukács, Georg, *Realism in Our Time*. New York: Harper, 1964.

Lyon, Janet, "Disability and Generative Form," *Journal of Modern Literature*, Vol. 38, No. 1 (2014), pp. v–viii.

Lyon, Janet, *Manifestoes: Provocations of the Modern*. Ithaca: Cornell University Press, 1999.

MacIntyre, Alasdair, *Dependent Rational Animals: Why Human Beings Need the Virtues*. Chicago: Open Court, 1999.

McMillan, Joyce, "Endgame," *The Scotsman*, 6 November 2007. Available at http://joycemcmillan.wordpress.com/2007/11/06/endgame/ (accessed 10 July 2013).

McNeff, Stephen, "The Threepenny Opera," in Peter Thomson and Glendyr Sacks (eds.), *The Cambridge Companion to Brecht*. Cambridge: Cambridge University Press, 2006, pp. 78–89.

McRuer, Robert, "Compulsory Able-Bodiedness and Queer/Disabled Existence," in
Lennard J. Davis (ed.), *The Disability Studies Reader*, Fourth edition. New York:
Routledge, 2013, pp. 369–78.

McRuer, Robert, *Crip Theory: Cultural Signs of Queerness and Disability*. New York:
New York University Press, 2006.

Majewski, Janice and Lonnie Bunch, "The Expanding Definition of Diversity:
Accessibility and Disability Culture Issues in Museum Exhibitions," *Curator: The
Museum Journal*, Vol. 41, Issue 3, 1998, pp. 153–61.

Manning, Lynn, *Private Battle and Other Plays*. South Gate CA: No Passport Press,
2014.

Mee, Charles, *the (re)making project*, www.charlesmee.org/casting.shtml (accessed
22 May 2015).

Memmi, Albert, *Dependence*. Boston: Beacon Press, 1984.

Mitchell, David and Sharon Snyder, *Narrative Prosthesis: Disability and the
Dependencies of Discourse*. Ann Arbor: University of Michigan Press, 2001.

Mitchell, David and Sharon Snyder, *Vital Signs: Crip Culture Talks Back*.
Documentary. Fanlight Productions, 1995.

Moore, John, "PHAMALy Actor Regan Linton Works Her Magic in San Diego," *The
Denver Post*, 3 February 2012, www.denverpost.com/ci_19880409 (accessed
22 December 2014).

National Library of Scotland, Theatre Workshop Edinburgh Accession Inventory
(Acc.13521) [2014]. www.nls.uk/catalogues/online/cnmi/inventories/acc13521.
pdf (accessed 31 May 2015).

Nottingham Playhouse, "Backstage Pass Members Pick the Winners,"
www.nottinghamplayhouse.co.uk/news/backstage-pass-members-pick-the-
winners/ (accessed 27 May 2015).

Nussbaum, Martha C., *Frontiers of Justice: Disability, Nationality, Species
Membership*. Cambridge, MA: Harvard University Press, 2006.

Oliver, Mike, "The Social Model in Action: If I Had a Hammer," in Colin Barnes and
Geof Mercer (eds.), *Implementing the Social Model of Disability Theory and
Research*. Leeds: The Disability Press, 2004.

Padden, Carol and Tom Humphries, "Deaf People: A Different Center," in Lennard
Davis (ed.), *The Disability Studies Reader* (Third Edition). New York: Routledge,
2010, pp. 393–402.

Pao, Angela, *No Safe Spaces: Re-Casting Race, Ethnicity, and Nationality in American
Theatre*. Ann Arbor: University of Michigan Press, 2010.

Paterson, Mary, "Reflections on *Access All Areas*," in Lois Keidan and C.J. Mitch
(eds.), *Access All Areas: Live Art and Disability*. London: Live Art Development
Agency, 2012, pp. 55–9.

Pearson, Nels, "'Outside of here it's death': Co-dependency and the Ghosts of
Decolonization in Beckett's *Endgame*," *ELH*, Vol. 68, No. 1 (2001), pp. 215–39.

Pepper, Penny, "Missing Piece Marvellous," *Disability Arts Online*, www.
disabilityartsonline.org.uk/missing-pieces (accessed 8 June 2015).

Phamaly Theatre website, www.phamaly.org (accessed 31 May 2015).

Piepenburg, Erik, "Parents and Kids Say They Appreciated Autism-Friendly 'Lion
King' Matinee," *New York Times ArtsBeat*, 3 October 2011, http://artsbeat.blogs.

nytimes.com/2011/10/03/parents-and-kids-say-they-appreciated-autism-friendly-lion-king-matinee (accessed 30 July 2015).

Poore, Carol, *Disability in Twentieth-Century German Culture*. Ann Arbor: University of Michigan Press, 2009.

Porter, Liz, "Graeae Theatre present The Threepenny Opera," *Disability Arts Online*, 18 March 2014, www.disabilityartsonline.org.uk/graeae-the-threepenny-opera-review (accessed 1 June 2015).

Prince, Michael, "Canadian Federalism and Disability Policy Making," *Canadian Journal of Political Science*, Vol. 34, No. 4 (2001), pp. 791–817.

Quayson, Ato, *Aesthetic Nervousness: Disability and the Crisis of Representation*. New York: Columbia University Press, 2007.

Rae, Robert, Robert Rae website, www.robertrae.co.uk (accessed 29 September 2015).

Ramamurthy, Sita, "Artistic Evaluation," Scottish Arts Council, 12 December 2007. www.scottisharts.org.uk/resources/Organisations/Theatre%20 Workshop/2007-08/Theatre%20Workshop%20Endgame%20SR%2006%20 11%2007%20pdf.pdf (accessed 10 July 2013).

Realwheels website, "Realwheels Mission and History," realwheels.ca/house-lights-on-realwheels/our-mission-and-history/ (accessed 9 June 2015).

Robbins, Bruce (ed.), *The Phantom Public Sphere*. Minneapolis: University of Minnesota Press, 1993.

Ryan, Frances, "We wouldn't accept actors blacking up, so why accept 'cripping up'?" *The Guardian*, 13 January 2015, www.theguardian.com/commentisfree/2015/jan/13/eddie-redmayne-golden-globe-stephen-hawking-disabled-actors-characters (accessed 13 May 2015).

Sabatello, Maya, "A Short History of the International Disability Rights Movement," in Maya Sabatello and Marianne Schulze (eds.), *Human Rights and Disability Advocacy*. Philadelphia: University of Pennsylvania Press, 2014, pp. 13–24.

Sandahl, Carrie, "Ahhhh Freak Out! Metaphors of Disability and Female-ness in Performance," *Theatre Topics*, Vol. 9, No. 1 (1999), pp. 11–30.

Sandahl, Carrie, "Considering Disability: Disability Phenomenology's Role in Revolutionizing Theatrical Space," *Journal of Dramatic Theory and Criticism*, Vol. 16, No. 2 (2002), pp. 17–32.

Sandahl, Carrie, "Queering the Crip or Cripping the Queer? Intersections of Queer and Crip Identities in Solo Autobiographical Performance," *GLQ: A Journal of Lesbian and Gay Studies*, Vol. 9, Nos. 1–2 (2003), pp. 25–56.

Sandahl, Carrie, "The Tyranny of Neutral: Disability and Actor Training," in Carrie Sandahl and Philip Auslander (eds.), *Bodies in Commotion: Disability and Performance*. Ann Arbor: University of Michigan Press, 2005, pp. 255–67.

Sandahl, Carrie, "Why Disability Identity Matters: From Dramaturgy to Casting in John Belluso's *Pyretown*," *Text and Performance Quarterly*, Vol. 28, Nos. 1–2 (2008), pp. 225–41.

Sandahl, Carrie and Philip Auslander, "Introduction: Disability Studies in Commotion with Performance Studies," in Carrie Sandahl and Philip Auslander (eds.), *Bodies in Commotion: Disability and Performance*. Ann Arbor: University of Michigan Press, 2005, pp. 1–12.

Sandahl, Carrie and Philip Auslander (eds.), *Bodies in Commotion: Disability and Performance.* Ann Arbor: University of Michigan Press, 2005.

Sandahl, Carrie, Aly Patsavas, Susan Nussbaum, and Salome Chasnoff (dirs.), *Code of the Freaks,* Personal Hermitage Productions, 2011.

Sealey, Jenny, "Introduction," in Jenny Sealey (ed.), *Graeae Plays: New Plays Redefining Disability,* London: Aurora Metro Press, 2002, pp. 9–14.

Sealey, Jenny, "Deaf and disabled artists: we will not let government cuts make us invisible," *Guardian* Theatre Blog, 13 April 2015, www.theguardian.com/stage/theatreblog/2015/apr/13/deaf-and-disabled-artists-we-will-not-let-government-cuts-make-us-invisible (accessed 27 May 2015).

Sealey, Jenny (ed.), *Graeae Plays 1: New Plays Redefining Disability.* London: Aurora Metro Publications Ltd., 2002.

Sealey, Jenny and Carissa Hope Lynch, "Graeae: an aesthetic of access: (de)cluttering the clutter," in Susan Broadhurst and Josephine Machon (eds.), *Identity, Performance and Technology: Practices of Empowerment, Embodiment and Technicity,* London, Palgrave Macmillan, 2012, pp. 60–73.

Sefel, John, "Finding Phamaly," *Stage Directions* (2012), www.stage-directions.com/4600-finding-phamaly.html (accessed 24 September 2015).

Shaban, Nabil, "Early History of Graeae" (2006), www.oocities.org/jinghiz53/The_Beginning_of_Graeae.htm (accessed 22 May 2015).

Shaban, Nabil, "The performer and disability," textbox under the entry "Disability" by Linda Moss and Sharon Jensen in Colin Chambers (ed.), *The Continuum Companion to Twentieth Century Theatre.* London: Continuum, 2006, pp. 212–13.

Shakespeare, Tom, "The Social Model of Disability," in Lennard Davis (ed.), *The Disability Studies Reader* (Third Edition). New York: Routledge, 2010, pp. 266–73.

Shakespeare, Tom and Nicholas Watson, "The Social Model of Disability: An Outdated Ideology? Exploring Theories and Expanding Methodologies," in *Research in Social Science and Disability 2,* Stamford, CT: JAI Press, 2001, pp. 9–28.

Shinn, Christopher, "Disability Is Not Just a Metaphor," *The Atlantic,* 23 July 2014, www.theatlantic.com/entertainment/archive/2014/07/why-disabled-characters-are-never-played-by-disabled-actors/374822/ (accessed 1 June 2015).

Shklovsky, Victor, "Art as Technique," in Lee T. Lemon and Marion J. Reis (eds.), *Russian Formalist Criticism: Four Essays.* Lincoln: University of Nebraska Press, 1965, pp. 3–24.

Siebers, Tobin, *Disability Aesthetics.* Ann Arbor: University of Michigan Press, 2010.

Siebers, Tobin, *Disability Theory.* Ann Arbor: University of Michigan Press, 2008.

Skotch, Richard, "American Disability Policy in the Twentieth Century," in Paul K. Longmore and Lauri Umansky (eds.), *The New Disability History.* New York: New York University Press, 2001, pp. 375–92.

Snowdon, Earl of, GCVO, "Foreword," in C. Wycliffe Noble and Geoffrey Lord, *Access for Disabled People to Arts Premises: The Journey Sequence.* Amsterdam: Architectural Press, Elsevier, 2004, pp. xi–xii.

Snyder, Sharon L. and David T. Mitchell, *Cultural Locations of Disability.* Chicago: University of Chicago Press, 2006.

Stanley, Sarah G. and Michael Rubenfeld, *The Book of Judith.* Co-produced by The Theatre Centre, Absit Omen, and Die In Debt Theatre on the Centre for

Bibliography

Addiction and Mental Health Queen Street site lawn, Toronto, Ontario, 19–31 May 2009.

Steinfeld, Edward and Jordana Maisel, *Universal Design: Creating Inclusive Environments*. Hoboken, NJ: John Wiley & Sons, 2012.

'Stop Changes to Access to Work,' http://stopchanges2atw.com/about/ (accessed 30 July 2015).

Sutherland, Allan, Chronology of Disability Arts, www.disabilityartsonline.org.uk/Chronology_of_Disability_Arts (accessed 30 July 2015).

Swartz, Matthew and Ali Zimmerman, "Distinguishing Sounds," *Theatre Design & Technology*, Vol. 41, No. 3 (2005), pp. 14–20.

Tait, James Fagan (playwright and director), *The Idiot*. Frederic Wood Theatre, University of British Columbia, co-produced by Neworld Theatre and Vancouver Moving Theatre and presented by the PuSh International Performing Arts Festival and Theatre at UBC, 20–29 January 2012.

Tajiri, Yoshiki, *Samuel Beckett and the Prosthetic Body: The Organs and Senses in Modernism*. Houndmills: Palgrave Macmillan, 2007.

That Uppity Theatre Company, "DisAbility Project," www.uppityco.com/dp.html?pnl=1_3 (accessed 22 May 2015).

Theatre Development Fund, "Autism Theatre Initiative, Making Theatre Accessible to Autistic Children and Adults," www.tdf.org/nyc/40/Autism-Theatre-Initiative (accessed 30 July 2015).

Theatre Workshop Scotland, "History," www.theatre-workshop.com/aboutus/history/ (accessed 31 May 2015).

Theatre Workshop Scotland, "The Threepenny Opera," www.theatre-workshop.com/events/2004/june/thrp_opera.html (accessed 7 June 2015).

Titchkosky, Tanya, *The Question of Access: Disability, Space, Meaning*. Toronto: University of Toronto Press, 2011.

Tolan, Kathleen, "We Are Not a Metaphor: A Conversation About Representation," *American Theatre* (2001), pp. 17–21, 57–9.

Tomlinson, Richard, *Disability, Theatre and Education*. London: Souvenir Press, 1982.

Trezise, Bryoni and Caroline Wake, "Disabling Spectacle: Curiosity, contempt and collapse in performance theatre," in Peter Eckersall and Helena Grehan (eds.), *"We're People who do Shows": Back to Back Theatre: Performance, Politics, Visibility*. Aberystwyth: Performance Research Books, 2013, pp. 119–30.

Trueman, Matt, "Threepenny Opera Review: 'All the More Furious from Disabled Actors,'" *The Guardian*, 18 March 2014, www.theguardian.com/stage/2014/mar/18/threepenny-opera-nottingham-playhouse-graeae-review (accessed 1 June 2015).

UK Government, "Access to Work," www.gov.uk/access-to-work/overview (accessed 27 May 2015).

UK Government, "Independent Living Fund," www.gov.uk/government/organisations/independent-living-fund/about (accessed 27 May 2015).

Vernon, Ayesha, "The Dialectics of Multiple Identities and the Disabled People's Movement," *Disability and Society*, Vol. 14, No. 3 (1999), pp. 385–98.

Vernon, Ayesha and John Swain, "Theorizing divisions and hierarchies: Toward a commonality or diversity?' in Colin Barnes, Mike Oliver, and Len Barton (eds.), *Disability Studies Today*. Cambridge: Polity, pp. 77–97.

Verrent, Jo, "Disability and the arts: the best of times, the worst of times," *The Guardian*, 23 March 2015, www.theguardian.com/culture-professionals-network/2015/mar/23/disability-arts-best-worst-of-times (accessed 22 May 2015).

Walsh, Maeve, "Theatre: On the Fringe," *The Independent*, 24 March 1999.

Williams, Tennessee, *The Glass Menagerie*. New York: New Directions, 1999.

Williamson, Aaron and Sinead O'Donnell, "In Alien Couch Territory," in Lois Keidan and C.J. Mitch (eds.), *Access All Areas: Live Art and Disability*. London: Live Art Development Agency, 2012, pp. 17–30.

Woolf, Virginia, "Shakespeare's Sister," from *A Room of One's Own*, in Sandra Gilbert and Susan Gubar (eds.), *The Norton Anthology of Literature by Women: The Traditions in English*, Vol. 2. Third edition. New York: W.W. Norton and Co., 2007.

Worton, Michael, "*Waiting for Godot* and *Endgame*: Theatre as Text," in John Pilling (ed.), *The Cambridge Companion to Beckett*. Cambridge: Cambridge University Press, 2005, pp. 67–87.

Wycliffe Noble, C. and Geoffrey Lord, *Access for Disabled People to Arts Premises: The Journey Sequence*. Amsterdam: Architectural Press, Elsevier, 2004.

NOTES ON CONTRIBUTORS

Michael Davidson is Distinguished Professor Emeritus of Literature at the University of California, San Diego, USA. He is the author of five books of criticism and the editor of *The New Collected Poems of George Oppen*. His most recent books are *Concerto for the Left Hand: Disability and the Defamiliar Body* (2008) and *Outskirts of Form: Practicing Cultural Poetics* (2011).

Ann M. Fox is a Professor of English at Davidson College, USA, where she specializes in modern and contemporary dramatic literature and disability studies. Her scholarship on disability and theatre has been supported by an American Association of University Women postdoctoral fellowship and published widely. She has co-curated three disability-related visual arts exhibitions; her current book project traces the representation of disability on the 20th century American commercial stage.

Terry Galloway is a multi-award winning writer, director and performer for stage, radio, video, and film. She started her long, eclectic career in theatre arts in 1968 after the University of Texas at Austin's Drama Department denied her admittance to its acting program. Since then she has received grants, fellowships and awards from, among others, the National Endowment of the Arts, the Texas Institute of Letters, the Mellon Foundation, and the Corporation for Public Broadcasting. Before her cochlear implant in 2010, Galloway was a deaf lip reader with a lateral lisp. Author of the powerful memoir *Mean Little deaf Queer*, Galloway is also the co-founder (with Dr. Donna Marie Nudd) and the Artistic Director of the Mickee Faust Club, a community theatre for the weird, queer, and differently abled community in Tallahassee, Florida. She has also been a visiting artist at the University of Texas, Austin as well as The California Institute of the Arts.

M. Shane Grant M. Shane Grant is a theatre scholar/artist whose scholarship focuses on contemporary queer representation in mainstream representation. His article " 'We're All Freaks Together': Whiteness and the Mitigation of Queer Community on 'Glee'" can be found in the *Queer In The Choir Room: Gender And Sexuality in Glee* (edited by Michelle Parke, McFarland & Co., 2014).

Notes on Contributors

Ben Gunter holds a PhD in dramaturgy from Florida State University. He translates scripts from the Spanish Golden Age, composes music for cabarets and queer plays, and writes about his experiences for publications ranging from *Shakespeare Plays the Classroom* to *The Southern Quarterly*. Ben serves as artistic director for Theater with a Mission, which brings everyday people face to face with living history through researching and performing such events as an Indian/Spanish Wedding in Spanish La Florida.

Carrie Sandahl, PhD, is an Associate Professor at the University of Illinois at Chicago, USA. She directs Chicago's Bodies of Work, an organization that supports the development of disability art and culture. Her own research and creative activity focus on disability as it intersects with other aspects of identity in live performance and film. Sandahl has published numerous research articles and an anthology she co-edited with Philip Auslander, entitled *Bodies in Commotion: Disability and Performance* (2005), which garnered the Association for Theatre in Higher Education's award for Outstanding Book in Theatre Practice and Pedagogy in 2006. She is currently collaborating on a feature-length documentary, *Code of the Freaks*, a critique of Hollywood's representation of disability.

Jenny Sealey, MBE, has been the Artistic Director of Graeae Theatre Company since 1997 and has pioneered a whole theatrical landscape with Deaf and disabled artists, placing them center stage, championing accessibility, and coining the aesthetics of access. Jenny co-directed the London 2012 Paralympic Opening Ceremony alongside Bradley Hemmings (GDIF). She also won the Liberty Human Rights Arts Award and was named on the Time Out London and Hospital Club h.Club100 2012 list of the most influential people in the creative industries. In 2009, she was awarded an MBE in the Queen's Honours and became an Artistic Advisor for the Unlimited 2012 Festival. Since 2012 Jenny has been awarded an honorary doctorate degree in Drama from Royal Conservatoire of Scotland, in Performing Arts from Middlesex University, and a Fellowship at Central School of Speech and Drama and Rose Bruford College.

INDEX

Index